HANDMADE HOUSEBOATS

INDEPENDENT LIVING AFLOAT

by Russell Conder

Houseboat *Tsunami*
New Zealand

 International Marine
Camden, Maine

International Marine/
Ragged Mountain Press

A Division of The McGraw-Hill Companies

10   9   8   7   6

**Library of Congress Cataloging-in-
Publication Data**
Conder, Russell.
    Handmade houseboats: independent
    living afloat / Russell Conder.
        p.   cm.
    Includes bibliographical references and
    index.
    ISBN 0-07-158022-0
    1. Houseboats—Design and
    construction.   2. Boat living.
I. Title.
VM335.C66   1992
623.8'223—dc20   92-13052
                                      CIP
Questions regarding the content of this
book should be addressed to:
    Ragged Mountain Press
    P.O. Box 220
    Camden, ME 04843
    207-236-4837

Questions regarding the ordering of this
book should be addressed to:
    The McGraw-Hill Companies
    Customer Service Department
    P.O. Box 547
    Blacklick, OH 43004
    Retail customers: 1-800-262-4729
    Bookstores: 1-800-722-4726

Printed by R. R. Donnelly, Crawfordsville, IN
Design by Patrice M. Rossi
Illustrated by the author
Production by Janet Robbins
Edited by J.R. Babb, Pamela Benner

Dedication

This book is dedicated to each and every houseboater who has ever fallen off his or her boat. It is also dedicated to William Atkin of the late, great *MoToR BoatinG* magazine, who probably did more to popularize houseboats than any other designer.

It is written in memory of Albert Bradlee Hunt, who edited *Houseboats and Houseboating*, published in 1905 by Forest and Stream Publishing of New York. I can best express my reasons for writing this book by quoting Albert Hunt:

To make known the opportunities American waters afford for enjoyment of the houseboating life. To present in an adequate measure the development which houseboating has attained in this country. And, chief of all, to set forth the qualities of the houseboat in such truthful picturing that a larger number of people may be prompted to prove for themselves its advantages and delights.

Contents

Acknowledgments

Much of this book owes its existence to the unrestrained generosity and enthusiasm of complete strangers, who responded to a mention in the editorial pages of *WoodenBoat* magazine that, down in New Zealand, a new book about houseboats was under way, and that any comments or photos would be warmly received.

The response from various people, organizations, and institutions has been unbelievable: John D. Corse, in Atlanta, Georgia, for example, entrusted to the mail a rare, turn-of-the-century book on houseboats. Roy Bisson, in N.S.W. Australia, posted three irreplaceable negatives. And Doug Harris, Auckland, New Zealand, painstakingly reproduced many of the photographs shown.

Unless otherwise noted, all quotations are taken from *Houseboats and Houseboating,* edited by Albert B. Hunt, Forest and Stream Publishing, New York, 1905.

I've also talked with many liveaboards, not one of whom has hesitated to share his or her experiences. I gratefully acknowledge all of these cooperative people. As much as anyone's, this book is theirs. And they are:

In New Zealand

Doug Harris, Creative Photography
Jackie O'Brien
Brian Donovan
Chris and Margaret Reeve
Les Robertson
Dan Reynolds
Ben and Thess Benneito
Leo and Karen Cappel
Joy and Arnold Engelberger
Ron and Monica Davey
Karen and Martin Barker
Raywyn and Ross Williams
John Scott
Boating NZ
Johanne Buchanan, *N.Z. Herald*
Joan McCracken, Alexander
    Turnbull Library

In Australia

Roy Bisson

Michael Norman, National Museum
    of Australia
John H. Watts, Leisureline Houseboats
Sunday Times, Queensland

In the United States

John D. Corse
The Parsons family
Henry J. Spruks
Richard W. Ramsey
Mary Lou Dietrich, *WoodenBoat*
Bernard Wides
David Sharps
James R. Babb, International Marine
Ed McKiernan, Sealand Technology Inc.
Paul Harrington, Holiday Mansion
    Houseboats
Waterways, New York

In Canada

Alex Whitfield

INTRODUCTION

Are You Crazy?

What a free life this opens up to the men and women of our crowded cities who live in 'heavenly' flats whose parlors and living rooms are deftly furnished with wonderful contrivances said to be mantel beds which have an inconvenient habit of inclosing the occupant... so many things that are all but what they seem. It is imitation comfort, and is neither a home, nor is it life— it is mere existence. For every man who is worn out with business cares or sick, with nerves unstrung or stomach out of order, we can recommend life on a houseboat as the best remedy in the world, whether it be in the North or the South.

This book is about how to build your own houseboat, and thereby sidestep the twin ogres of twentieth-century survival: mortgages and landlords. If you can hold these pages open, dear reader, then you have the manual dexterity to hold a hammer. If you can do that, then armed with this book and a smidgen of imagination, and at least a little gumption, you can build your own floating home, and be comfortably ensconced inside it, within a few weeks.

What exactly is a houseboat? Oddly, that's a difficult question to answer. A harbormaster I know once said, "If you can define a houseboat, you're a better man than me, mate, and I've heard people trying to do it for 50 years." The quest to define the term may be pursued at length, but put simply, a houseboat is a house that floats. No matter whether you call it a houseboat or a raft house or a floating home, it's a house that needs no expensive real estate under it. It can look like a million dollars, as in the collection of turn-of-the-century houseboats at Henley-on-Thames in Figure I-1, or it can look like an abandoned tree hut that just crashed down

Figure I-1. **A favorite houseboat reach just below Henley Bridge in turn-of-the-century England.**

through the leaves into the river. What it looks like doesn't matter much, for in the eyes of yachting purists, most houseboats are an affront to common decency.

At the turn of the century, Edward Field, of the Society of Naval Architects and Marine Engineers, sniffed that, "Houseboats, as the name is commonly applied in our country today, can pertain to almost anything, from a raft half aground with a house erected on it containing possibly one large room, to the beautifully equipped and spaciously appointed vessels capable of accompanying a yacht club squadron cruise and finishing well up with the best of the ten-knot yachts. . . ." Recently, the sentiment was more forcibly expressed in the novel *The Tidewater Tales* by John Barth where, " . . . there steamed in one day to its new home berth, to complete the rape of Sherritt Cove, neither a natty sailing yacht nor a gleaming cabin cruiser, but—how to utter it?—a huge *houseboat.* . . ."

Compared with sleek yachts and gleaming cabin cruisers, houseboats may occasionally look like poor country cousins, but they have one distinct advantage over their tonier kindred: comfort. None of this constantly bending double, or knocking knees on protruding tables. Houseboats are homes. More than that, they're economical homes.

Of course, people live aboard boats of all kinds, and have done so for years. However, while a boat can be a house of sorts, a house can never be a boat, not even remotely of sorts. Push a house into water, and it'll sink unhappily beneath the waves—unless, of course, it has a raft beneath it—in which case, it has become a houseboat. The point is: A houseboat is, first and foremost, a boat.

> **D**an Beard, father of Boy Scouts, wrote a book years and years ago; a charming book about boats and camps, and guns, and fields, and brooks, and lakes. In this book are plans of simple and very small houseboats. Always I have looked at the illustrations and plans of these boats with interest, and not without longing. There is one built upon logs, another on a scow. Standing among reeds or being swept upon the current, these boats call to boys, yes, and men, to seek the outdoors. No rent to pay, no taxes to consider if you live on a houseboat. No telephone, nor light rates. No neighbours to bother about. Only the water, with perhaps another boat or two. I tell you, shipmates, here is a mode of living that deserves serious consideration.
>
> William Atkin, "Selected Popular Motor Boat Designs," *MoToR BoatinG*, 1947.

An ordinary houseboat is infinitely cheaper to build than a conventional house. A houseboat requires no expensive dirt and stones and worms beneath it, no water and electricity umbilically siphoned into its insatiable maw, no lawns to manicure, no weeds to worry. Furthermore, it offers freedom from rent, mortgage, most taxes, and all but the most intrepid vacuum-cleaner and encyclopedia salespersons. And if the neighbors become obstreperous? Up anchor and be off!

Perhaps of most importance, houseboats require no use of bulldozers, trucks, excavators, concrete-mixers, asphalt-layers, or other machines that rip apart and "develop" the countryside. Houseboats ride unobtrusively, drifting to and fro, above the natural environment that's been around for millennia, an ecologically sound form of housing that even fish seem to like. (Certainly enough of them hang around, looking for handouts.)

So let's get on with it. As I type these words, the wind is howling outside—not a fit night for man or beast. Inside, the fire flickers in the chip oven, and a pot of spaghetti bolognaise simmers its aroma throughout the house. The cats and the dog struggle for possession of the floor mat, valiantly trying to restrain their noses as their eyes drift repeatedly to a fresh flounder—tomorrow's breakfast—hanging from a nail inside the back door.

The following chapters don't pretend to be anything more than words of enthusiasm and encouragement from a small house afloat on a small creek somewhere in the middle of a small country. Their true worth lies in whatever spark they may kindle in the reader's imagination. And if you just can't imagine life on the briny, don't worry: Check out houseboat charters. Devote your next Escape From Routine Toil to living afloat, aboard any of the excellent rental houseboats that may be hired. It'll soon become obvious why houseboaters don't go off on vacations: There's nowhere better to go.

CHAPTER ONE
Wherefrom

We advise every one that the beauties of nature are lost to them unless they try living on the water. A cottage in the country is monotonous compared with the ever-changing landscape of the water—there is beauty everywhere, the air is pure, the nights are cool, the mosquitoes do not bother you, and there is a restful tone of comfort and happiness about a houseboat which can be had in no other abode.

When Cleopatra drifted down the Nile, Marc Antony cooing and mumbling sweet-nothings in her ear, she wouldn't have wanted every Egyptian for miles around peering at their shenanigans. She would have wanted privacy. Let's face it, she would have demanded, as well, a regal standard of comfort. Lying in the bilges of an odorous, leaky, papyrus-and-cord sailing vessel would have dampened anyone's ardor. Cleopatra's royal barge was undoubtedly a pre-Christian houseboat.

Another early houseboat, pre-Christian (but heading in that direction), was Noah's ark. The grand patriarch of the Old Testament may have been thought crazy by his neighbors, but he had enough sense not only to build a houseboat, but to cram a farmyard, an aquarium, an aviary, and a zoo inside as well.

TURN OF THE CENTURY

Carrying livestock around in a houseboat isn't all that novel. Wherever there are rivers, animals have been carted up and down them. A sumptuous, late nineteenth-century Florida houseboat, the millionaire Pierre Lorillard's *Caiman*, was accompanied by a stableboat. For the convenience of his guests, the secondary boat held carriages and horses to draw them, as well as dogs and their kennels. Hunting to hounds, riding, or trips to the nearest township were always available.

Herbert Corse, while towing the houseboat *Summer-time* to the East Canal in 1915 with the cruiser *Lady Anne II*, remarked in the log: "With them they were moving their livestock, and the *Summer-time* was an example of what can be loaded on a houseboat. A cow and 2 fat pigs occupied the back deck, 20 chickens in a coop on the top of the back awning, and 6 beehives on the roof of the cabin, plants in pots and various other paraphernalia; towing the outfit were 3 small launches."

Animals would not have been welcome on the opulent houseboats of Kashmir, originally built to circumvent Moghul laws that restricted foreign ownership of land. The British colonial administrators of India flocked north each year to escape the oppressive summer heat of the south and sojourn in the cool air on Dal and Nagin lakes. In *Houseboats and Houseboating*, Albert B. Hunt observed rather poetically, "Tired British

Figure 1-1. The good old *Summer-time*, Fort George Inlet, 1912.

India looks forward to the month in a houseboat among the floating is-lands of the Lakes of Srinagar as almost the nearest thing to physical happiness which he can find on the wrong side of the parallel dividing Europe from Asia."

While the British relaxed in Kashmir, their countrymen back home looked forward to an annual event on their own houseboats. The Royal Regatta at Henley-on-Thames was a highlight of the "season," when stately houseboats (more than 300 in 1904) were towed by horses on shore from their winter moorings, to be arranged along each side of the canal, and from which hordes of gentry would cheer for their favorite rowing crews, as the latter battled for trophies, ribbons, and cups. There were also keen competitions on board the houseboats themselves, as each vied with its neighbors to sport the most resplendent and colorful arrays of flowers, which cascaded from awnings, railings, and decks.

These houseboats were not self-sufficient. Gentlefolk did not prepare their own food; tenders tied alongside provided cooked meals, champagne, and the servants' accommodations.

The servants would have been busy. In 1905, Albert B. Hunt wrote: "My Lord and Lady, His Grace the Duke, and her Serene Highness, all keep open house, or rather, houseboat. It is no unpretentious entertaining that the Britisher does in his floating residence during Henley week. His great retinue of servants is there in full force—butlers and footmen and grooms. There are elaborate dinner parties in the long, gorgeously furnished saloon. There is music in the spacious drawing rooms. On deck the beaux and belles of the Empire step through the mazes of the cotillion, or wander through those tropic gardens which give the boat the appearance of a vast floating island to beholders on the shore."

Some of these houseboats were splendidly grandiose. In 1902 the river authority, the Thames Conservancy, listed in their registrations such vessels as *Cigarette* at 119 feet; *Ibis*, 113 feet; *Kittiwake*, 95 feet; and *Kismet*, 90 feet.

Possibly the first houseboat in England was built, and settled in, at Oxford. Originally a horse-towed barge, she was retired from commercial service in 1858 to have a house built atop her. Although only 17 feet 9 inches wide (actually quite wide for a canal barge), Salter's green barge, as she was known, was 107 feet long. The idea caught on, and soon other barges were also taken to Oxford to have houses and college boat clubs built atop them.

The Keble College Barge, built in 1899, was probably a very radical design at the time—it still is. The clubhouse looks as if it were designed to commemorate a Phoenician galley and Drake's flagship. It was 68 feet 6 inches long by 14 feet 6 inches wide, and featured, as shown in the plans, a 26-foot reading room, showers, toilet, lockers, and a dressing room for the convenience of the undergraduates.

Figure 1-2. **The Thames houseboat** *Vinia*, **1905.**

Across the stormy Atlantic, houseboat owners in North America were just as dedicated to "the season" as their English cousins, and hundreds of handsome vessels were brought out for the summer from their winter moorings. In California, for example, members of the San Francisco Yacht Club could sit amidst their papers and drinks and contemplate the houseboats floating in Belvedere Lagoon. Working professionals, doctors, brokers, and bankers—anyone who was anyone—would commute to the city, and at close of business, be back aboard their houseboats for the evening's entertainments. The parading of the houseboats in San Francisco, now but a memory, was a colorful and festive phenomenon.

So where did they go? Belvedere Lagoon was eventually overtaken by development, and the houseboats vanished, a few winding up ashore as gift shops and restaurants. A similar fate befell the houseboats at Larkspur Boardwalk, originally settled 75 years ago, but swept away in 1967. A few are preserved on private land.

The best-known colony of houseboats today, at Sausalito, California, comprises more than 600 floating homes. The area was used as a shipyard during World War I; Arques Shipworks repaired barges there, and employees took to living in them as well. Later, when the San Francisco Bay bridges

Figure 1-3.
**The Keble
College Barge,
Oxford, 1905.**

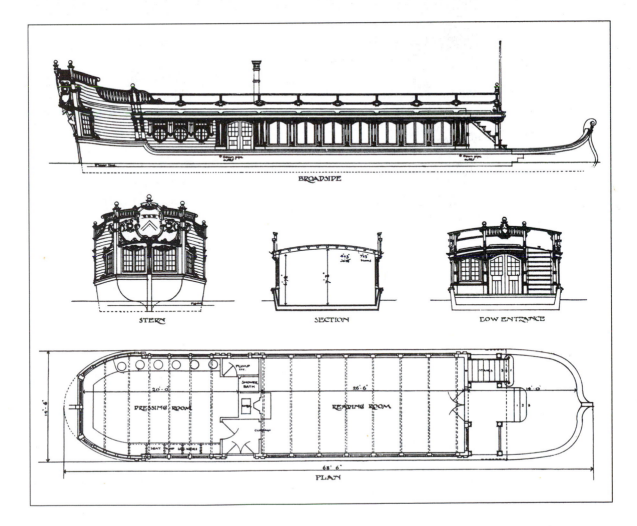

BROADSIDE

STERN   SECTION   LOW ENTRANCE

PLAN

were opened to traffic and ferryboats became redundant, a handful—like the *Vallejo* and the *Charles Van Damme*—were beached at Gate Five. Like moths to a beacon, houseboats appeared alongside, and today a quarter-mile of the cove hosts the largest houseboat community in North America.

Ninety years ago, Seattle glitterati were equally enraptured with their summer retreats on Lake Washington. In later years, houseboats there were taken over by the nouveau riche, who proceeded to live in them all year round. This shocking state of affairs wasn't to last, though. It took 40 years, but they died out, except for one houseboat, built in 1909, that is still on adjoining Lake Union, serving today as a boat rental office. Now a new community of houseboaters is slowly emerging on Lake Union.

In Portland, Oregon, houseboats regularly moved along the Willamette River; eventually, one of the biggest collections of shantyboats—a far cry from the gilded floating palaces of San Francisco—grew up in the appropriately named Scowtown. In 1906 the humble houseboats of Middle Scowtown (one of three sites) were ordered moved for the development of wharves, just as their Belvedere cousins had been.

Oregon, too, had its season when the wealthy came out onto the Willamette. *Raysark*, for example, was a houseboat of 2,240 square feet, in which, "In 1903, a few select friends were invited to join the *Raysark* on a maiden voyage. She was towed from Portland, over the swirling waters of the Columbia River Gorge, through the Government Locks to a summer home near Lyle, Washington. A 178-mile excursion, just to find 'picturesque' surroundings!" wrote Ben Dennis in *Houseboat.*

Earlier, the houseboat *Vagabondia* had traveled 350 miles, from Jacksonville, Florida, to Lake Washington at the head of St. Johns River. She then journeyed another 96 miles to Mosquito Inlet, but not by tow: The houseboat was equipped with a recessed stern wheel, "which style is necessary in order to successfully navigate the narrow and tortuous rivers."

Meanwhile, on the other side of the continent, houseboats were definitely *de rigueur* for those who could afford them. The sedentary used stationary houseboats as floating summer cottages, while more adventurous folks explored the coastline from Louisiana to Maine in waterborne mobile homes. "It is not surprising that in Florida we should find the highest type of houseboats . . . with a jolly company on board, the owner of a Florida houseboat snaps his fingers at the crowded hotels and pursues his even way through the beautiful backwaters," enthused *Munsey's Magazine* in 1906.

Albert B. Hunt wrote in *Houseboats and Houseboating*, ". . . it is down on the Indian River, however, that one may find a houseboat colony flourishing under ideal conditions, and, in its social features, coming

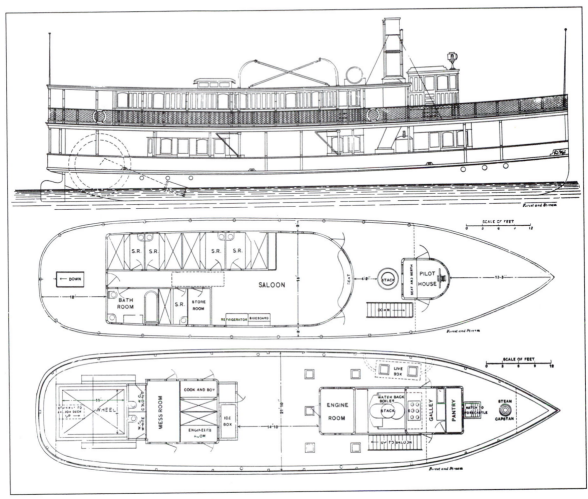

Figure 1-4. Outboard profile and cabin and deck plans for *Vagabondia.*

nearer to the houseboat life on the Thames. . . . Since the time when the late Pierre Lorillard towed the first houseboat into those waters, a whole fleet of craft has sprung up. . . . The more venturesome of the houseboatmen, when they have grown weary of the quiet of the sluggish lagoon, trail out into the ocean and thence to Lake Worth and into Biscayne Bay, through the Cards Sound and along the tropic shores of Key Largo . . . rounding Northwest Cape and floating into the White River Bay, and from there right into the heart of the Everglades."

Pierre Lorillard's first houseboat was eventually destroyed by fire, but he immediately ordered another from a New York boatbuilder. The 125-foot-long *Nirodha* displaced 137 tons and had two decks, two modern 20 h.p. engines, an electrical generator, and separate rooms for the doctor, captain, cooks, servants, waiters, and steward, as well as five staterooms for guests.

Mr. Lorillard had an interesting extended family, as remembered by Joseph Parsons in "Excerpts from Recollections of Wassaw Island," a private memoir: "Once when I was a young lad my father sent me down to the South End with a gift of game to Mr. Lorillard, whose yacht was lying there, and when I explained my errand, he asked me aboard and introduced me to his companion, Mr. Baldwin, and also to two young ladies as his cousins. When I got back and told my father and mother that I had met aboard the yacht Mr. Lorillard's two nice young lady cousins, I realized by the twinkling of eyes they exchanged that there was something funny about those cousins."

A few houseboats in the fleet of craft in these Southern waters scorned gasoline or steam engines in favor of traditional sails. *Savanilla*, built in 1903, was 84 feet long and 24 feet wide, yet needed only 2½ feet of water for her inland cruising. Her topsail schooner rig made her a beautiful sight when under way—and comfortable at anchor. A compatriot, the 87-foot houseboat *Clarina*, had been built in 1865 as the topsail schooner *William Butman*. In 1900 she was converted into a stately houseboat with six

Figure 1-5. Savanilla, a sailing houseboat.

staterooms and four cabins for crew. To provide for all amusements, a bicycle room was fitted between the sail room and the chart room, with space for five or six of the wildly popular new machines.

The shallow waters of the southern coast demanded that any houseboat be shallow in draft. *Whim Wham*, for example, a 91-foot-long vessel with two accommodation levels and a promenade deck, drew but 30 inches of water, while the 90-foot-long (including stern-wheel paddle), two-storied *Buckeye*, with a roof garden on the upper deck complete with potted palms, orchids, wicker furniture, and hammocks, drew only 26 inches.

Figure 1-6. **Whim Wham, a large motorized houseboat.**

> **B**ut the Florida coast is only one of many regions. . . . Within twenty-five miles of the New York City Hall, there is ten times the extent of coast line available for houseboating. . . . An ideal place for a houseboat is on Barnegat Bay, where there are miles of landlocked water. . . . There are already a good many houseboats in this region, and new ones are added every year.

Another sailing houseboat plied Great South Bay. *Sommerheim*, built in 1897, hoisted a yawl rig for extended cruising. She was not a yacht, but a 20- by 70-foot, three-bedroom house that happened to have a mast through the roof, and a mizzenmast astern.

Figure 1-7. **Sommerheim, a beamy sailing houseboat on the Great South Bay.**

The Ohio and Illinois rivers have their houseboats. A favorite home of the summer houseboat is on Georgian Bay and among the Thousand Islands of the St. Lawrence River. Some of these houseboats, both on Georgian and Alexandria Bays, are most elaborately appointed and decorated, and really are quite equal to many a summer villa or cottage.

Houseboats were everywhere. In Buffalo, New York, at the Niagara border, an artist purchased a discarded Erie Canal cable boat, named his new houseboat *Bohemian*, had it pulled by horse to Albany (in the English manner), then towed down the Hudson River to New York—the artist sitting at his easel, under canvas awning, sketching the passing parade as he drifted along.

There are a large number of houseboats on the Shrewsbury River, and each year there will be additions to the fleet. . . . On the Shrewsbury, at Pattersons Cove, in the vicinity of Little Silver, there have been houseboats for many years. Lake Hopatcong is another place where houseboats are yearly built and occupied. . . .

The boats are pretty and comfortable, but cottagers are very properly exacting about pollution of the lake, so that disposal of waste is a serious problem. Up along the shores of the Sound, on the Long Island and Connecticut coasts 'the house on logs' is frequently to be observed. Where only a few boats were to be seen five years ago, today there are scores; showing that the fad, if the sport can be so called, is growing rapidly.

Large, mobile houseboats cruised the Chesapeake Bay and Long Island Sound, like 100-foot *Rancocas*, and *Ruffhouse*, which was 96 feet overall. These spacious, extremely comfortable houseboats—on a par with today's millionaire yachts—dwarfed their working-class cousins to the south, where functional vessels drifted down rivers like the Ohio, the Cumberland, or the Tennessee.

Figure 1-8. *Ruffhouse*, a gasoline-powered houseboat.

In the early 1800s, pioneers made their way into the Midwest aboard rough-hewn flatboats. Many of these boats were dismantled on arrival, to be rebuilt as the settlers' first cabins. The ones left intact, and lived on afloat, were the precursors of what we call *shantyboats* today—part traveling home, part livelihood, usually exotic. As the liveaboard owners settled, the shantyboats grew into houseboats, until by the end of the century, as Hunt noted, "In the Middle West, where the waters are sheltered, houseboats are not by any means an unknown quantity. Several very elaborate and comfortable craft with numerous smaller boats are anchored on the beautiful lake, Minnetonka. The Mississippi, whose strong current is somewhat of an obstacle to happy houseboating, has nevertheless one of the handsomest houseboats in this country. A wealthy lumberman has had built for him a luxurious summer home, and propelled by a sternwheeler steamer. All through the summer this houseboat, filled with jolly parties of guests, wends its way up and down the great river, anchoring where whim suggests, moving on when will dictates."

That houseboat was *Idler*, owned by Mr. Lafayette Lamb. Although *Idler* was some 117 feet long, she drew a phenomenally scant 1 foot 9 inches. Spectators might have been excused if they presumed she had an engine, for two stacks protruded from the stern awnings. In fact, one was a vent for the kitchen, while the other was from a steam boiler that ran the electrical plant, heated the rooms and the bath hot water, and drove the filtering pumps. The sternwheel steamer *Wanderer* was used very rarely to push the houseboat along, for the heat and smoke of the former were deemed most disagreeable.

DEPRESSION ERA

All these jolly parties were soon to be rudely interrupted, however. The Depression that started in the back offices of Wall Street brokers and spread around the world sounded a deathknell for the ostentatious enjoyment of wealth that had been displayed on the rivers and bays. The floating summer homes of the formerly wealthy were sold or left to decay on their winter moorings.

Ironically, these deserted playgrounds were appropriated by refugees from the collapse. The newly poor needed homes, and they quickly set about building them. Shantytowns sprang up in various waterways on both sides of the continent, but these houseboat dwellers were a hardier lot. They lived aboard their boats through summer and winter alike, and adapted to the demands that the seasons made upon them. The ice surrounding *Nomad* would have dampened the spirits of any jolly party goer.

Canadians, in an earlier century, also lived aboard houseboats. The waterways of British Columbia were used as highways to float logs to sawmills, and it was realized that a number of logs could be strapped together, creating a very stable platform—a platform that could support ample, mobile accommodations for workers. Soon houses, stores, depots, and even hotels plied the waterways. The lumberjacks were joined by their wives and children, and eventually there were whole neighborhoods afloat.

Houseboat colonies were well established on Kootenay Lake in Kootenay National Park by the turn of the century, having been conceived and built by the railroad companies to attract hunters, fishermen, and anyone else wanting to rough it in comfort—after arriving, of course, by rail.

Figure 1-9. Nomad.

Figure 1-10. A houseboat on Kootenay Lake.

In their heyday, more than 100 small communities of houseboats were scattered throughout the vast waterways of British Columbia. When the Depression came to Canada such communities flourished, just as they did in the United States. The largest gathering was in False Creek, Vancouver. In his book *Houseboat*, Ben Dennis reported the result of a 1938 survey carried out by Vancouver City: "Population ever-growing. More than two hundred houseboats at present. Some four hundred and fifty adults and one hundred children. . . . The people contacted seem contented and happy, most of them expressed satisfaction at living on the waterfront and a desire to remain there. There was apparently no sickness anywhere!"

WAR'S END

If the Depression flung the needy out onto the water, so did the conflagration of World War II. At war's end, veterans built houseboats in England and North America from surplus landing craft and barrage-balloon barges. Perhaps afflicted with what we would recognize today as post-traumatic stress disorder, many were disinclined to settle down immediately, but were drawn to the healing effects of life afloat. The Bohemian lifestyle, with its attendant questioning of established values, was being forged.

This memo, from Herbert M. Corse to a Lieutenant Commander at the naval fleet base at Green Cove Springs, Florida, offered a partial solution to the problem of housing demobilized service personnel:

A Proposal to Develop a Type of Houseboat; first, to assist in relieving the present housing shortage, and subsequently, to use as privately-owned recreation units on coastal and inland waterways.

The establishment of the U.S. Navy Reserve Fleet Base at Green Cove Springs, Fla. on the St. Johns River has produced an acute housing shortage in the area extending as far as Palatka, St. Augustine, and Jacksonville.

It is proposed that Navy Surplus boats and barges of approximately 45 to 50 feet in length be converted into living units for married couples. These quarters would be a floating counterpart of the automobile house car trailers, some of which are now in use in Navy housing. For economic use of a given length and breadth, the houseboat has an advantage over the trailer in that it can be made 2-storied by using a canopy covered upper deck.

The docking facilities necessary for a houseboat community would consist primarily of shallow water docks from which connection for electricity and water could be made to the houseboats. . . . Sites near the mouths of tributary streams and highway bridges appear especially suitable. If such sites are developed by the Navy for houseboat communities, they could be passed on to the National Park Service or the State Park Commission.

Ultimately the houseboats should be sold to private individuals. . . . It will help develop the health of the future generations of prospective Navy personnel.

Meanwhile, the damming of inland rivers, like the Ohio and the Tennessee, had created a whole series of huge lakes that were ideal for houseboats. By the end of the 1950s, small, self-contained houseboats—the type popularized by *Popular Mechanics* magazine and designer William W. Atkins—were everywhere.

These easy-to-build houseboats, intended primarily as small but comfortable retreats, eclipsed and eventually replaced some of the cruder shantyboats that had wandered the rivers—but not all of them, as evidenced by this contemporary reminiscence by James R. Babb, editor and guardian angel of this volume: "I grew up on the Tennessee River, and serious houseboaters—River Rats was the pejorative local term for them—were my friends and idols when I was a kid. Many of the shantyboaters in my hometown were retired steamboat captains who lived on the decaying remnants of their old commands. One guy had moved an old log cabin onto a barge; another had just the pilothouse from a steamboat nailed down to

(continued on page 18)

Figure 1-11. Coolwater, **featured in** *Modern Mechanix* **magazine.**

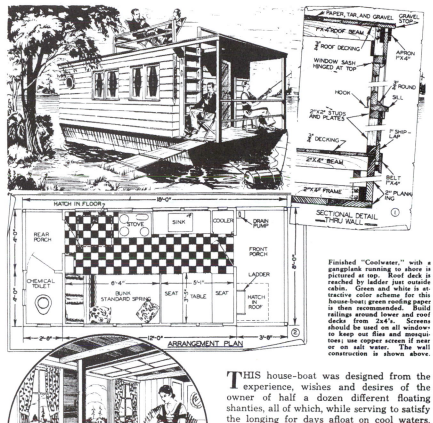

Vacation In A Houseboat

Spend next summer on a houseboat. "Coolwater" can be built for about seventy dollars, including all furnishings, by careful selection of materials.

PAPER, TAR, AND GRAVEL   GRAVEL STOP
1"X 4" ROOF BEAM
¾" ROOF DECKING
WINDOW SASH HINGED AT TOP
APRON 1"X4"
HOOK
¾" ROUND
SILL
2"X 2" STUDS AND PLATES
¾" DECKING
1" SHIP-LAP
2"X4" BEAM
BELT 1"X4"
2"X4" FRAME
2" PLANKING

SECTIONAL DETAIL THRU WALL   ①

ARRANGEMENT PLAN

HATCH IN FLOOR   18'-0"
STOVE   SINK   COOLER   DRAIN PUMP
REAR PORCH
FRONT PORCH
CHEMICAL TOILET
LADDER
BUNK STANDARD SPRING   6'-4"   SEAT   TABLE   5'-1"   SEAT   HATCH IN ROOF
2'-8"   12'-0"   3'-8"
8'-0"
②

Finished "Coolwater," with a gangplank running to shore is pictured at top. Roof deck is reached by ladder just outside cabin. Green and white is attractive color scheme for this house-boat; green roofing paper is then recommended. Build railings around lower and roof decks from 2x4's. Screens should be used on all windows to keep out flies and mosquitoes; use copper screen if near or on salt water. The wall construction is shown above.

One corner of "Coolwater" house-boat showing kitchen range, sink, icebox. Windows are hinged to swing upward.

METAL SHIELD   ③

THIS house-boat was designed from the experience, wishes and desires of the owner of half a dozen different floating shanties, all of which, while serving to satisfy the longing for days afloat on cool waters, did not entirely fill the requirements of one who likes to spend long lazy days under the water willows in the summer and busy days scouring the marshes for wildfowl during the winter. The house-boat *Coolwater* fills these requirements nicely.

It combines a maximum of comfort with a minimum of expense—a good vacation boat.

Coolwater will afford pleasure and profit to the whole family, as a permanent or temporary mooring can be found in almost any marsh or along a beautiful river bank free of

107

Figure 1-11
continued.

Slide Finished Houseboat Into Water on Skids

charge. There is no property to buy and no taxes to pay. If the owner will do the work of simple carpentry himself, it will be hard to find a better way to spend the 60 or 70 dollars that it costs to build and furnish this craft. First decide on your building and launching site, which need not, of course, be permanent as an outboard motor and a skiff can easily move a boat of this size.

We start with two sides of the scow, 2x6's and 2x12's clear lumber, backed as shown in Fig. 8. Get this lumber sided and edged and it will come about 1½ inches thick. The edges must be fitted very neatly and dressed with a slight bevel to allow for the caulking. The two frames come next, Fig. 8. These are built up of 2x4's rough lumber. Use only galvanized spikes and nails in all construction unless you care to go to the expense of

galvanized bolts. Now lay your frames and sides upside down on a flat level place and put on your end planking. Don't forget to notch out the limber holes, as in Fig. 5, to

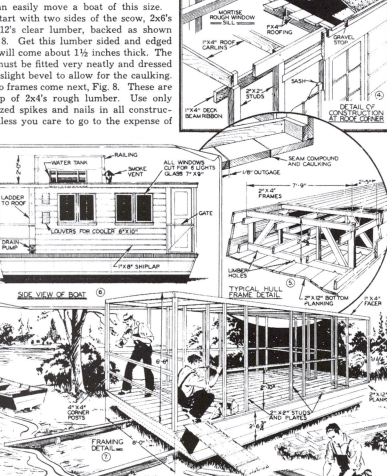

Build houseboat on shore, then slide into water on skids as shown above. Other sketches show details of roof and frame construction. Chemical refrigerator will be found ideal for "Coolwater," but ordinary icebox is simplest where only week-end visits are made. Use lever to slide boat onto the skids. Grease the skids where shoreline has little pitch.

Figure 1-11
continued.

"Coolwater" Bunk Takes Standard Size Spring

Pump is needed to pump out bilge water. Design shown above is easy to build, and will be found satisfactory for this purpose. Keep piston and chamber oiled.

allow for all leakage to drain to the pump, before putting on the bottom planking.

The general way to make scows waterproof is to caulk the seams with long strips of oakum and then run hot tar all over the inside and up to the water line on the outside. A half a barrel of tar, an old mop and an iron bucket are all you'll need. Keep the tar bubbling hot and brush it well into all corners and seams.

Now lay your decking, not forgetting the hatch and pump hole, and you are ready for the house. The 2x2 plates are laid first. The studs and upper plates are laid out on the floor and the door and window openings framed in before you raise the walls. The rafters are sawed from 1x4 hard pine, giving about a 1½ inch pitch to the roof. The roof, Fig. 4, is covered with 1x4 tongue and groove boards, and tar and gravel roofing paper in a color to match your final paint scheme.

The house is sheeted with 1x8 shiplap trimmed out flush with the window and door openings. The corners are mitered or covered with 1x2 battens. ¾-inch quarter-rounds serve as stops for doors and windows. Next, put in your finished window sills and

hang your sash as shown in detail, Fig. 1. The windows swing up and can be hooked to ceiling. Screens can be hung on outside.

The doors should come next. The port lights let into them, while not absolutely necessary, give a very shippy appearance. Any glazier will cut the glass circles for you. The frames are band-sawed or fret-sawed from some soft ¾-inch material.

In the interior layout the bunk takes a full size spring and mattress. By lowering it a trifle another bunk could be built in above. Lockers under the bunk and under the seats must be ventilated or dry rot will soon set in. The cushions for the seats are made from an old pad and covered with a bright chintz to match the curtains.

A sink is very handy even if water must be carried to your boat. A shallow well dug six to ten feet from the river bank will nearly always yield good water and a tank could be mounted on the roof (see Fig. 6) with a hand pump and length of hose to pump it full. Failing that, a pair of clean 5-gallon kerosene cans with wooden handles will give you a week-end supply.

(continued from page 14)

a platform supported by oil drums. These were extremely cool people, who made their own liquor, stayed up all night fishing and coon hunting, and could expectorate a dragonfly right out of the air."

Shantyboats were unknown in England; they simply weren't the done thing. Instead, the rivers were famous for their canal boats, gaily painted in traditional patterns that indicated where each boat came from. The narrow boats that plied the country's canals carrying freight were rediscovered by the disaffected of the 1940s; as in the United States, workboat-to-houseboat conversions were common. These houseboaters set in motion the idea that dwelling in floating homes was a gypsy thing to do—it fit in well with the Bohemian, then beatnik, then hippie lifestyles.

TODAY

This counterculture aura still surrounds houseboats, but, although it is one that many houseboaters like to foster, it isn't necessarily accurate. Modern store-bought houseboats are durable, efficient, and fast, and, compared with more traditional forms of watercraft, they're even nominally affordable—at least for some. They are also extremely popular, especially in the United States. Representative houseboats of this type—known as family cruisers or coastal cruisers (which are more up-market)—are the Barracuda and the Aqua Home.

Figure 1-12. **A Barracuda houseboat in search of summer.**

Figure 1-13. **Aqua Home 460, formerly a Chris-Craft model.**

The spring 1989 issue of *Family Houseboating* included a letter from Hod's Boats, Portland, Oregon, which described a journey to Alaska and back again in a Barracuda: "Generally speaking the weather was just beautiful as was the scenery. However, crossing Queen Charlotte Sound is never easy. Going up the wind was NW at 25—swells to 7 feet and about a 3-foot chop . . . Coming back the wind was SE at 35 gusting to 45—swells to 10 to 11 feet and a good 4-foot chop . . . Jack, I don't see why people buy conventional boats when this one has every ability they have and about 50 percent more room."

On the other side of the world, in the far-flung remnants of the British Empire that had been colonial New Zealand and Australia, houseboats are still a rarity. In Australia, the original houseboats were required to navigate the many shallow waterways that riddle the eastern coast, and were usually equipped with stern- or side-paddle wheels driven by steam engines. Often, houseboats were made from retired paddle steamers, like the *P.S. Enterprise*, beached at a place called Mannum for some 30 years.

Figure 1-14. The *P.S. Enterprise*, idle at Mannum for 30 years.

Houseboats are enjoying a surge in popularity today, as Australians rediscover the pleasure of privately traveling their rivers. The only difference now is that the houseboats are made of aluminum and powered by hefty outboard or inboard/outboard motors.

Figure 1-15. A modern single-hull houseboat.

Figure 1-16. A popular twin-hull vacation houseboat.

In the late 1980s a multimillion-dollar hotel boat, a huge, grandiose thing, was anchored off Townsville, Queensland, to cater to tourism generated by the picturesque Great Barrier Reef and outlying islands. A hotel boat is a natural development of the houseboat, as are the very common restaurant boat and the very uncommon bowling-alley boat. Hotel boats regularly convey discerning vacationers up and down the network of canals in Europe today. Check in in one town, and wake up in another.

In New Zealand, local entrepreneur Alexander Hatrick had a hotel boat built in 1904 to provide accommodations for tourists traveling from the ski fields of Chateau Tongariro to the township of Wanganui. The visitors proceeded downriver by paddle steamer, navigating several whitewater rapids on the way, where the maneuvers often involved running a rapid backward and swinging the boat's bow around, halfway through. Originally moored at the mouth of the Ohura, on the Wanganui River, the hotel was later moved to the Retaruke Stream, where it would be out of the way of drifting logs and fast-flowing river currents. Electricity was brought aboard from a generator ashore. Wrote Arthur Bates in *The Pictorial History of the Wanganui River*, "It was an idyllic spot and when the weather was right the tourists loved the area and word of the attractions . . . soon spread among the intrepid Edwardian tourists. Huts were built above the flood level for the crews manning the boats. A spring supplied water which was stored in a large square tank on the roof towards the stern. The roof was covered with rubberoid. Visitors were impressed with the bird songs, peace and early morning mists."

Figure 1-17. "The Houseboat" moored at Retaruke Stream in the late 1920s.

Known simply as "the houseboat," because it was the only one in the country at the time, there were 20 two-berth cabins along the lower deck, and a dining saloon, social hall, smoking room, and lounge on the upper level. The rooms were lined with waxed native timbers, and the silver, glassware, and linen were reputedly of excellent quality. In 1933, fire overwhelmed the houseboat, and despite frantic efforts to bore holes in the hull and let the boat sink in order to extinguish the flames, it was lost.

Many houseboats have succumbed to fire, wind, or unforgiving waves, but houseboating as a unique way of life lives on. Houseboats quietly but effectively mold the human beings who live inside them into people who welcome change. The changing winds, the tides, the set of the waves, and the fluid scenery all remind the houseboater that change is the natural order of things, that he or she is but a part of the dynamo that is the world. For the houseboater, the real world is just outside the back door, lapping at the edge of the porch.

I *had no theories to prove. I merely wanted to try living by my own hands, independent as far as possible from a system of division of labor in which the participant loses most of the pleasure of making and growing things for himself. I wanted to bring in my own fuel and smell its sweet smoke as it burned on the hearth I had made. I wanted to grow my own food, catch it in the river, or forage after it. In short, I wanted to do as much as I could for myself, because I had already realized from partial experience the inexpressible joy of so doing.*

Harlan Hubbard,
Shantyboat: A River Way of Life. Lexington: The University Press of Kentucky. Copyright 1953 and 1981 by Harlan Hubbard.

CHAPTER TWO
• • • • • • • • • • • •

Staying Afloat

For the man who is cooped up in the city, amid the hustle and bustle of business life, having little chance to see the blue sky, the green fields and waters and all the beauties of nature, the houseboat will supply just the needed rest and freedom from care.

〰〰〰〰〰〰〰〰〰〰〰〰〰〰〰〰〰

For houseboaters, staying afloat, keeping the family heirlooms dry, is important. It's not easy vacuuming the lounge if fish are nibbling away at your toes or crabs, eyes atwinkle, are inching toward them. The fastest, most convenient, and definitely the most economical way to keep a house afloat is to build a raft, like Huckleberry Finn. Under the raft, anything buoyant can be stuffed. A stroll along a riverbank or beach will reveal the remarkable variety of flotsam and jetsam that drifts around on the waves— things like bottles and cans, plastic, chips of GRP, driftwood—all subject to the physical law that if it weighs less than an equivalent volume of water, anything will float. Nothing floats because it wants to; it's the weight of the object in relation to the weight of the water it displaces that determines its buoyancy.

If a bathtub with a plug in the plughole were pushed into a lake, it would float. Most of the volume of the bathtub would be air, which is relatively weightless. The volume of water *displaced* would be heavier than the weight of the air-filled tub, and the tub would have enough buoyancy to float. Remove the plug, however, and the bathtub would lose the air within it as the water coming in the plughole forced it out. The tub would sink, but not because of the incoming water; it's the air going out the top that does it. If the air were trapped, as it would be if the bathtub had a lid welded on, then the container would remain afloat.

There's one more condition at work in our floating fixture scenario: the weight of the container, which must be deducted from the total buoyancy. The net buoyancy of a lead can, for instance, would be less than that of a plastic one of identical size. They might both hold the same volume of air, but lead weighs more than plastic, so the buoyancy of the cans is different.

AIR

As any sailor will tell you, it is imperative to keep the air trapped inside anything intended to float. The houseboat in Figure 2-1 illustrates what happens when water unexpectedly replaces air. The raft-type hull was

Figure 2-1. The dangers, albeit rare, of a single-hull houseboat. When water forces entry, down she goes.

kept afloat by trapped air, but when gale-force winds spilled the boat to one side, the air spilled out with predictable result.

For an object to float reliably, air must be contained. There are three ways in which to accomplish this: Use materials like freshly felled logs or blocks of Styrofoam, which have air trapped inside them in minute cells; seal air inside appropriate materials, using fiberglass or concrete; or inject air into something like a rubber tube. This gives us three options:

- cellular air
- quantitative air
- compressed air

Cellular

Tree trunks, felled and turned into trimmed logs, are the most universally used natural means of flotation. In pre-plastic North America, cedar logs were the most common choice. As they slowly became waterlogged, a fresh log or two would be rolled underneath—an occasion to hang out balloons and have a party. Some houseboats acquired, over the decades, inverted pyramids of logs beneath them.

Once a log dragged laboriously into the water starts to float, it becomes frisky and easy to maneuver. We can work out what a log should support by deducting the weight of an equivalent volume of water from its own weight. Formulas for volume are scattered throughout the ensuing pages.

The Buoyancy of Timbers
Deduct the equivalent volume of water, which is 64 lbs./cu.ft. for seawater, and 60 lbs./cu.ft. for fresh (or rain) water, from the weight of the volume of timber.

Timber	Weight/cu.ft.
Ash (fresh)	52.81
Ash (seasoned)	43.12
Beech (fresh)	53.37
Beech (seasoned)	43.12
Birch	49.50
Box	60.00
Cedar (fresh)	56.81
Cedar (seasoned)	47.06

Timber	Weight/cu.ft.
Elm (seasoned)	36.75
Fir (New England)	34.56
Fir (Riga)	47.06
Mahogany	50.00
Oak (English)	58.37
Oak (Africa)	60.75
Pine (fresh)	28.81
Teak	41.06
Walnut	41.94

Admiral Sir Frederick Bedford, *The Sailor's Pocket Book: A Collection of Practical Rules, Notes, and Tables, for the Use of The Royal Navy, The Mercantile Marine, and Yacht Squadrons.* Portsmouth: Griffin and Co., 1898.

In *The Sailor's Pocket Book: A Collection of Practical Rules, Notes, and Tables, for the Use of The Royal Navy, The Mercantile Marine, and Yacht Squadrons*, Admiral Sir Frederick Bedford of Portsmouth wrote in 1898, "To calculate the floating power of spars: To ascertain the weight, multiply the square of the mean diameter in inches by 0.7854 to find the area; multiply the area by the length to find the cubic contents; and the product by the weight of a cubic foot of the material." This information-packed book was too thick and heavy to carry in a pocket, but it did provide some esoteric cases—for example, a floating topmast of Norwegian pine, 64 feet long and 21 inches in diameter, would support 4,293.5 pounds if floating. Any reader with access to nonnative (and thus choppable with a moderately clear conscience) forest may find this method of flotation most convenient and economical.

Styrofoam, a lightweight material encapsulating millions of tiny air pockets, is used as the base, or core, in surfboards, life buoys, and even yachts, and makes wonderful floats. Uncovered Styrofoam will slowly absorb water, however, so to avoid having a houseboat sink, common practice is to sheath an entire block with a nonporous covering—anything that keeps water out and air in. Fiberglass, coal tar, and concrete are often used for this purpose. The procedure is straightforward: The material is sprayed, rollered, brushed, or plastered all over the Styrofoam block and allowed to cure, dry, or harden. The process is then repeated on the bottom, after which the block is ready to be pushed into the water. At least one Canadian manufacturer produces off-the-shelf concrete-encased Styrofoam pontoons for houseboats.

Quantitative

If the block of Styrofoam is replaced with nothing but air, we still have the buoyancy that keeps things afloat. We have a hull. We can build a house upon that hull, and we have a houseboat. The hull has to be watertight and is often subdivided into partitions, or watertight bulkheads, each of which is sealed off from the other. Should water find a way in, it will only compromise one partition, so long as the partitions go all the way to the deck. (The ill-fated *Titanic* was designed with so many watertight compartments that she was called "unsinkable," but the ice mountain that ripped her open gave the seas access to too many compartments. If the tear had not been quite so long, she would have survived. There's no such thing as a guarantee on water.) Access may be made to each independent compartment for inspection and/or pumping out, and this is sound boatbuilding practice.

Wood, fiberglass, concrete, or steel hulls offer mobility along the lines of a conventional motor vessel, like a period Egyptian houseboat or a more sedentary concrete pontoon houseboat. Twin hulls can also be used. Figure 2-4 shows a houseboat being built over two box-shaped plywood hulls.

Figure 2-2. The Egyptian houseboat *Dahabiyeh Scarab* in 1905.

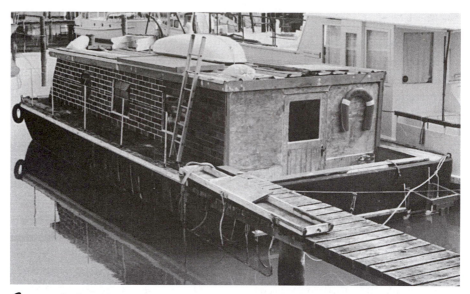

Figure 2-3. **Concrete hull and brick veneer, Milford, New Zealand.**

Figure 2-4. **Twin plywood hulls serve as flotation.**

There are, however, qualifications for this hull business. A houseboat, like any boat, has to be built properly. Who knows where it'll end up? If it found itself flexing in ocean waves, would it know how to hold itself together? In thus entering the realms of you-have-to-know-what-you're-doing boatbuilding, the reader is best advised to refer to the early works of Bill Atkins, *Popular Mechanics* magazine, or the books listed in the bibliography. The initial chapter of Harlan Hubbard's *Shantyboat* includes details of his shantyboat's hull.

The humble bathtub has great potential: A number of them may be fitted beneath a wooden frame and permanently bracketed or bolted into place. To purchase a quantity of new bathtubs, however, would be expensive, and the money would be better spent on one hull, or on barrels. But who knows; the reader may work in a bathtub factory.

Steel pipes, welded closed at each end, can be used for flotation, especially under a houseboat intended to be motored frequently from place to place. (As soon as a steel pipe is pushed into the water, it's called a pontoon if it floats—or a spud if it doesn't.) Enquiries at a steel-welding pipe manufacturer may prove worthwhile. Several lengths of 3-foot-diameter pipe may provide just the strength you're looking for. Alternatively, concrete drainage pipes, suitably capped at each end, or a great many large-diameter PVC pipes, could be used to support the raft.

Steel buoys, welded together like giant marbles, are a popular option. A frame is built above the buoys to lay the raft platform on, and then the house can be built according to whim. Buoys were originally built to mark channels and other navigational need-to-knows for ships; they'll stay afloat. Figure 2-5 shows a welded structure of framework and buoys being moved to a waterway with a forklift. Note the steel struts welded on top to frame the house.

Figure 2-5. **Another source of flotation—steel buoys welded together.**

Compressed

Compressed air has the virtue of permitting the deflation, collapse, and transportation of whatever it has been pumped into; for example, inflatable fairground playrooms, or, more simply, an inner tube that is thrown into water and sat upon. This option should be contemplated by designers who are already experimenting with inflatable tents and small houses.

The compartments beneath an inflatable houseboat would need to be made of a durable material if the houseboat were intended to settle periodically on a foreshore. A reliable air compressor would also need to be carried aboard. When the materials have been developed, there can be no doubt that this may prove to be a very worthwhile, transportable form of housing. Until then, we're stuck with what we've got, and if that means inner tubes, say, from tractors or trucks, then why not? Their only immediate drawback is the potential damage from sand, shingle, or rocks on the seashore—and in the owner being laughed at.

BARRELS

The same building process will apply no matter what flotation is installed beneath the raft, and the reader is encouraged to experiment with any form of getting—and staying—afloat. But because it's the cheapest and easiest for most of us, the option we'll use is to strap together a great many independent compartments, each automatically insulated from the other, interchangeable, replaceable, and economically obtained—barrels, in other words. Forty-four-gallon, 55-gallon, and 60-gallon barrels are common, but any readily available size will do.

Barrels are very efficient at trapping air. Since they are designed to transport everything from diesel fuel to wine—none of which can be allowed to seep out—barrels are leak-proof. And because the average houseboat sits atop a great many barrels, your buoyancy eggs are distributed into many baskets.

Steel barrels are the cheapest option; however, they will eventually rust away. Where wind and water meet, there is enough readily replaced oxygen being thrown promiscuously about to equip the intensive-care unit of any hospital. Oxygen is one of the most corrosive elements known, and it will attack steel houseboat barrels with glee. Not only do the drums deteriorate, but flakes of rust fall into the mud and sand, poisoning the benign environment where miniscule creepy-crawlies used to live, before the kamikaze debris started raining down. If you have acquired a houseboat with steel drums, they'll undoubtedly need replacing soon. If you are building a new houseboat and choose steel for reasons of economy, you are

Figure 2-6. Barrels beneath a raft frame support the 54-foot houseboat shown in Figure 2-7.

Figure 2-7. Houseboat *Jessica* in Rangihoua Stream, Waiheke Island, New Zealand.

simply putting off the painful necessity of opening your wallet and buying plastic barrels, which will last as long as the houseboat does.

Please consider plastic as a friendly alternative right from the start. Stainless steel barrels used in the dairy industry are equally good, but they're expensive. Ordinary plastic barrels are readily found, and they are strong and durable. Due to their rounded shape, they will support the weight of a house, on the shore or afloat. The plastic barrel compresses as load is applied; that is, it transfers the load away along its curve, rather than attempting to support the weight in one place and then breaking, like a flat surface will. All a plastic barrel requires in the way of consideration is that it be placed out of, or protected from, the direct rays of the sun: Ultraviolet light will eventually weaken the material and cause it to become brittle. That should not be a problem with houseboats, for the barrels are placed underneath the raft, in the shade.

Capacity

When Archimedes sat in his bath, soap in hand, and noticed how water slopped over the rim, he suddenly realized that the volume of his body had displaced an equal volume of water; if he could measure the water so displaced, then by inference, he would know the volume of his body. We still use that discovery today. By measuring the volume of air in one of our barrels (if they're all about the same size) we can find out what volume of water it will displace. We have two alternatives for measuring the volume: gallons or cubic feet.

Gallons

Technically, one Imperial gallon of distilled water, measured at 62 degrees Fahrenheit, weighs 10 pounds. A U.S. gallon of water weighs 8.342 pounds. If we know the gallon capacity of a barrel (or of any other kind of container), all we have to do is multiply by 8.342 (or 10, depending on your relative distance from imperialism) to find the weight of the volume of water the barrel will hold, which is the same as the volume of water displaced, which is the same as the weight the empty barrel will support. In a word, its buoyancy. To make the math easier, we'll use Imperial gallons for our calculations; multiply by 8.342 to find the equivalent in U.S. gallons.

If a 20-gallon barrel full of fresh water weighs 200 pounds, an empty 20-gallon barrel will have a buoyancy of 200 pounds; a 44-gallon barrel will have a buoyancy of 440 pounds; a 60-gallon barrel will have a buoyancy of 600 pounds; a 200-gallon barrel will have a buoyancy of 2,000 pounds. Easy, isn't it?

Because of its salt content, seawater is a little more buoyant than fresh water, but not by much; the difference is less than 6.7 percent.

Cubic feet

A cubic foot of fresh water weighs about 60 pounds (actually, it's 62.39816 pounds, Imperial or otherwise, for those who care), and the same amount of seawater weighs about 64 pounds. Therefore, if we displace one cubic foot of water, we will have a buoyancy of the same amount—it will take 64 pounds of houseboat to push aside one cubic foot of the ocean.

There are only a few formulas we'll need for finding volume in cubic feet, as described in these "useful rules in mensuration" in the aforementioned *The Sailor's Pocket Book*: "IV. To find the volume of a cylinder, the diameter and length being given. Multiply the square of the diameter by .7854, to get the area of the section, and then multiply this area by the length. . . . VI. To find the volume of a sphere. Multiply the cube of the diameter by .5236, and the product will be the volume required. VII. To find the volume of a cone. Proceed as in IV, and divide the result by three."

These formulas are used to find the volume of a buoy or a barrel and then to figure its buoyancy. A rectangular block's volume equals length times breadth times depth. Some examples:

I: A Styrofoam block 30 feet long by 15 feet wide by 4 feet deep.

Volume   = Length × Breadth × Depth
           = 30 × 15 × 4
           = 1,800 cubic feet
Buoyancy   = Volume × Weight of seawater
           = 1,800 × 64
           = 115,200
           = 57.6 tons (51.43 long tons)

II: An 8-foot-diameter steel buoy.

Volume   = Cube of Diameter × 0.5236
           = (8 × 8 × 8) × 0.5236
           = 512 × 0.5236
           = 268.08 cubic feet
Buoyancy   = 268.08 × 64
           = 17,157.12 pounds
           = 8.58 tons (7.657 long tons)

III.   A barrel 4 feet long by 2 feet in diameter.

Volume   = Square of Diameter × 0.7854 × Length
                      = (2 × 2) × 0.7854 × 4
                      = 4 × 3.1416
                      = 12.566 cubic feet
Buoyancy   = 12.566 × 64
                      = 804.22 ÷ 2,000 pounds
                      = 0.40 tons (.36 long tons)

If we wanted to be persnickety about it, we could convert cubic volume into gallons to double-check our figures, by multiplying cubic feet by 144 to get cubic inches and then dividing by 277.27: "To calculate the capacity of a cask, multiply half the sum of the areas of the two inferior circles, viz, at the head and bung, by the interior length, for the contents in cubic inches; which, divided by 277.27 (the number of cubic inches in a gallon) reduces the result to that measure." It hardly seems worth the bother, though.

Application

One 60-gallon barrel will support 640 pounds of houseboat in seawater, and 600 pounds in fresh water. A quarter of a ton is a lot of weight, but that represents a barrel totally immersed. We want half immersion. So, dividing our buoyancy in half, we can reckon on supporting 320 pounds per barrel in seawater, and 300 pounds in fresh water.

Number of barrels	Seawater	Fresh water
10	1.43 tons	1.34 tons
20	2.86 tons	2.68 tons
30	4.29 tons	4.02 tons
40	5.71 tons	5.36 tons
50	7.14 tons	6.70 tons
60	8.57 tons	8.04 tons
70	10.00 tons	9.38 tons

Table 2-1. **Buoyancy of 60-pound Barrels (in long tons, 2,240 pounds).**

Thus, if we were to build a raft with a house that weighed about 5 tons, then we could float it easily with 40, 60-gallon barrels. For that matter, we could use 40, 44-gallon barrels. We would ride in the water a little over the halfway mark of each barrel—our own Plimsoll lines—but we still could have a wild party aboard, with lots of people eating and pushing each other overboard, and not worry about sinking.

Fortunately, the builder does not have to weigh the houseboat before building the raft. It just so happens that the weight of the average single-level houseboat is well supported, at half-immersion of the barrels, with a barrel for every 3 feet of length and 4 to 5 feet of width (Figure 2-6 shows this arrangement). Thus, for every 12 to 15 square feet of raft area, we

Figure 2-8. A secluded spot for *Home Life,* 1905.

should allocate one barrel. An average raft of perhaps 40 feet by 15 feet is 600 square feet, which would require 40 to 50 barrels. The whole thing would probably weigh, if built as in the ensuing chapters, between 15,000 and 17,000 pounds.

But don't become cavalier. Weight should be minimized in a houseboat. Strict building codes designed to withstand earthquakes ashore have no relevance on the water. The codes that govern good boat construction *demand* lightweight building materials.

Strength will be built into the houseboat by other means than the use of massive materials. For one thing, the rooms will be smaller than those of a house ashore, and the walls correspondingly more efficient at holding the structure together. The roof will be lighter and spread over a smaller area. Nonetheless, framing and construction codes are imitated where applicable, for they are sensible when properly adapted to the sea.

CHAPTER THREE

Room to Breathe

To the artist or the lover of nature this kind of boat furnishes a summer home that can always have a change of scene—new landscapes, fresh views of the water, beautiful sunsets, and an unequalled chance to study the heavens on starry nights, at peace with all worldly thoughts, free from the noise and turmoil of the madding crowd. The placid waters furnish a natural park that you can enjoy as though you were the possessor of the mighty acres of an earldom.

Houseboats, because they are not designed primarily for navigation, can be as spacious, flamboyant, wayward, awkward, and bizarre as imagination allows. If you want a home with a sunken swimming pool or a discotheque or a movie theater aboard, like Sam Sardinia's converted 200-foot car ferry, last seen heading for Florida, then more power to you.

What you get is what you put down on paper before you start building, so it's worth taking the time to think through what you need. To feed your imagination, check out the enormous variety of accommodation layouts for launches, yachts (particularly catamarans), recreational vehicles, trailer homes, and even cottages. Pilfer freely, mixing and matching ideas as you like. A few representative plans are scattered throughout this book, but because space is limited and tastes differ, we'll concentrate on providing the bare essentials. How the elements get put together will be up to you.

ESSENTIALS

A houseboat needs spaces for lounging and sleeping, for cooking and eating, for storage, and for attending to one's private toilette. In a land house, that means a lounge, a bedroom, a kitchen, a dining room, cupboards, and a powder room. Sometimes, on land as well as afloat, these spaces are rolled together and made to do several things at different times. Recreational vehicles, trailers, and yachts often contain good examples of multiple-use spaces: For instance, a dining table may drop down to form a double bed in what was a lounge—and a cupboard may appear, as if by magic, from beneath it.

As Albert B. Hunt noted, "A large houseboat is far more comfortable than any large craft even approaching it in size. It is 'house' first and 'boat' next. In other words, no room is taken up with propelling machinery, stores, keel, shaft, masts or other things needed in a yacht. All the space goes to accommodation." If we can utilize that space to its maximum advantage, then so much the better. We'll have comfort and room to breathe.

Lounge

The bigger the better, especially if surrounded by windows. Otherwise, a cozy and snug feeling can be induced in smaller areas. We want space for one armchair as an absolute minimum, with another chair, or better yet a settee, for visitors. A fireplace, potbelly stove, or chip oven will create a cheerful atmosphere and ensure a warm and dry environment. A stereo, television, and ship-to-shore radio or cellular telephone provide links with the outside world.

Figure 3-1.
The luxury of
a living room
aboard a
Kashmiri
holiday
houseboat.

Figure 3-2.
Opulence is
clearly indicated
in the interior of
a period
American
houseboat.

Figure 3-3. **A compact, slightly more functional kitchen in a—how to put it—budget-conscious houseboat.**

Top it off with bookshelves and indoor plants, odd pieces of furniture like sideboards or harpsichords, barometers and the obligatory prints of sailing boats on the wall, and tide charts and binoculars and wind-up clocks. And don't forget a basket for the dog.

Bedroom(s)

This is the inner sanctum, where the cares of the day can be put aside. An average double bed is 6 feet 6 inches by 4 feet 6 inches, and a single bed is 6 feet 6 inches by 3 feet. You might want a portmanteau, dressing table, armoire, or wardrobe; these are usually about 3 feet wide, but measure before lugging anything aboard. When allocating space, which we'll get to, allow room for drawers and doors to be opened. A wardrobe against the bed is useless if you have to jigsaw an access hole through the top. Shelves for books, knickknacks, candle stubs, and the like are essential. A mirror on the wall can be used to give the illusion of greater space.

An opening window or other form of ventilation is desirable. Oxygen depletion in the middle of the night is not pleasant, especially for children. They can be troublesome enough as it is.

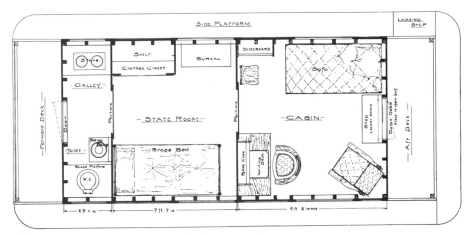

Figure 3-4. **Hostess, an English narrow boat.**

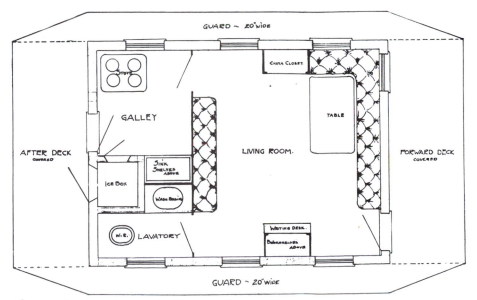

Figure 3-5. **Kelpie, a chubby American craft.**

Figure 3-6.
**Interior
arrangement
of a 25-foot
shantyboat on
a scow, 36 feet
long and 12 feet
wide.**

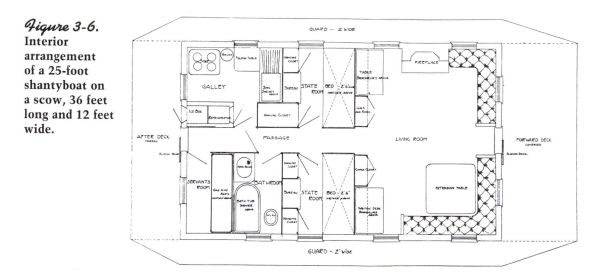

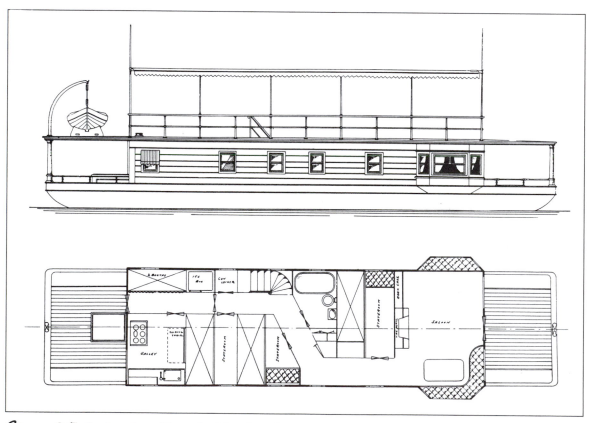

Figure 3-7. **Outboard profile and cabin plan of a 45-foot houseboat.**

Galley

The galley, like a kitchen ashore, should include a stove/oven (either the one in the lounge or a gas range), a work surface, and a sink and drain. Shelving will be necessary to store (or "stow," as it's called when you're afloat) packets of herbs, coffee, tea, baked beans, etc.

You'll need cup-hooks to hang garlic and onion braids, pots, frying pans, colander, whisk, and cups. Extra stowage may be found under the sink. Sliding drawers are a tidy way to put away utensils, especially sharp knives. A suitable chest of drawers may be converted for galley use.

Dining Room

It's difficult to justify space for a dining room. How often do we eat? However, the dining table can be made to pay its way if it does double-duty as a desk or study area. A drop-leaf table can be extended for guests, and the leaves can be dropped when you need more floor space.

Unless the decor is Japanese-inspired, you'll need chairs, too. You may also want to add storage space for dishes and glasses, unless there's enough room for them in the galley.

Bathroom

This, the most private of rooms, is where we rearrange our sleep-disfigured features every morning before facing the world. If economy is applied anywhere, it must not be here. This is the room that separates livable houseboats from briefly occupied ones.

My craft would have a head worthy of the name: an ample compartment at the head of the boat, with full-sized toilet, operated by push-button. There would be leg room and head room. A rug on the deck, magazine rack on the bulkhead, with a cigarette compartment and matches, built in, and within easy reach. Good reading lights and a reclining back. Why not!

Rube Allyn, *Water Wagon*. Saint Petersburg: Great Outdoors Publishing Co., 1952.

A hand basin is essential, and so is a shower—a hot-water shower, by the way; no yacht-type water buckets suspended from a nail. The toilet may be a portable chemical one, a marine toilet, or a modified land-style flush toilet. Don't forget a toilet-paper holder. A shelf or a medicine cabinet to hold pharmaceuticals, potions, pills, and pick-me-ups may be fitted to a wall. You'll also need a mirror to monitor the awakening process.

All Together Now

We have the ingredients: now to mix them about. To do that, we have to know sizes. Measure minimum spaces in any house ashore, and you'll determine just how little you can live with. It's an interesting process, which usually works like this: Arrive at sizes you think are the bare minimum you can function in, work out the sums, find you can't afford that much space; go back to the minimums and reduce them. The budget is the final determining factor, and no house design rules can circumvent that. Our personal minimums are determined largely by how much money we've scraped together.

Browse through the ideas presented here, then try drawing your own plan. You might like a lounge completely surrounded by other rooms, isolated as it were in its privacy within the heart of the houseboat. You might prefer it to be at one end, where the views can best be appreciated.

High ceilings demand walls that are a long way away from each other. Hallways have to be wide and airy. Bedrooms have to be big enough to swing not one cat, but three, holding tightly to one another's tails. It's all a question of prestige, of course; nothing to do with what we actually need.

What we really need is enough room to do the things we want, and to do them comfortably. If the final result is inadequate, it's a simple matter to knock up another raft, build another room or two aboard that, and tie the two houseboats together. One raft can become the bedroom/utility side of the house, and the other the lounging/rumpus/den side. If they're still inadequate, knock up yet another raft.

CRITERIA

A good design will combine the rooms we want, like random elements, into a functional, efficient whole—or an inefficient funhouse. Look at the rough drawings of your houseboat, and imagine the flow of the people who will inhabit it. They rise, moving from the bedroom to the bathroom, then back to the bedroom and into . . . where? The galley? The lounge? If someone else is admiring the contents of the fridge, is there room to get by?

The bedroom in Figure 3-8, apart from indicating a basic minimum size, shows how space is allocated for rising, opening drawers, and exiting the room.

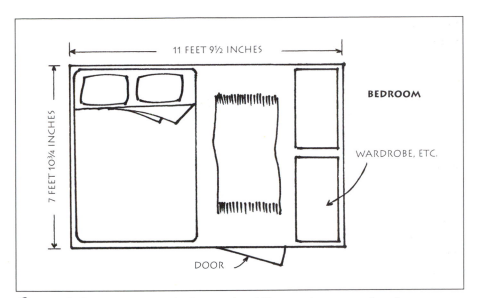

Figure 3-8. Ideally, your bedroom should be spacious enough to keep you from bumping your head on the way out, or when rising, and allow you to open dresser drawers with ease.

Is the design of the galley conducive to traffic flow? Or is it a bottleneck? If so, maybe it should be at one end, away from the main door, where there won't be flow.

Can someone laden with Bloody Marys and Margaritas, straws and garnishes all adangle, get easily from the lounge to the front deck? Did they have to come through the bathroom to get there?

Imagine yourself living on the houseboat, doing these things. Will it be easy? Will it be fun?

The three alternative kitchens in Figure 3-9 show the effects of different layouts. The first has the space to fit a dining table, extra work space, or even a door, at the lower wall. The second is functional, with more room for the cook to work. The third restricts traffic flow, so it could not comfortably be placed between a front door and a living area. It provides an area to the right of the oven to eat from and work on, however. As in the first example, a door could be installed on the lower or end wall.

Important point: It's always a good idea to put the toilet area at a distance from the galley and the lounge (for obvious reasons). Land-based regulations (which don't affect us, but may have some merit buried in them and are worth a glance) usually require two separate doors between toilet and kitchen.

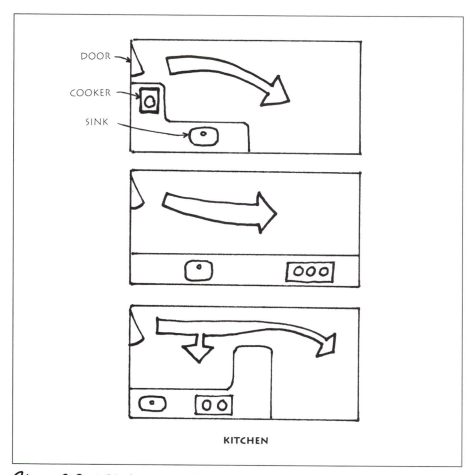

DOOR

COOKER

SINK

KITCHEN

Figure 3-9. **A kitchen can be functional, leaving lots of room for culinary experimentation, or you can build one that leaves more space for dining and entertaining. Keep in mind both the flow of work and the flow of through-traffic.**

Intentions

Is the houseboat intended for a narrow creek or stream, or for the big world of rivers, bays, and lakes? The creek craft would be as narrow as practicable (the English "narrow boats" are only a little over 6 feet wide), while the lake vessel can be as chubby as it likes.

Some people think a narrow houseboat is more nautical looking, but for that to be true it has to be moving. When stationary, I think they look better chubby. Anyway, houseboats needn't try to look nautical—they already are.

In the narrowest houseboats, the width is no greater than the widest
room and side deck. The widest room usually is determined by the
modular size in which plywood is sold: 4 by 8 feet. Three sheets of plywood
would measure 12 by 8 feet; when a few feet are chopped off the top, those
three sheets represent one end wall.

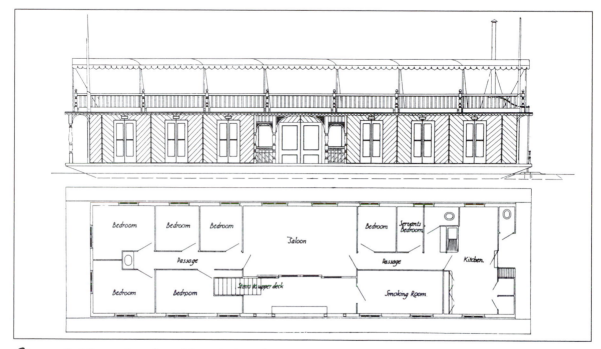

Figure 3-10. **Outboard profile and plan of the Thames houseboat** *Kelpie,*
showing center saloon arrangement.

Figures 3-11 through 3-14 are concerned with narrow designs intended
for use in a stream. Snug Houseboat was meant to be a small but cozy
retreat. It was built in six days. Most storage was overhead, with twine
netting slung between rafters to hold books, camera, socks, dog biscuits,
and the like. Further storage was provided by a wardrobe, and by shelving
on the walls. The settees could have been lift-up types with more storage
space beneath them, like sea chests, but economics demanded junkshop
furniture instead, and that's what we got. Naturally, anyone blessed with
cabinetmaking skills would revel in the opportunity to transform the
interior of a small houseboat into a puzzlebox of intricate storage units,
but such skills are not easily achieved.

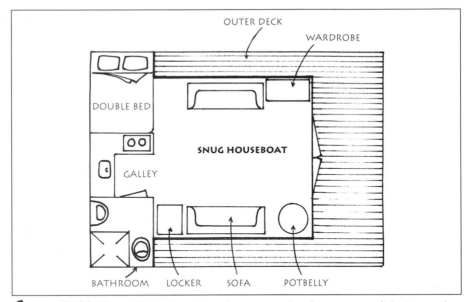

Figure 3-11. Snug Houseboat is a clear example of economy of design and space.

The double French doors that open onto the forward deck allow a view of the surrounding scenery from anywhere inside, while along the side walls, vertical strips of 6-inch, dark-tinted Plexiglas let in light—and lend a one-way view of the neighbors. Thirty barrels were used for buoyancy, but they were not distributed evenly. More than half were clustered at the stern to support the extra weight of internal walls and fittings.

An overhead loft, reached by a ladder from what had been the bedroom, was added later. It became a library by title, but junk area by deed.

The bathroom door needs to be rehinged to swing the other way; at the moment, exiting parties risk plunging anyone in the galley hard into the sink.

The potbelly fire could have been better sited, too. It prevents any movement into that corner, and no chairs can be drawn in front of it to warm one's toes. It could have been fitted beside the gas oven (with the gas bottle securely outside) on the left side of the passage; a steaming kettle would be within reach, and heat could spread equally to both settees. Notwithstanding that, the houseboat is exceptionally cozy in the grip of winter, yet cool in summer.

The next design, Spacious Houseboat, is equal in width to Snug Houseboat but much longer, some 54 feet instead of 25 feet. Half-wall dividers between the lounge and the galley/dining room and between the galley and the second bedroom lend a sense of spaciousness. The lounge is at one end of the boat to exploit the unique views. The bathroom between the two bedrooms turns those rooms into a suite.

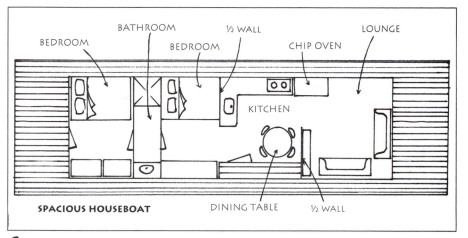

Figure 3-12. **Nearly 30 feet longer than Snug Houseboat, Spacious affords considerably larger living quarters.**

The lounge of *2-rite* has been placed center stage to isolate the bedrooms from each other, yet provide an arena in the middle of the boat for normal social interaction. Great for a family, where the kids get shunted off one end.

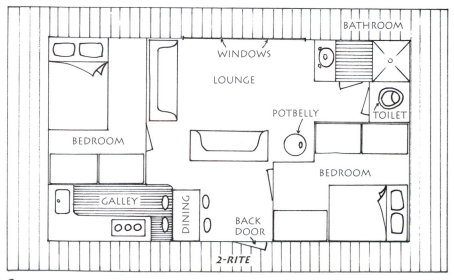

Figure 3-13. **2-Rite leaves lots of space for the family.**

T'idyll was designed as a vacation home for two couples, not for all-year living. Costs were kept to the bare minimum.

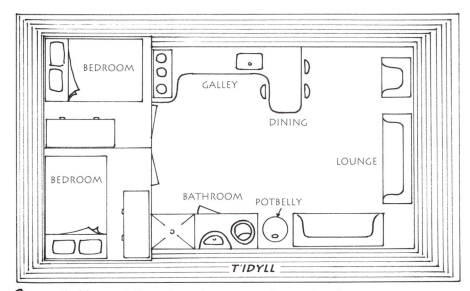

Figure 3-14. **T'idyll is relatively compact, but perfect for one or two couples on a weekend retreat.**

The A-frame houseboat in Figure 3-15 was prepared for a large family living aboard permanently. Double beds are shown in the lower level bedrooms, but bunks were finally installed. The upper bedroom has been kept narrow to provide a spacious upstairs sun deck. Views always improve the higher we go, and what better view in the world than from the upper deck of a houseboat?

An A-frame is stable, strong, and easy to erect. It does suffer from ineffective use of space however, so dormer windows are a good addition. Dormers project from the sloping roof, both upstairs and downstairs, to give full headroom to the outside walls on one side of the boat without sacrificing structural strength. Both sets of dormers have been kept to the lee-side of the prevailing weather; so, where it is predominantly northerlies that bring foul weather, the dormers face south. Of course, as houseboats are easily moved, one could enjoy the view to the North as long as the weather was fine, then swing 180 degrees when the forecasters started commenting on approaching lows and squally, rainy belts.

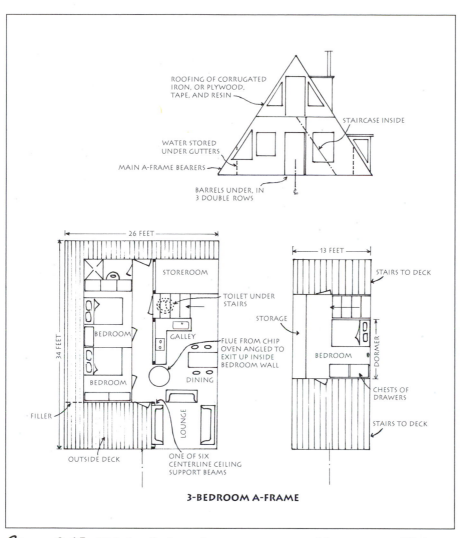

ROOFING OF CORRUGATED
IRON, OR PLYWOOD,
TAPE, AND RESIN

STAIRCASE INSIDE

WATER STORED
UNDER GUTTERS

MAIN A-FRAME BEARERS

BARRELS UNDER, IN
3 DOUBLE ROWS

26 FEET

STOREROOM

TOILET UNDER
STAIRS

GALLEY

FLUE FROM CHIP
OVEN ANGLED TO
EXIT UP INSIDE
BEDROOM WALL

BEDROOM

34 FEET

BEDROOM

DINING

FILLER

OUTSIDE DECK

LOUNGE

ONE OF SIX
CENTERLINE CEILING
SUPPORT BEAMS

13 FEET

STAIRS TO DECK

STORAGE

BEDROOM

DORMER

CHESTS OF
DRAWERS

STAIRS TO DECK

3-BEDROOM A-FRAME

Figure 3-15. **This family houseboat was constructed for year-round living.**

Octopus, the hexagonal, split-level houseboat in Figure 3-16, is an exercise in packing variety, and even charm, into a small space—and maximizing the opportunity to appreciate interesting views.

A door on the lowest-level porch leads into the galley. The houseboater could collect a cold beer, then step up a level to the dining table. Finishing, the glass left on the table, he could step up another level to flop into an armchair in the lounge. The bedroom to the left is down another step. The bathroom is isolated from the bedroom; the only access to the bath is from the porch.

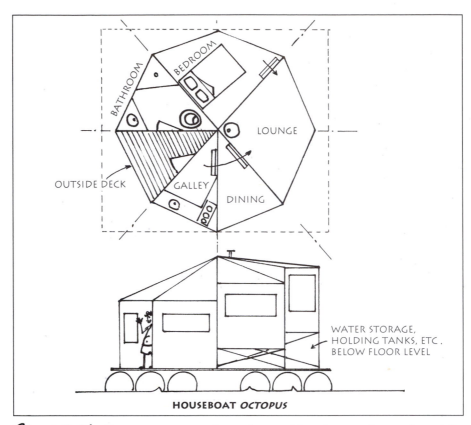

HOUSEBOAT *OCTOPUS*

Figure 3-16. ***Octopus*** **accommodates the need for vistas and space in a tight design.**

Water, holding tanks, tools, and whatnot are stored beneath the house floor. The side frames below floor level could be covered in plywood, and a door added for security.

So there we are: simple ideas for simple houseboats. You may have noticed that there are no rules for houseboat design—they're as much an expression of sculptural freedom as they are utilitarian homesteads. Tony Holt's bamboo houseboat in Queensland, Australia, is a good example of allowing for dreams in the prebuilding plans.

Browse, sketch a few ideas, look in a few books about boats, recreational vehicles, and apartment renovation—but don't be too long about it. Although a great number of people get enthusiastic about building and living in a houseboat, few actually do it. The main snag for a lot of would-be houseboaters is that they can't settle on the right design; they're forever holding out for the elusive perfect design. It doesn't work that way. The only well-designed houseboat is one that's been built.

Figure 3-17. **This bamboo houseboat is a fine example of a builder's freedom to blend style and personality when designing a handmade houseboat.**

After all, it doesn't matter how it looks or acts. It doesn't matter how many stupid features or cranky quirks it has. What does matter is that it exists at all, that it's a haven, that it's a step into a new era.

Some of these houseboats, both on Georgian and Alexandria Bays, are most elaborately appointed and decorated, and really are quite equal to many a summer villa or cottage. They are so large as to contain twelve to fifteen sleeping rooms, in addition to drawing, dining, and smoking rooms, and kitchen and servants' quarters, and are generally two stories high, with a roof garden on the flat top of the second story.

This is a crucial point in the evolution of a human being from land-based creature to houseboater. Of course it'll be hard. When you're up against the brick wall of a lifetime of conditioning; when the wall can't be climbed or drilled into or dug under or walked around, it's understandable to stop, procrastinate, and look for more understanding and guarantees. It takes a phenomenal surge of faith to look at the wall and know it's not there—to walk through it.

The idea that first took hold, the vision of a freshly painted houseboat sitting proudly above the waves, its owner/builder standing on its deck, grinning from ear to ear, is itself the very thing that will endow the energy to begin. It is the only thing. That idea has to be kept secure; it's still a fledgling in need of quiet nurturing. The quickest way to destroy it is to thrash it about with friends and neighbors and in-laws.

CHAPTER FOUR
. . . .

Galvanized and Steadfast

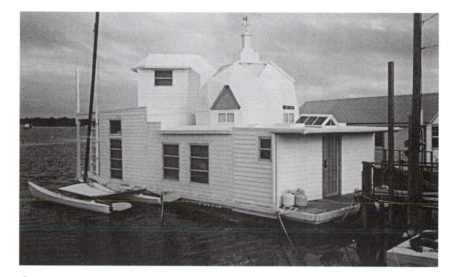

In the pleasant summer evening, lazily swinging in the hammock or ensconced in easy chairs on a houseboat, could anything be more delightful to the tired man or the lazy man than this cottage on the water, with view of the country meadows outlining the blue waters. Like Robinson Crusoe he is 'monarch of all he surveys'—he can move when he likes and take his home with him.

Like Huckleberry Finn, your time has come to enter the pages of history, to build a houseboat. Unlike Master Finn, however, it won't be to leave home, but to get there.

TOOLS

To do that, you have to bolt and hammer a raft together. But first, a quick word about tools: It always pays to have decent ones. Blunt saws, hammers with splintered handles, chisels with nicks in 'em—forget it. After reading this book, anyone who decides to build his own home is strongly urged to put aside a little money right at the outset to buy, at least, one professional ripsaw, one professional crosscut saw, and one professional builder's apron. Into the apron, put a medium-weight hammer, a new chisel, a new rule, a new builder's pencil, and a nail punch. Put a new brace to one side and buy the bits as you need them. Screwdrivers, too, can be purchased as the need arises. Consider it money well spent.

If power is available, a circular saw and an electric drill will ease the work. Rechargeable battery-powered tools are particularly useful, especially after the houseboat is built and you've severed your ties with the mains. Makita and others make battery chargers that work from the houseboat's 12-volt DC system. Some cordless tools can be plugged into the houseboat's 12-volt supply directly.

STABILITY

Even the finest tools will do you no good unless you understand what it takes to keep your handiwork upright. Common sense implies that a top-heavy structure would glance at a slightly choppy sea, immediately swoon, and topple over. Boats are built low whenever possible. If a boat must be high, like a freighter or a car-ferry, substantial ballast is added in the bilges to keep weight low.

A boat will turn over only when its center of gravity (determined by weight distribution) overcomes its center of buoyancy (determined by hull shape). These centers don't exist as concentrated points, like miniature Bermuda Triangles where compasses go all awry and airplanes disappear; they are but mathematical expressions. In Figure 4-1a, you can see how the two centers align.

In a normal boat, the Center of Gravity (CG) is below the Center of Buoyancy (CB). The position of the centers is supposed to make the boat right itself automatically if tossed over by rogue waves, because the Center of Gravity tries to return to being beneath the Center of Buoyancy—and the Center of Buoyancy is frantically trying to get above the Center of Gravity. In a houseboat, there's no such guarantee—in fact, the centers are the other way around. There's more of the boat out of the water than there is in it. However, before anyone turns green at that thought, here are some saving graces.

In Figure 4-1b we can see what begins to happen as the houseboat rocks on a swell. The Center of Buoyancy moves outboard. An imaginary line plotted vertically from the new position of the moving center will intersect a line from the Center of Gravity at a theoretical point above them both. Called the metacenter, this is something like the top of a swinging pendulum, with the houseboat at the bottom of the arm. The more extreme the swing, the shorter the arm becomes (Figure 4-1c). When the metacenter falls below the level of the Center of Gravity, gravity wins. Over she goes, with people, plates, budgies, and all, into the water.

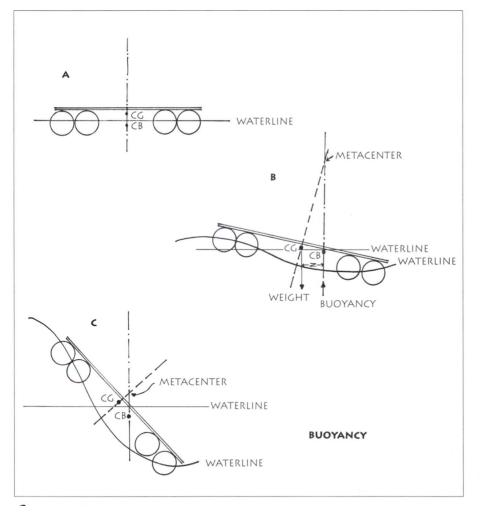

Figure 4-1. **A houseboat's Center of Buoyancy tries to remain *below* its Center of Gravity, making it more vulnerable to capsizing than a power- or sailboat. The Righting Moment can counteract this—if you keep weight *low*.**

Don't worry, it won't happen. There is a force called the Righting Moment at work to prevent the pendulum from swinging. As the boat rolls and the Center of Buoyancy moves outboard, it tries to lift the houseboat out of the water. The Righting Moment, a product of the weight of the Center of Gravity and the distance (Z) between the theoretical lines that drop from both the Center of Gravity and the Center of Buoyancy, acts as a guardian angel. The farther the pendulum swings, the more intensely and energetically the Righting Moment tries to correct it.

If, for example, a 10-ton houseboat should roll, so that the Center of Buoyancy moves across 2 feet, we would say that the Righting Moment, working on the Center of Buoyancy to correct the swing, was 20 foot/tons. This force increases as the distance Z increases. That's a substantial force.

In practice, the theory won't be tested. Any waves large enough to set up the roll in the diagram would be accompanied by strong winds, winds that would push a houseboat rapidly sideways like a huge, fixed sail. Anyone who would be out in gales and waves that large wouldn't own a houseboat in the first place. They'd be gardening behind very tall walls, attended to by people in white uniforms.

RAFTS

The raft under your houseboat will need a latticework of support beams to create pockets for the barrels, and to provide something for the decking to be nailed to. There are two kinds of support beams: *joists*, which run across the raft, and *bearers*, which run the length.

When the joists are bolted to the bearers, as shown in Figure 4-2, we effectively prohibit the barrels from rolling sideways and from sliding forward or backward. Their inherent buoyancy pushes them directly upward, and the weight of the houseboat pushes down, locking them into their pockets. The joists are bolted at a distance determined by the barrels. If the barrels are 3 feet 2 inches long, then the joists will be positioned to leave a space of 3 feet 3 inches, and if they're 2 feet 10 inches long, then the joists will be 2 feet 11 inches apart.

The bearers are also placed at specific distances across the raft, but to know where, we have to answer some questions:

- How wide is the house compared to the raft supporting it?
- How many rows of barrels are there?
- Are the barrels in single file or doubled up?
- How thick are the bearers?
- How wide are the barrels?

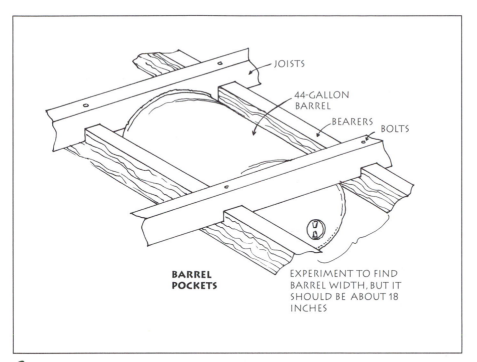

Figure 4-2. When constructing a raft for your houseboat, attach joists and bearers so that they form a pocket to hold the barrels. If the barrels are 3 feet 2 inches long, for example, position the joists and bearers to leave a 3-foot 3-inch space.

Barrels

There should be a row of barrels under the walls of the house, irrespective of the width of the raft, or anything else (see Figure 4-3). We can then support the wall frames over the bearers, and we have something solid to which to nail them. These two rows of barrels become starting points for other row positions. If the plan calls for side decks, bring the starting rows in from each edge. If there are no side decks, the starting rows will be flush with the raft edges.

When barrels are installed flush with the edges of the raft, they act as a buffer should the houseboat ever drift up against pilings and other debris. When installed farther under the raft edges, it is possible that the raft can float over a piling, and when the tide drops, get caught on the damned thing. In that case, barge boards along the outer edge might provide some protection.

If we use a row of barrels for every 4 feet of width, we will have more than enough buoyancy. If a raft is 20 feet wide and the walls are flush with the edges, then five single rows would provide equal, and even, buoyancy.

If a raft is 20 feet wide, but with two, 2-foot side decks (for a house width of 16 feet), we're committed to starting the rows under the walls 2 feet in from each edge.

In Figure 4-3b, a double row of barrels has been fitted on each side. We have the same number of barrels as in Figure 4-3a, but the weight of the raft has been reduced because four fewer bearers are needed—the two barrels side by side only need two outer bearers to hold them in place. This reduction in weight could be substantial.

We can also fit a double row along the centerline, as in Figure 4-3c, with no extra bearer weight. However, this should be done only when the inside of the houseboat has furniture and walls spread evenly across it as weight. Imagine arrows of force pointing upward from each row of barrels. If there's only a little weight pushing down in the middle of the raft, compared to the sides carrying walls, doors, windows, and furniture, then it's drastically uneven, and the buoyancy will try to curve the floor up. In practice, if this happens it's easy enough to pull a few alternate barrels out.

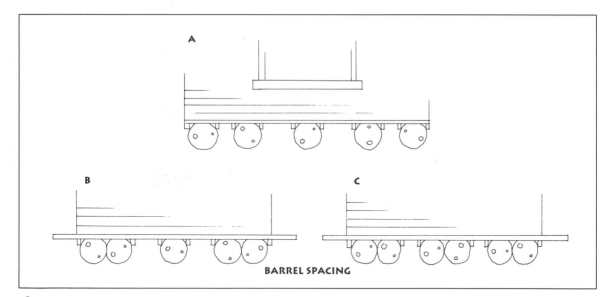

BARREL SPACING

Figure 4-3. **Placement of the barrels is critical in constructing a raft for your houseboat. Ideally, there should be a row of barrels for every 4 feet of width. Start by placing a row of barrels under the walls to support the wall frames over the bearers. These outer barrels also act as a buffer.**

In building the house, we'll be creating a three-dimensional structure with as much bracing as practicable. This is why it is inadvisable to fit a lot of barrels under an outer decking. With no weight bearing down except for the occasional houseboater or pussycat walking on it, the barrels will try to force the decking up.

Bearers and Joists

Now, how thick will the bearers be? Conventional, land-based building codes call for massive hunks of lumber that may or may not be appropriate for our purposes. Because the raft will be floating on a moving surface, and because it's a two-dimensional thing (at present), it is impossible to construct it so rigidly that it will not move. It will become rigid only when the three-dimensional house goes on top. Our question becomes, not how much, but how little can we get away with?

The heavyweight raft in Figure 4-4 was constructed with 2×8 bearers and 2×8 joists bolted together. These were reinforced with 4×4 beams. More joists went on top, this time 2×4s, with 1-inch tongue-and-groove planking laid on top of that. The structure was bolted and nailed and Z-nailed, until it was nearly a metallic raft. As if that weren't enough, a layer of ¼-inch plywood was nailed over the entire accommodation area, virtually the whole raft.

Figure 4-4. **This particularly sturdy raft was constructed with 2×8 joists and bearers, followed by 4×4 beams, additional 2×4 joists, planking—bolted and Z-nailed—and a final layer of plywood.**

When the time came to crane the raft onto a beach (it had been built in a vacant lot handy to a tidal inlet), and it was lifted into the air, it hung, sagging like a wet noodle, from the crane strops. We exchanged nervous glances with the crane driver and watched as the raft was lowered onto the shingle of the foreshore.

The tide eventually rose, and the raft vibrated in the water like a guitar string. One person jiggling at one end sent tremors pulsing along it. However, when the wall frames went up and the sheathing went on, the houseboat locked itself rigid, and it never moved again.

The next raft we built was an experiment in the other extreme: There were no joists at all. The bearers were 2 × 4s in three parallel pairs, each pair 15 inches apart, held in place by 1-inch planking on top. It was as structural as a piece of wet paper. It was heaved onto a beach; as it floated, barrels were rolled underneath, where they slammed (such is their buoyancy) up between the bearers. When the wall frames and plywood walls were erected, the wobbly floor tightened up, but it was never as good as it should have been—the side decks flex.

Figure 4-5. **This extra front deck is sagging because it was inadequately braced.**

Using these two extremes (and other examples), we arrive at a rule-of-thumb: joist beams and bearer beams should be 2 × 4s up to a length of about 16 feet, 2 × 6s up to about 30 feet, and 2 × 8s up to 45 feet. These are common lumberyard sizes (unplaned). The bearers can be strengthened by laminating, or even bolting, two lengths together, but that shouldn't be necessary. The real strength of the houseboat is in the rigidity supplied by the wall frames, both along the length and across the house. That's why it's a good idea to build as many walls across the houseboat as possible.

What we do now is stand a barrel on end on the ground and lay a piece of wood against it. That will represent a joist beam. If a double row of barrels is being installed, stand two drums side by side. If the bearers are to be, say, 6 inches, stand a piece of 2 × 6 square against the joist beam, touching the barrel. Mark the joist beam and repeat on the other side. Those two marks are the chord shown as (x) in Figure 4-6—the correct placements for either single or double rows.

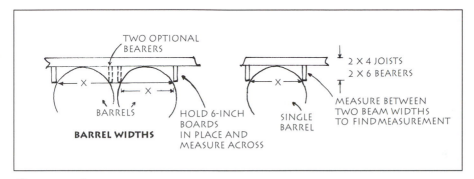

Figure 4-6. **Spacing is crucial to the design of your raft. Whether you plan on single or double rows of barrels, finding the chord (x) will determine how the barrels should be spaced.**

There is one other point. If the builder chooses to chisel notches in the joists and bearers at the intersection, as in Figure 4-7, the chord (x) will be affected. To compensate, trim an equivalent amount from the bearer when measuring the chord. If we plan to notch 1 inch from the bearer and 2 inches from the joist, the bearer actually will protrude only 3 inches alongside the barrel. Therefore, make the test piece of wood 3 inches.

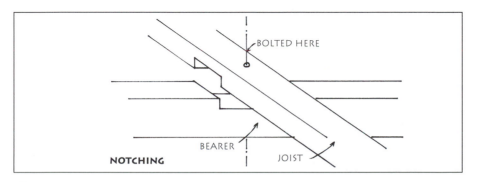

Figure 4-7. **For added strength, you can notch the joists and bearers, but remember that this will affect the chord. Trim the length of the bearer accordingly (see Figure 4-8).**

The difference between un-notched and notched beams is shown in Figure 4-8. In each case, the barrels will be locked against the bearers, with a gap equal to the width of the joist beam between them, and the side of the barrels barely resting against the bottom of the deck planking. This is always a good idea. If measurements get a little sloppy, or construction isn't absolutely precise (well, we're not trained builders, are we?), we don't really want barrels pushing up through the floorboards, right?

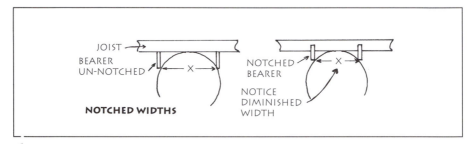

Figure 4-8. **Here you can see how notching the bearers and joists diminishes the width of the chord (x).**

So now we're ready to build—well, almost. If the raft is longer than the longest pieces of lumber you can find, you'll have to scarf together the bearers.

The ends of two lengths are cut, then bolted together across the width—called *scarfing*. The professional method of scarfing is to mark a length four times the width of the plank, then cut diagonally across. Galvanized carriage screws are used, with the head of the bolt at the side where the floor will be. It will pull down into the wood and not interfere with the planking. Extra strength can be added across the joint with a strip of plywood, or even a hunk of wood the same thickness as the plank. Keep it to the outside of the pocket for the barrel, however.

You do have the option of ordering the joists at an exact length. You might pay a small percentage extra, but you won't get a piece a fraction too short, nor will you be paying for the extra bits you might have to cut off. It seems to work out that you get both, too short and too long, if you don't ask for exact cuts.

Assembly

So, let's get started.

It's very helpful if you have a friend (or can acquire one) who is willing to let you lay the raft out on his lawn or back lot. The raft can be measured and cut, notched and drilled using power tools. On the side of a riverbank,

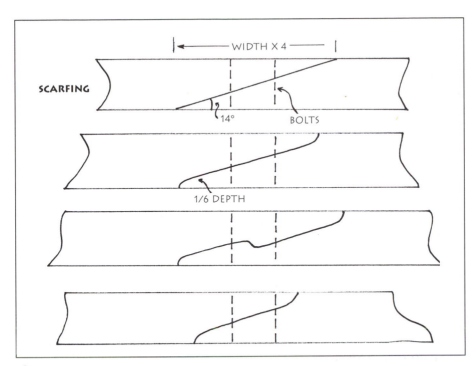

SCARFING

WIDTH X 4

14°

BOLTS

1/6 DEPTH

Figure 4-9. **If your bearers aren't long enough, you'll have to scarf them.**

it's all hand tools unless you have quality cordless ones, like Makita's, or hire a generator—that would alert neighbors to what you're up to. If the raft is prebuilt, marked for ease of construction, disassembled, and transported, it'll be reassembled and out on the water before the neighbors can get to their phones to call the authorities. By then it's too late—you're up and running.

The first thing to do is scarf the necessary number of bearers. Lay them out on the ground; they'll look too short, but it's just an illusion. Ignore it.

Assemble the joists in one place and mark them where the intersections for the bearers will be; that is, so far in for the first beam, then the chord of the barrel(s), then across to the next beam, the chord again, and so on. At each mark, remember to allow for the thickness of the beam that will be crossing it.

The result might be, for a houseboat with 18-inch side decks, three rows of barrels, and 8 feet of accommodation width, something like this, scribed along the joists:

16.0"	Side deck	Nothing underneath
2.0"	Bearer beam	Beneath wall/Intersection
15.0"	Chord	Barrel pocket

2.0"	Bearer beam	Intersection
23.5"	Inside floor	Nothing underneath
2.0"	Bearer beam	Centerline intersection
15.0"	Chord	Barrel pocket
2.0"	Bearer beam	Centerline intersection
23.5"	Inside floor	Nothing underneath
2.0"	Bearer beam	Intersection
15.0"	Chord	Barrel pocket
2.0"	Bearer beam	Beneath wall/Intersection
16.0"	Side deck	Nothing underneath

With the joists marked, we turn our attention to the bearers. They are scribed, as mentioned before, at a measurement a little more than the length of the barrels. Again, allow 2 inches, or whatever is suitable for the thickness of the joists.

All beams can be notched now, but this is not essential. Notching locks each beam into the other, but the bolts will suffice until the floor is laid, and then the whole platform won't move anyway.

Stand each joist beam on top of the bearers, aligning all the marks (so painstakingly arrived at), then drill down through both beams at each intersection, using whatever diameter drill or auger is suitable for the bolts you have. (Galvanized ⅝-inch will do well.)

When the holes are drilled, number each intersection with a marker, then disassemble the whole structure if you intend to trailer the materials to their construction site. Re-erect the platform, following the numbers, and the whole thing can be bolted together and on the water in an hour.

Flotation

At the site, there are two ways to proceed. One is to bolt the edifice together where you know the tide will come in and float it, assuming you're in a tidal area. The barrels are then slipped into the water and manhandled into their pockets while the raft floats obediently at hand. That's the theory, anyway. What generally happens is that the raft floats away while you're trying to push a barrel underneath, or that the barrel won't cooperate—they have to be lined up carefully square to the edge of the raft, and leapt upon, to make them roll under. Once they've begun to roll, they will keep going until they hit the first bearer beam in their way, which they will overcome with a nudge—and then will slam into the pocket. If that row is a double row, the next one will follow when the first has been rolled to its side of the pocket.

This is not as hard as it sounds, and can be great fun in the summer. It's also one of the ways to replace rotten or rusted barrels. The old one will sink out, leaving a vacant pocket to roll the new barrel into. Or you could wait until the tide is out and dig a hole in the mud or sand to get at the old barrel. To replace a complete row of barrels, the whole houseboat can be jacked up with a couple of house jacks, truck jacks, or floor jacks. This requires a shingle, or compact sand shoreline, on which to lay some planks for the jacks.

The other assembly technique looks more professional, and you won't get wet. Prop the two inside bearers up on a couple of barrels and bolt on the first and second joist beams. Swivel one of the barrels into the pocket created. Go halfway along the raft-to-be and stand the same bearers on two more barrels. Bolt on two more joists and swivel another barrel into place. Repeat at the end of the bearers and swivel the third barrel in. Now start bolting on all the joists and swivelling in more barrels. You should finish with a row of barrels supporting two bearers, with joist beams flopping about on each side. Start working along one side with the next set of bearers and barrels, then come around to the other side for bolting on and swivelling in the final set. That's it; she's ready to float, and we might as well put the floor on.

In the event that the houseboat is being built for a freshwater setting, whether stream, river, or lake, and tidal flows aren't conveniently available, it simply means building the raft completely, and then manhandling it into the water. There are several ways to do that. The least exertive, and most expensive, is to phone someone with a mobile crane and have them lift it into the water.

Alternatively, the raft—if it has been constructed on top of some planks left lying on the ground—can be pushed along the planks and launched. The pushing can come from a horde of people or an automobile, which would be easier. No damage can ensue. The friction of barrels and raft frame (the raft decking will go on later) will be minimal, and oil or grease smeared on the planks will help even the most reticent raft to budge.

Rollers can also be used. If massive blocks of stone could be rollered to build the Great Pyramids, we need have no hesitation in rollering a relatively light-weight raft across the ground and into the water. We would still need the planks underneath the raft, and the rollers would go under the planks.

Now, before the deck goes on, is an opportune time to tie the barrels into their pockets with twine. If you are using steel barrels (for shame!), use steel wire as well; replacing rusty barrels is easier if you don't have to crawl beneath the house to cut twine, and the steel wire will have rusted away as effectively as the barrels themselves.

Plastic barrels are very effectively strapped into place with the plastic parcel-wrapping straps big department stores and transport companies use. Beg, borrow, or steal—no, better not steal—the small hand-held machine that wraps the straps around things and then fastens them with a clip. Then again, why bother? The barrels aren't going to go anywhere unless you take the houseboat into the teeth of gale-force winds and waves—or suspend it from a tree.

DECKS

Decking is a straightforward and extremely satisfying job. Planks of 1½-inch or 1-inch pressure-treated lumber are nailed along the raft from joist beam to joist beam. Get your supplier to provide the longest lengths possible; this will save quite a bit of cutting, as you trim each plank to fit between the beams.

As soon as you begin the decking process, fit a bollard to a corner of the raft. A bollard is a hitching post, something to tie ropes to, and it may be square or round or the foot sawn off an old piece of furniture. Notice that a bolt is inserted down through it, the deck, and a large plate underneath to fasten it securely. Don't just bolt it to a deck plank—it'll rip out.

Glancing at Figure 4-11, you will see that decking can be as varied or as plain as time and patience allow. The inside section is the accommodation area; if carpet or other flooring is to be laid, it can be as boring as we like.

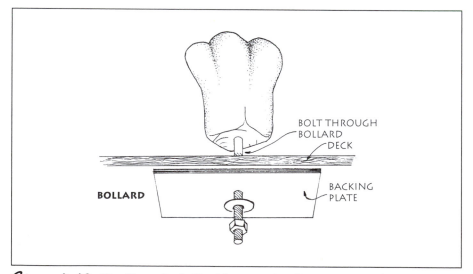

BOLT THROUGH
BOLLARD
DECK

BOLLARD

BACKING
PLATE

Figure 4-10. **You'll need a bollard for securing lines to your raft. This one is made from a salvaged piece of claw-foot furniture.**

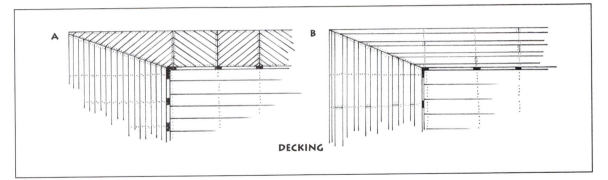

DECKING

Figure 4-11. Decking can be as fancy or plain as you like. The outer deck is your chance to show off your handiwork. Be sure to leave spaces to drain away water.

The outside decking, however, gives us the opportunity to experiment with different patterns, types of lumber, and plank widths.

Observant readers will have noticed in the illustrations that a gap has been left between the inner and outer deckings. An inch will suffice, and the gap, or scupper, begins on the outside of the accommodation area, including the width of the walls. The gap will let rainwater and seawater falling aboard flow immediately overboard. We don't want it creeping into the structural beams. Seawater is okay—it pickles wood—but rainwater causes rot.

Referring to Figure 4-12a, an extra, shorter joist beam has been added an inch or so away from the beam that will carry the end wall of the house. The decking across the end of the raft is then brought only to the new beam, and the scupper is thus allowed to run completely around the house. Figure 4-12b shows how the completed decking would look, and includes an optional barge board, nailed along the ends of the joists, which tidies the raft and protects the end grain of the joists. Figure 4-12c is a reminder that where planks have been cut to follow the right angle of the deck, a diagonal joist beam must be nailed in first to receive the ends of the planks.

When laying the decking, start at the inside accommodation area. The planks should be nailed together as tightly as possible. Lay each new plank next to the one in place, drive a nail in a little way, and then hammer a chisel into the beam next to the plank. By levering the chisel towards the plank, you will move it hard against its neighbor and the nail can be driven home. When cutting for length, remember to measure halfway across the joist beam. There has to be room for the end of the next plank to fit on there as well.

A purist would insist on tongue-and-groove flooring, where a concave surface on the edge of one plank fits into a convex surface on the edge of

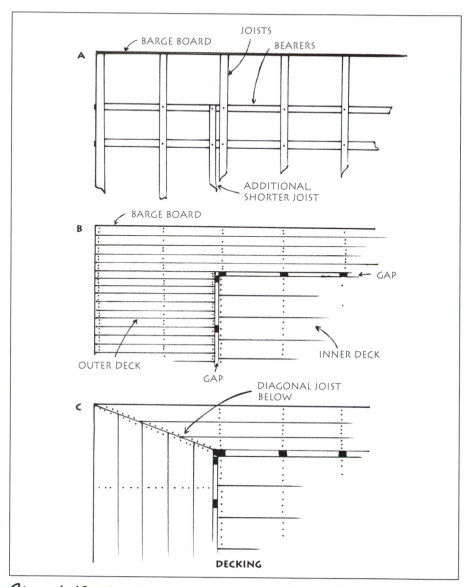

Figure 4-12. **A bargeboard trim protects the end grain of the joists, while a diagonal joist supports mitered deck planks.**

the one next to it. Tongue-and-groove flooring is moisture-free and draft-free. If you can afford it, go ahead.

For those of us using the cheapest rough-sawn planks we can find, an extra degree of comfort and security can be added by laying sheets of plywood over the planking and nailing them down. To keep the houseboat absolutely protected from rising dampness, a layer of clear plastic may be spread over the floor before the sheets of plywood are nailed on, to sandwich the moisture-repelling material between the layers of wood. Tar-impregnated builder's paper is equally efficient.

On the outer decking, it is not important to push the planks tightly against each other. Gaps will let water drain away.

At this point, dear builder, you can pause to reflect on what you're doing. Are you crazy? All this money and time. . . . It's okay. Open a cold beer and pour it over the raft. Christen it, in its infancy, as a damn good idea. Then open another beer, and sit on the floor of the raft of the houseboat that will soon be your home. It may not be as luxurious as *Summerholme*, but it won't cost as much either.

Figure 4-13. **Summerholme—when boaters wore boaters.**

It is impossible of course to describe . . . all of the comforts and pleasures of houseboating. But the few unpleasant moments and discomforts which are bound to fall to the lot of those who live on a houseboat can be dismissed in a very few words. To begin with, partitions on houseboats are not like brick walls. They do not stop sound, and the houseboater is liable to awake in the morning before he is called by hearing the cook grinding coffee in the kitchen or sweeping the dining room overhead. Then there are sometimes rainy days when houseboating is not very agreeable indoors or out. On stormy nights, windows, doors, and even the walls creak, you are liable to be kept awake long past your regular bedtime.

CHAPTER FIVE
....

Quick and Easy

E*asiest of all methods to obtain a summer home afloat is to purchase an obsolete canal boat—an old-timer—renovate and fumigate; cut out large windows in its side, place skylights in the deck, made so that the windows can be raised to catch all the air possible; partitions inside to suit the size of the family, and all is ready. . . .*

~~~~~~

This is a fun sport: to build a houseboat, but to do it quickly and on the cheap.

Once you've built a raft, anything that people live in ashore can be pushed, dragged, or craned aboard to create an instant houseboat. Camper trailers are the most popular converts—who could argue with a home afloat for only $600?—but house-truck bodies, recreational vehicles, VW buses, full-size buses, old houses, garden sheds, garages, even surplus railway carriages can all become boats—all it takes is a little lateral thinking. There's not a new thing in it, however: The oft-quoted Albert Hunt remarked of a boat he saw in San Francisco Bay at the beginning of the century, ". . . a decrepit ocean steamer *The Tropic Bird*, serves as one summer cottage, while another is made of four horse-cars of the variety known as bob-tail set on a float. It is a life of good health and good fellowship."

Trailer homes that have been allowed to deteriorate to the point where they are no longer roadworthy, with rusting wheels, peeling paint, and mildewed walls, can be acquired for next to no money, or even for free. If you jack one into the air and cut the underframe (axles, springs, and towing assembly) away with an acetylene torch, you can transport the remaining accommodation to the raft and slide it aboard.

This approach solves at one stroke the weary dilemma of where to park. Oceans, rivers, and lakes are the world's biggest trailer parks, even if you can't put a letterbox out. With an outboard mounted on the stern or bow, the houseboat can be taken anywhere.

Prefabricated garages (usually made of aluminum) have been erected on rafts and converted to very cozy domiciles. Purchased in kit form, available everywhere from large lumberyards to Sears, they are easily constructed and immune to the ravages of most weather. They are often supplied with roll-up doors, which make ideal storm shutters over floor-to-ceiling windows or French doors.

Cabooses, guard's vans, surplus freight containers, and even railway cars can be very successfully converted. The ultimate acquisition would, of course, be a sleeping car. Railway cars are prewired for power and preplumbed for water. Once the bogies underneath have been gas-axed off by the railway workshop, the weight drops drastically. One might even hope to find old brass fittings and leather seats, memories of another era. In West New York recently, a railroad barge, LVRB 79, was converted by the Serious Foolishness Company from a 100-foot derelict scow into a museum/theater/gallery. Anything is possible.

Of course, the easiest way to acquire an instant houseboat is to peruse newspaper classified ads in search of houses, cottages, or sheds being offered for removal. When property developers buy up land with old houses on it, intending to build new, tall, ultramodern things thereon, the old homes have to go. The options are either to bulldoze them or have them removed (look in the Yellow Pages under House Removals); they're often available for free, or at nominal fees. As I type these words, a three-bedroom, perfectly adequate but geriatric house within walking distance has been sold for $375, and is being jacked up so that a trailer can be backed under it.

HULLS TO HOUSES

A houseboat can also be built from an existing boat, either monohull or multihull. The groundwork has already been done, in that the hull has been assembled; all that remains is to ensure it'll float. That may require learning the skill of caulking, of hammering hemp and tar into the seams between the hull's planks, to keep out the sea. Figure 5-1 shows just such a hull, an ex-freighter: 102 feet of potential home.

The couple in Figure 5-2 have lived aboard their 1912 lighter, *Kaka*, for 35 years. In 1984, during the barrage of Cyclone Bola, the houseboat was slammed into some decaying mooring poles that holed the boat; the tides now flow in and out of the lower levels of the hull, but it was an easy matter to move the bedroom to the upper level, shut the lower-level door, and ignore it.

The barge shown carrying a horde of campers in the 1950s was recently converted—once the people had been pushed off—into the author's houseboat *Tsunami*, but the process was not as quick and easy as the builder had imagined it would be; as the houseboat would endure ocean swells, the lessons of professional boatbuilding had to be arduously learnt.

Figure 5-1. If you don't want to start from scratch, you can look to existing hulls, such as this ex-freighter.

Figure 5-2. *Kaka*, built in 1912. . . . "They said I was crazy thirty years ago!"

Figure 5-3. *Hone*, a sister lighter to *Kaka*, has been given another level of accommodation.

Figure 5-4. **The barge that used to ferry holiday-makers in New Zealand in the 1950s now serves as the author's abode, houseboat *Tsunami*.**

It was suggested by *Mechanix Illustrated* in 1953 that a spacious catamaran could be built by slicing an existing monohull boat down the middle with a circular saw (along the centerline keel) and then nailing some planks over the open sides of each half. The idea was to finish up with an overall width of 1 foot per 3 feet of length. The right-hand hull section went to the left, and the left-hand hull section went to the right. This created two curving inner hulls and flat outer hulls, with a venturi-like effect between them as the water was compressed. Compressed water, like air, speeds up. A platform could then be bolted between the two hulls. Bedrooms, storerooms, workshops, etc., could be fitted into the hull sections, while the central platform could be used for a lounging area, galley, and master bedroom.

Raft-style houseboats are close cousins to sailing multihulls; in both cases, instead of using barrels along each side of the main platform, two or three sealed pontoons are used. Ex-sailing multihulls can be salvaged and converted directly into houseboats. Strengthening should be installed, like a strongback or lengthwise bulkhead for each hull, to carry the loads that will be placed on top. Two young men in New Zealand recently built a house on top of a catamaran. The idea was good, but the weight of the house split the hulls; they had been designed to carry a light cabin, a mast, and sails, not 4 × 4s, 2 × 4s, rough-sawn planks, and furniture. It was eventually abandoned. If you use existing hulls, ensure that the house materials are appropriate to the strength available; if not, add more strength.

HULL MATERIALS

Although some boatbuilders screw up their faces when they hear the word ferrocement, it is not beyond the capabilities of any reader with more time than money to design a ferro-houseboat—a complete concrete shape. Maybe it would look like a barrel—a gigantic 4,444-gallon concrete barrel, with 19.84 tons of buoyancy. A poured concrete floor inside, over some scrap iron, would provide ballast—that is, weight to keep the barrel rightside up. It would be horrific if it started rolling, like a barrel going over Niagara Falls. On the other hand, it might as well have a conventional shape.

Ferrocement hulls are virtually maintenance-free. Another benefit is that the wire armature over which plaster is applied may be sculpted into any imaginable shape. It's certainly cheaper than GRP (glass-reinforced plastic), and more convenient to work with.

Speaking of GRP, a large fiberglass swimming pool, removed as unwanted from the ground, was once launched into the water with a house built inside, where swimmers had previously floated on inflated mattresses, soaking up sun. It was an easily affordable fiberglass hull, and once internal bracing had been fitted, it was extremely strong. Another idea tested was building a house inside a GRP mold that had been used to fashion sleek yachts. The mold, in which GRP hulls had been laminated and then lifted out, was buoyant and had a sharp end and a blunt end. Despite having some steel reinforcing rods running around its exterior, it was cavernous, and a small house was quickly dropped inside it. It awaits an engine.

Now, the stuff that will have the average reader staring in disbelief: papier-mâché. Before the advent of the automobile, European coach builders discovered that papier-mâché, when made of paper and *varnish*, was unbelievably strong, extremely light, and waterproof, qualities houseboat builders can exploit to advantage. The new miracle material may be space-age rayon or Kevlar, but I'm left wondering if we ignore our rich experimental past to our detriment. If the good citizens of Austria, say, were willing to risk their necks in one-horsepower carriages made of a strong, light material, rattling along hard cobblestones, maybe we should start learning how to play with the stuff again.

MOVING HOUSE

Finally, a word or two about actually moving the raft and the houseboat once they've been built. Where the water is shallow enough to wade in, it's also shallow enough to walk along the shore, pulling—or pushing—the houseboat. When afloat, most things are easily moved, and that includes homes full of furniture, cats and children. A push is enough to overcome inertia (nothing in the physical world likes to be disturbed); from then on, a push now and again is enough to keep the boat moving.

Figure 5-5. Moving day.

If it's too cold or deep to wade, a boat is just as easily moved by poling. If you stand on deck and push against the bottom with a pole, the boat will move; walk back along the deck, pushing all the while, and you'll build momentum. At the far end of the boat, get the pole out of the water (without losing it, or being left hanging from it), stroll quickly back along the deck, and repeat the process until you're where you want to be. Beats sitting in an office, anyway.

Two men in a rowboat can move the average houseboat without great strain, and poling works wonders: but the canny houseboat skipper relies upon wind and tide for much of his work. Your true housekeeper is altogether too willing to wait upon tide and wind. He is going nowhere. He has forgotten the meaning of the word 'hurry'. All he asks is that the views from his deck chair or hammock may be beautiful, that as he looks from his dining room window he may see long vistas of shimmering water and woodland greenery, or watch water and trees and sky drift by, slowly, gently, cloud-like, while he steals through a network of marshes, still lagoons, or shallows, winding creeks, rivers or canals.

Then there's towing, or motoring. An outboard motor may not be aesthetic, but it's just the thing if the wind is blowing or the tide has turned against you.

An outboard can be installed on the stern of any houseboat and used to push the vessel forward, but it's infinitely better mounted on the front deck. Trying to push and steer a nondirectional vessel like a houseboat is like trying to push a trailer ahead of a car. Steering is difficult, if not downright impossible. We'd transfer the trailer to the rear towbar to pull it; likewise, by moving an outboard motor to the front deck and, because now it's facing the wrong way, putting it in reverse, we can pull the houseboat. Steering is a breeze, and we can see where we're headed, instead of trying to look through the house from the back deck. Of course, outboards have only a fraction of their rated power when operating in reverse. If you have a small outboard and a large houseboat, you may have to try something else.

If the outboard motor is attached to a dinghy, or indeed if any motorized vessel is used to tow the houseboat, attach a bridle with a pair of ropes coming from one point on the stern of the motorized vessel, splitting and

Figure 5-6. **A NZ Royal Navy houseboat.**

spreading back to each side of the houseboat. Then, should the houseboat veer left, the right rope will restrain it, and vice versa. If the crew of the towing vessel is new at this, remind them that you have no brakes; if they slow or stop, you'll run them over. When slowing, a tow-er should smartly nip to one side of the tow-ee's course; the boat under tow will then pass safely to one side. A second person in the first boat should be nominated to haul aboard any slack ropes to keep them out of the propeller. Ring up the local Coast Guard office too, and ask what lights or flags have to be flown when a vessel is under tow.

Ultimately, there is nothing exotic about houseboats. Even the New Zealand Navy uses one. The houseboat in Figure 5-6 is a twin-level diving school, with classrooms below and lockers and kitrooms upstairs. The houseboat, berthed in Defense Department waters, has been built into a pontoon-like ferrocement hull.

CHAPTER SIX

Up She Goes

It is a fact that can be demonstrated by inquiry of sailors and men who follow the water, that few people living on board a boat are known to have rheumatism, typhoid, bad colds or the common ills prevalent on land. On shore the summer boarders may be tantalized with mosquitoes, or they may be unable to sleep in beds in their warm rooms, and try to get air by spreading mattresses in front of windows, but a few hundred yards out on the water where the anchor light gleams on the houseboat, everyone is slumbering, cool and comfortable.

With the raft floating happily in a creek, river, or lake—or sitting dry on a foreshore—the house awaits construction. The building of an entire house might at first seem a bit overwhelming, but don't worry. Building the house may be the most challenging job, but by moving, step by step, through the whole process and reducing each daunting job to a series of small tasks, you'll soon have a houseboat. The first step—and one that should not be slighted—is planning.

WALLS

Houses are walls with a roof on top to keep out the rain. Walls are sections of framing, the bits of wood that we'll cut and nail together to hold the wall sheathing in place. Before we actually start building, however, we have to draw up wall-frame plans, sketched with the sole purpose of reminding you where everything goes. These needn't win architect's prizes for draftsmanship; what matters is that the builder can understand them. And if the builder is you, the person who drew them, how can we go wrong?

A wall frame consists of a *bottom plate* that runs along the floor, with *studs* projecting upward like pillars to support a *top plate* running along the top, as in Figure 6-1. Wedged between the studs is *blocking*, or *noggins*, to reinforce the studs and keep them straight and true. Over the holes where the doors and windows go are *lintels*, which compensate for the studs missing from the door and window holes. These are supported by a pair of extra studs. At the bottom of the window holes are *sills*, which support the weight of the window frames.

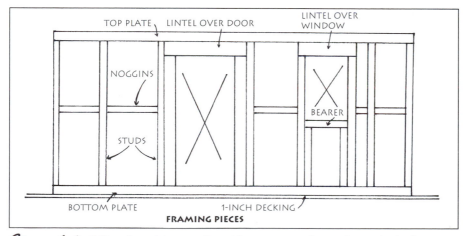

Figure 6-1. When framing your houseboat, space the studs on 24-inch centers, except where there are doors and windows.

So far this is all reasonably conventional; houses ashore are constructed the same way. Where we will differ is in the use of lighter lumber, which not only will be an enormous cost saving, but will save weight as well. If the reader is of a mind to increase his or her feeling of safety and would prefer to use thicker, wider, heavier lumber than I recommend, be my guest. It should not be replaced by lighter grades, however, even if you want to squeeze every last ounce out of your flotation. What follows are minimum sizes; one column gives land usage, the other gives the houseboat equivalent.

Framing	Land	Water
Studs	2 × 4	2 × 2
Blocking (Noggins)	2 × 4	2 × 2
Plates (top)	2 × 4	2 × 3
(bottom)	2 × 4	2 × 2
Lintels (average)	2 × 6	2 × 3
(extraordinary)	2 × 8	2 × 4
Sills (average)	2 × 6	2 × 3
(extraordinary)	2 × 8	2 × 6

These dimensions are for rough, unplaned lumber. The table below shows the difference between unplaned, nominal dimensions and the dressed (or planed) dimensions common to the corner lumberyard. For the raft and the house framing—in short, all structural work—the builder is best advised to use unplaned, raw timber as delivered straight to the saw yard, which will provide more strength at less cost (and the dimensions are easier to figure).

Nominal Dimension in inches	Dressed Dimension in inches
1	¾
2	1½
3	2½
4	3½
5	4½
6	5½
8	7½
10	9½
12	11¼

Houses built on terra firma have to withstand not only the rigors of building inspectors, but of earthquakes. Houseboats don't. They have to survive on water, where a different set of rules applies. There's a waterquake every minute or two—and there's nothing to sink foundations into. We have to build light, but we also have to build strong.

We mustn't forget charming and comfortable, either. As Albert Hunt noted: "The houseboat offers probably more change and refreshment than could be obtained by spending an equal sum on any other means of living, accommodation and amusement. Only one thing must be taken for granted or made a condition. The life ought to be more or less a lazy one. There can be no energies and activities of a very positive kind."

On to drawing plans of the wall framing. As we already know the length and width of the house that is going on the raft, all we need now is the height. Stand against a wall somewhere in a conventional house and see how much height is wasted. High ceilings create space high overhead, but besides spiders, who needs it? For a rule of thumb, side walls of 6 feet to 6 feet 5 inches will be more than adequate. A peaked roof will provide more headroom in the main area, and who stands hard against a wall anyway? Besides, there'll be shelves and furniture against them.

Boats have low cabins because designers know that when people are below, they're either sitting or lying down 90 percent of the time; headroom can be traded for sleekness or speed. We won't go to that extreme. We're building a *house*boat, not a house*boat*. And we're building to suit ourselves, too.

If your design calls for a peaked roof that extends beyond the walls over the deck, you'll need a higher wall frame, as in Figure 6-2. Make the overhanging edge whatever height is suitable (measure your tallest friend), and adjust the height of the inside frame accordingly. An alternative is to install the cantilevered frame shown in Figure 6-3, but the inside framing required to carry the weight of the overhang, while not heavy, might look unattractive if you're planning to leave the beams exposed.

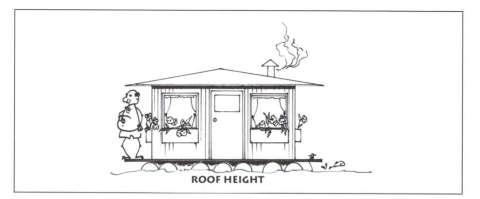

ROOF HEIGHT

Figure 6-2. **If your roof has an overhang, make sure you and your friends will fit underneath.**

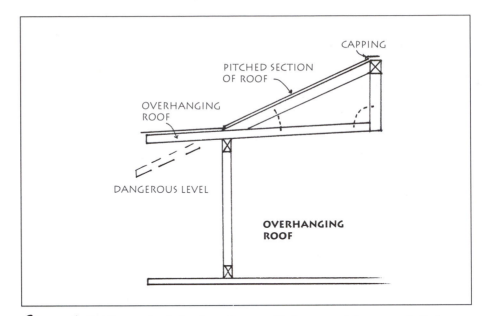

Figure 6-3. Plywood reinforcing plates, called gussets (shown as dotted lines), should be fitted to keep the secondary rafters rigid.

For example, let's say you want the side walls 32 feet long and 6 feet 5 inches high. On a piece of paper, draw a line 32 inches long to represent the bottom plate. You've started a scale drawing, at 1 inch equals 1 foot.

Make two right-angle lines at each end to represent the end studs. These sit on top of the bottom plate and hold up the top plate, and so will be 6 feet 5 inches less the combined widths of the plates. In this case, that's 5 inches. Therefore, the studs will be 6 feet long. The top plate is then represented with the final line completing the rectangle. Obviously, the top and bottom plates of the actual frame will be too long to be cut from one length of timber. The simple solution will be to abut two or three lengths together, with the joints above and below one of the wall-studs. At the joint, drive nails diagonally through the ends of the top lengths, in the case of the top plate, down into the end of the stud.

The alternative is to scarf the lengths together, as discussed previously, to create one extra-long top plate. For this purpose, it's unnecessary overkill and will prove difficult to erect.

Plywood is supplied in modular sizes, each sheet being 4 feet by 8 feet, so it's convenient to work in multiples of four, as in 24 feet or 28 feet. Therefore, mark a vertical line (in pencil) between the top and bottom plates every 4 inches to represent the edges of the ply, and then again at every 2 inches to represent every stud (remember, on our plan 1 inch equals 1 foot). The studs, as you can see, are spaced on 2-foot centers—one at the edges of each sheet of ply, and one in the middle. Plywood is very strong laterally but will flex in and out without the central stud's support. These studs will actually be 2 inches wide (if using 2 × 2s as suggested), so note that the actual gap between the studs will be 1 foot 10 inches, and the studs themselves will be *centered* on each 2-foot mark. Our hypothetical 32-footer will have 17 studs on a side.

By the way, if for some reason you are using planed lumber, which is ½ inch thinner than unplaned lumber, the gap between the studs (still on 2-foot centers) would be 1 foot 10½ inches (2 feet, less one-half stud on one side, less one-half stud on the other side; that's 24 inches, minus ¾ inch, minus ¾ inch equals 22½ inches). This rule will apply throughout: If using the lighter, less substantial lumber, you'll have to substitute 1½ inches where you read 2 inches—and the extra calculations'll be your own fault. The one wall that I built with 1½-inch studs proved wholly unsatisfactory.

Windows

Now we're ready for the windows, or rather we're ready to draw in the window holes on our plan. Windows come in all shapes and sizes. For houses ashore they're usually made of wood or aluminum. While the latter may be lighter and last longer, they are much more expensive than wooden ones bought from a demolition warehouse. And aluminum windows can't be scraped back and sanded and varnished to glow quietly along the walls. By now, the resourceful reader will have scoured the country for cheap windows and doors and stored them away in a friend's garage. With a list of their dimensions, you're now ready to plan the window holes.

When discussing windows, the overall dimensions will include the window *and its frame*, if it's intended to be an opening one. If it isn't, framing is optional.

Let's say that we've got two windows to go in the wall—one 2 feet wide and the other 6 feet 6 inches wide. Every window hole will need a stud on each side. You can save a little work and lumber by siting a window hole right next to an existing stud.

Having decided where the holes will go on the plan, allow 1 extra inch for the window frame and draw it in (i.e., for the example windows we'd mark on the plan's top plate where a 2-foot 1-inch hole will be, and where a 6-foot 7-inch hole will be). The window frames will find that extra inch very handy when they're installed; it'll provide room to move and adjust and tweak them into square so that the window sash actually opens.

Now, a lintel will go under the top plate, but it won't be much help if it just sags down on top of the window. It has to be supported free of the window frame, so there are two lintel studs at each end to do that. The

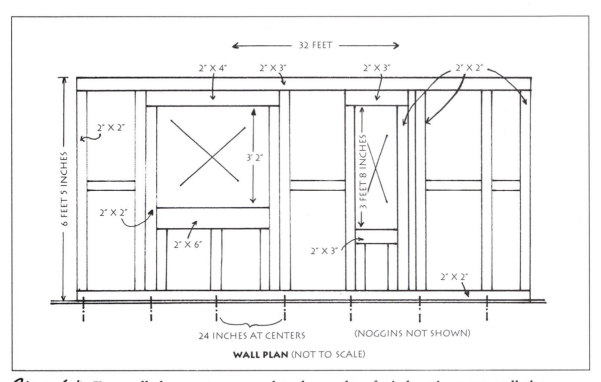

Figure 6-4. Your wall plan must accommodate the number of windows in your overall plan, including the window frames. To avoid waste, keep in mind the modular 4-foot dimension of plywood.

lintel is the length of the window holes plus the combined width of the two studs. As we're using 2-inch studs, the example lintels will be: First stud width plus window hole plus second stud width, which works out as: 2 inches plus 2 feet 1 inch plus 2 inches equals 2 feet 5 inches; and 2 inches plus 6 feet 7 inches plus 2 inches equals 6 feet 11 inches long. So far, so good, but how deep?

The 6-foot 6-inch window will need a minimum 2×4 lintel. Most houses ashore have the windows aligned along the top edge, but there's no reason why we can't line up all the bottom edges instead. So here's a hard decision: which way to go, normal or strange? If you go strange (let's say creatively exotic), then you'll lower the lintels to where you want them and drop the studs from the top plate to fill in the upper gap.

If you go normal, however, you will need to use 2×4 lintels above every window around the house. So instead of using a 2×3 for the 2-foot-wide example, we go to 2×4 here as well.

Draw in the holes for your windows on the wall plan and erase the stud lines now inside the window hole. Measure down each extra pair of lintel studs drawn next to the window holes to mark the overall depth of the windows—adding an extra inch for each window frame. That mark represents the top of the sills that bear the weight of the window. The extra-wide and extra-heavy window will need a 2×6 sill and the other one a 2×3, so measure down and mark those dimensions of the sill on the plan.

Finally, the sills are supported by short studs at each end, and possibly studs in the middle (as is the case in the extra-wide window). How long should these be, assuming we've done our arithmetic properly? Let's say our example windows are, respectively, 3 feet 2 inches and 4 feet deep. From the top, then, we have:

top plate	4 inches
lintel	4 inches
window frame	3 feet 2 inches
allowance	1 inch
sill	6 inches
bottom plate	2 inches
Total window	**4 feet 7 inches**

The overall wall height is 6 feet 5 inches, so the sill studs will be 1 foot 10 inches long, and are marked accordingly on the plan.

The windows, in most cases, will extend pretty well up to the top of the wall. This is brought about through the low ceilings, and in order to secure the light and air where most needed this is necessary. The windows will be broad and kept up pretty well from the floor.

The windows are a very important feature and the best kind and type to use must be regulated by conditions that prevail, and as these vary in almost every case, no hard and fast rule can be laid down.

William W. Atkin,
MoToR BoatinG.

Doors

For the doors we can follow traditional building practices, or we can adapt them for the houseboat. If we use a standard door, which usually is about 6 feet 6 inches high with frame and clearance, and add a 4-inch lintel and the top and bottom plates, the overall height of the wall frame is up around 7 feet 5 inches—which is getting tall. If that's acceptable, the door and frame are installed the same as a window, leaving out the bottom bearers of course. The door frame sits directly on the bottom plate, next to two studs that support a 2×4 lintel up under the top plate. These studs should be heavier than others in the wall, for the door is the main escape route in the event of catastrophe; we don't want it jamming at inopportune times. Use 2×4 studs, perhaps with additional 2×2s nailed alongside.

If, on the other hand, it's thought that the wall frames will be too high using this approach, we can employ a shortcut. We'll forget about the lintel and the door frame and run a Skilsaw across the bottom of the door to make it the height we want. If we stand two 2×4s end on where the door frame will be, that is, notched 2 inches around both the bottom and top plates so that the 2×4 projects 2 inches out onto the deck past the plates, we can screw the door hinges directly to these projecting studs. The door will then close against the top plate and the bottom plate. A pair of 2×2s nailed against the 2×4s serve as additional supports within the wall structure (total 2 by 6 inches), and provide a nailing surface for the plywood wall sheathing.

Sides and Ends

If the roof is going to be flat, the side walls and the end walls are built much the same way. With a pitched roof, however, the end-wall frames will need additional pieces to support the *ridge beam*, which runs the length of the house and forms the spine of the roof. In Figure 6-5 we can see how one central stud flanked by extra studs supports the ridge beam. The two flanking studs are made long enough to overlap the ridge beam completely on each side (they can be measured and cut on site). Notice also the packing material tucked into the pocket at the top of the studs; this ensures that the ridge beam is held tightly in place.

Each internal wall that cuts across the raft should support the ridge beam, too, providing extra strength and rigidity. These thwartship walls are called *bulkheads* on a boat—and a houseboat, too—and will look similar to the end-wall framing shown in Figure 6-5, although of course you'll have to allow for doors in the bulkheads to allow passage from room to room.

A rectangular houseboat, as in Figure 6-6, will require plans for four outside walls—two side walls and two end walls—as well as plans for the interior bulkheads. An octagonal houseboat will require five wall plans. A dome won't need any.

There's no need to build the wall in one continuous section. The wall can be divided into manageable lengths (room lengths are convenient), and can be figured out on the plans. Later, the walls for each room are built in

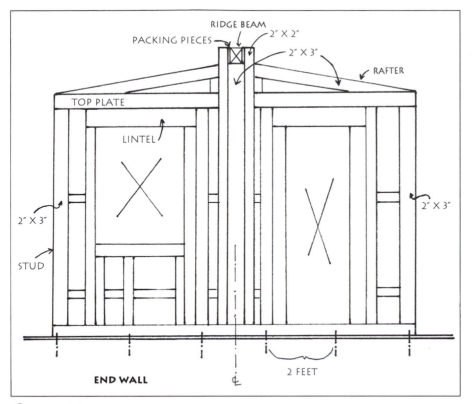

Figure 6-5. If the roof is pitched, the end-wall frames will require extra studs to support the ridge beam.

Figure 6-6. A rectangular houseboat, with an eclectic assortment of windows and doors. Your wall plan (two side walls, two end walls, and the interior bulkheads) should be drawn *after* you've decided what goes where.

stages, lifted into place, and nailed together in a steady progression along the raft.

One final point: Where two wall frames meet at right angles, that is, at corners, one of the end studs remains a 2 × 2 and the abutting one on the other wall frame should be a 2 × 3 or 2 × 4. This gives us something to nail the inside wall material to. If it's forgotten, it won't matter, as a packing piece of 1-inch lumber can be nailed on later.

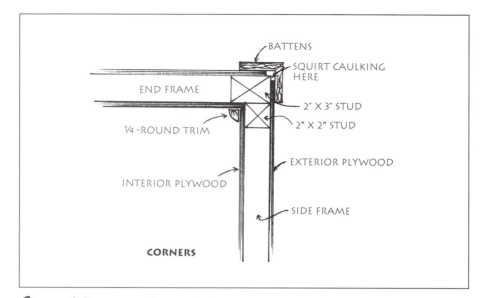

Figure 6-7. **Exterior sheets of plywood with their protective battens and the trim on the inside of the corner. Stuff insulation inside the cavities of the wall frame and staple on a plastic vapor barrier before sheathing the inside walls.**

HAMMER TIME

Now armed with freshly sketched plans for each wall, the builder can proceed to build. Just follow the instructions; it's as simple as painting by numbers.

Well, okay, it's not always simple. If you just can't fathom all this, despair not. Give the overall dimensions of the house, windows, and doors to a builder (*not* an architect), tell him which windows you want where, and I'm sure that, for a fee, you will be handed back a set of working plans, even if they're as basic as pencil sketches on yesterday's lunch wrapping.

Building the frames entails standing on the decked-in raft, sawing each piece of lumber to its correct length, then nailing each in place wherever the plans demand. Lay a stud on deck at right angles to the top plate (*always* use a 2-foot carpenter's square to make sure), and drive a 20d galvanized nail or two through the top plate into the end of the stud. Next drive two smaller nails (10d or 12d) through the sides of the stud at an angle (called toenailing) into the top plate. Nail on the bottom plate, on to the next stud, and thus one progresses; the lines on the plan transform into actual frames. No amount of words will replace the satisfaction of driving the first nail of a frame. You're building your own home, not someone else's, and not a tree hut or a shack either. A *home*.

Hint: It is astonishing the number of times a piece of wood winds up getting securely nailed to the wrong side of a pencil mark. When cutting or nailing, try annotating each pencil mark you make with an X, which means "waste this side" or "nail this side."

Another hint: Don't cut every piece of wood immediately; cut only when you need the next piece. That way, if your arithmetic is faulty you'll discover it before a stack of wood is wasted. Start building from the top plate down, fitting the studs, lintels, etc., generally working down to the bottom plate; when it's time to fit the last pieces of the jigsaw puzzle, a quick check with a ruler will confirm (or deny) the validity of your sums.

As each frame is completed and slid across the deck to its proper place, it can be lifted up and edged into the exact spot where it will live—with nails being driven through the deck and into the beams underneath to hold it in place. Nail a temporary length of lumber to the opposite end of the deck, lay the other end across a bearer or against a stud in the newly lifted wall, and when you're sure the wall is plumb, nail it to the stud to hold the wall in place. You can't use a level, because if you're afloat, you're probably rocking; if you're aground, the shoreline probably slopes. Instead, try this useful bit of Euclidean geometry: 4 measures along the deck and 3 measures up the wall frame coincide perfectly with 5 measures joining those two points. In a triangle, the ratio 3:4:5 produces a right angle at the base.

Now raise the adjoining wall frame and nail them together at the corner. When all the frames are standing and nailed together and the inside wall frames are in place, it's time to install the ridge beam. Now it looks like a house. Like the deck, however, the area within the house framing will look *far too small* when it first goes up. Resist the urge to rip it down and build bigger. It'll be fine.

THE ROOF

A flat roof is easy to erect: Just nail 2×3 or 2×4 rafters from one side wall across to the other every 2 or 4 feet along the top plates. The roof may terminate at the wall edges or extend out over the side decks. A flat roof, covered in corrugated iron, will shed water just as readily as a peaked one and will provide a lower, perhaps more nautical profile. A flat roof, by its very nature, can only move in one direction—that, unfortunately, is downward, and materials overhead, other than iron, like plywood, should be regarded with caution if not disdain. A flat but insubstantial roof will soon sag, and a sagging roof will very quickly lead to leaks. A sagging roof with snow on it will very quickly lead to collapse. *Builders in areas with snow or heavy rains, however, should opt for the extra strength and weather-shedding ability of a peaked roof.*

Ridge Beams and Barge Boards

The central element of any peaked roof is the ridge and its ridge beam, each end of which is supported by the end frame. If the roof isn't intended to extend past the end walls, the ridge beam will be the same length as the outer wall frames. It is cut to length (if you scarf timbers together, as discussed in Chapter 4, to make a long one, the joints should be made over an internal wall) and then manhandled into position. Lift each end up to a top plate on a side frame; then, with builder and companion sitting on top of the frame at each end, lift it up and drop it into the pockets in the end frames.

If the roof is intended to extend over either end deck to create outside areas protected from sun and rain, it will require additional support. Figure 6-8 shows how this is done. It may look complicated, but it's worth tackling. The ridge beam is cut to the required length and installed as mentioned above. When the rafters are fitted (which we're coming to), the ones destined to sit atop the end frame are cut into segments, leaving, as in the example, 2-inch gaps on 2-foot-or-so centers. These will house 2 × 4 pieces that run parallel to the ridge beam and extend from the preceding rafter (on the right) out over the end wall the same length as the ridge beam. A set of barge boards is then nailed across the ends of the protruding beams to tidy the appearance and to protect the end grain.

If you can find them, use Z-nails to secure these overhanging pieces of wood (and the rafters, too). Z-nails look, not surprisingly, like Zs. One end is driven horizontally into a beam; the other end is driven into the adjoining plate. If you can't find Z-nails, use rafter ties—twisted metal plates perforated for nails (check lumberyards).

Rafters

Rafters act as A-frames, components of a structurally strong triangle that compress together as load is applied to the roof. Rafters made of

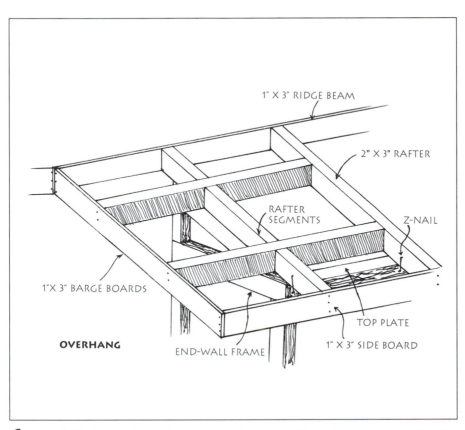

Figure 6-8. If you plan to have an overhang, you'll need extra support for the roof.

2 × 4s should be strong enough for most sensibly sized houseboats. You could use 2 × 3s, but only if the walls are reasonably close together, say no more than 9 feet.

You may want the rafters to extend out over the side decks. This makes a sheltered area where one can pull on gumboots and a raincoat before venturing forth into the elements. It also protects the sidewindows from driving rain. When measuring the lengths of rafters, cut one first to use as a template, or pattern, because you'll have to trim the end of the rafter to the angle at which it abuts the ridge beam (see Figure 6-5).

Cut off the protruding end, or tail, of the rafter at the same angle as the end against the ridge beam so that it is plumb. That is, if the ridge beam end is cut at 30 degrees, then cut the outer end at 30 degrees, too. This is easily done if you make a cardboard pattern (or even better, use a mitering block, which can be adjusted and tightened as a permanent gauge). Once you get the pattern to fit properly (try it at several places along the walls, on *both sides of the ridge beam*), cut your rafters to shape.

How many rafters, you ask? Not as many as there are wall studs, because unlike the walls, the roof carries little weight, unless you're in snow country. A rafter every 4 feet—every 2 feet or even 16 inches if you're expecting snow—will be ample. Mark the top plates and the ridge beam (you did bring a ladder didn't you?) at 4-foot intervals. Again, the marks indicate the centers of the rafters, so add two marks an inch out on each side of the center mark. Do the same along the top plates.

The rafters are now lifted up and nailed in place, hard against the ridge beam and on top of the top plates. Finally, to fill the gaps along the top plate between the rafters, cut and fit lengths of 2 × 4 blocking. You may want to leave several open to use as ventilators. Add a small hinged flap on the inside (when you're finished framing). Leave them open in summer or whenever the houseboat is unattended, and shut them in the winter.

The entire frame has been built at this point, and merely awaits covering. If it seems a little floppy and loose in the wind, don't worry. The plywood sheathing in the next chapter will lock everything into place.

At this point the builder has the option of splashing creosote or another wood preservative, such as Cuprinol or WoodLife, along the frames, particularly at floor level. These products are very good at repelling water, so you might want to use some in the bathroom area, too. Most of them—particularly creosote—stink for a while, though, and they're hazardous chemicals, too.

Decision time.

CHAPTER SEVEN
· · · · · · · · · · · · ·

Filling In the Spaces

*W*hat makes the life so particularly jolly in England is the fact that there are so many people who are taking their leisure so truly leisurely, and who have houseboats on which entertainments are given for the delight of other houseboaters as well as the occasional guest from the city. Evening hops on deck, smokers' parties, musicales and chafing-dish regalements are more than delightful under these al fresco conditions.

~~~~~~~~~~~~~~~~~~~~~~~~~~~~~~

If the local weather forecast is for rain (or even worse, blizzards), it's a good idea to start thinking about roofing. Even if the walls are still bare frames, it is uncommonly pleasant to be able to work on the raft in most weather; if it rains or if it shines, the builder cares not one jot.

97

In what my grandfather would call "the good old days," most house-boats used tongue-and-groove (T&G) planking for both the roof and the walls. The most commonly used sizes and treatments for roofs were as follows:

- ¾ × 8 T&G pine or spruce, with 10-ounce canvas and paint
- 1 × 4 T&G pine, with tar and gravel roofing paper
- 1⅛ × 3 T&G cedar, with 10-ounce canvas and glue
- 1 × 3 T&G spruce, with 10-ounce canvas and glue
- ⅞ × 3 T&G fir, with 12-ounce canvas and paint
- ¾ × 3 T&G pine, with 8- or 10-ounce canvas and paint

ROOFING

There is no reason a builder today couldn't revisit the past and use individual tongue-and-groove planks cut and nailed in place along the rafters, then covered with canvas and paint or marine glue. "Marine glue—one part india-rubber, twelve parts mineral naphtha or coal tar; heat gently, mix, and add twenty parts of powdered shellac. Pour out on a slab to cool; when used, to be heated to about 250 degrees Fahrenheit," saith the indefatigable *Sailor's Pocket Book*. We can obtain far more strength per weight, however, by using plywood. It's also extremely quick and easy to install.

Particle board or oriented strand board (Aspenite is a common trade name) is marginally cheaper than plywood, but it is heavier, not as strong, and of dubious durability in a wet environment. Softboard or even cardboard *could* be used, because it's even cheaper still, but it would have as much strength as a dead haddock. It wouldn't lock any strength into the house.

What goes over the ply (or the tongue-and-groove, for that matter) is entirely the builder's choice. You might like tiles, canvas, tarpaper, shingles, thatch, or brushed-on epoxy resin protected from the sun with paint. You could even glue on thin sheets of aluminum printing-press plates discarded by newspaper printers. Look around the neighborhood to see what is the preferred method ashore, and then adapt it to the watery element.

In most areas, the cheapest, fastest, and most permanent way to waterproof the plywood roof sheathing is to use corrugated metal sheets. This is not a job to undertake when the wind is blowing, however. The sheets are lethal if they get ripped from a builder's hands to scythe their way across the shore.

For that matter, if you are confronted by a windy season when building or are of a nervous disposition, put on the wall sheathing before going any further. Aerodynamicists will notice the resemblance the sheathed roof bears to an airplane wing. If you are building in settled conditions or if you adore a challenge when it's blowing, put the roof on before the side walls. There's really only one advantage in saving the wall sheathing until later, and that's being able to clamber up and down the framing like a monkey as you work.

Plywood

A houseboat is basically a series of interconnected shapes made of plywood. With this material we can make anything—any shape or configuration, any length or width, any design or lack of design. We need only cut the plywood to the shape of our fanciful construct and stick pieces of framing timber underneath the edges to nail things to—and if the framing happens to conform to land-based building codes, then so much the better (provided we remember we're trying to save weight).

Plywood is available in many different grades, thicknesses, types, and timbers, including teak, spruce, Fijian kauri, fir, mahogany, or plain old concrete-form ply. Rather than waste space listing them all, I'll leave it to the reader to inquire of the local timber merchant, who will know what is available to suit your needs in your area. In most cases, ½-inch plywood will be strong enough for anything short of hurricanes and high-velocity encounters with tropical reefs. That is not to say that heavier grades can't be used. In fact, using ¾-inch or even 1-inch ply would allow you to reduce the total number of studs in the wall framing, the middle studs becoming superfluous.

Although you can use premium plywood made of rare veneers, I have seen houseboats made of the cheapest grade plywood available, namely ³⁄₁₆-inch car-case ply used for crating imported automobiles. The houseboats are still going strong. But if absolute economy is not a factor, use a good grade of exterior sheathing ply. Plywood that has been pressure treated with wood preservative (Tanalized is one trade name) is preferable to untreated plywood in the rigorous marine environment, particularly for walls, which are nearer the water. A warning: Pressure-treated wood is pressure treated with poison. Wear a dust mask when cutting and wash the sawdust off exposed skin.

Roof Sheathing

Generally, the plywood sheets comprising the roof sheathing will be laid over the rafters, forming the inside ceiling. It's a good idea to paint or varnish their interior surfaces before putting them up; it beats getting a crick in the neck painting or varnishing them when they're overhead. Before the sheathing goes on, the rafters can also be varnished, painted, stained, creosoted, or even hand-carved.

To get started, the ply is nailed on along the ridge beam so that each edge meets over the beam, with no cracks visible from inside. Working carefully along each side of the plywood, drive in 1½-inch galvanized nails, but don't sit on the sheet as it's being nailed: this forces the plywood to assume a permanent curve.

Nail each sheet down each rafter, and along the top plate. If the distance from ridge beam to top plate is more than 8 feet, the length of a normal plywood sheet, and there's a great gaping hole left to fill, then nail on extra lengths of 2 × 2 lengthwise between the rafters to accommodate the edges of the next sheet that will be joined there.

When the roof is sheathed, we're ready to cover it with something weatherproof and permanent. By now you should have decided what you want to use. Composition shingles or roll roofing can be applied directly over the plywood by scrupulously following the instructions packed with the roofing material. If you're using the recommended corrugated metal sheets, however, you've got a little more carpentry to do. You'll need to add *purlins*, framing members that run the length of the roof to which we nail the corrugated metal.

Figure 7-1 shows the basic roof structure: The rafters sit atop the top plates, the ply sits atop the rafters, the purlins sit atop the ply, the corrugated metal sits atop the purlins, the ridgecapping sits atop the corrugated iron, and no doubt seagulls will then sit atop them all. Notice also the barge boards nailed on the ends of the rafters, with 2 inches or so of metal roofing projecting over all to form a drip edge.

A good rule of thumb is to have an aggregate of 6 inches of timber up there. Thus if the rafters are 2 × 3, use 2 × 3 purlins; if the rafters are 2 × 4, use 2 × 2s or even 2 × 3s if you like.

The first purlin down from the ridge beam is positioned to provide a nailing surface for both the top edge of the metal roofing and the ridgecapping. If the capping measures, say, 9 inches from edge to center, fit the first row of purlins 8 inches from the ridge beam. Fit another row where you think the top plate will be, visible by the rows of nails along the ply. A professional carpenter would probably climb down, measure the distance from the plywood's edge to the top plate, then climb back up again, mark it out properly, and snap a chalk line so that the purlin over the plate goes in arrow-straight. It's an option. Then, add more rows through the middle of the roof at whatever intervals you like, say from 2 to 4 feet—whatever divides the space equally. No particular reason; just to

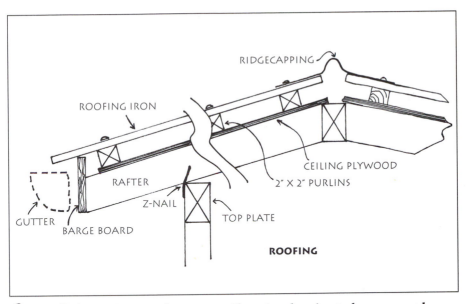

Figure 7-1. **The basic roof structure. If you're planning to have exposed rafters, lay down a vapor barrier over the plywood decking, then stuff insulation between the purlins.**

be consistent and tidy. If the space were 7 feet, for example, then one more row, 3 feet 6 inches down, would be fine.

Ideally, you should now stuff insulation between the purlins to insulate the houseboat's interior from the weather outside and the noise of the rain, which can be thunderous on a metal roof. Flip ahead to Chapter 11 for a discussion of insulation choices, but anything with air bubbles in it will do, from old egg cartons to Styrofoam.

Corrugated Metal

Corrugated metal is ordered in two dimensions, length (the length of the rafter *plus* 2 inches), and *cover*—which is not the width of a sheet, but the area of sheet remaining after overlapping 1½ corrugations with the adjoining sheet. Rather than force customers to work out all this convoluted math, lumberyards only need to know the distance from ridge to eave, and the total length of the roof (i.e., the net area covered). With those figures in hand, they'll be able to tell you how many sheets you'll need.

You'll need two other items, the aforementioned ridgecapping and endcapping (you won't need ridgecapping if you've chosen to build a flat or single-pitched roof). As we've seen, the ridgecapping sits proudly atop

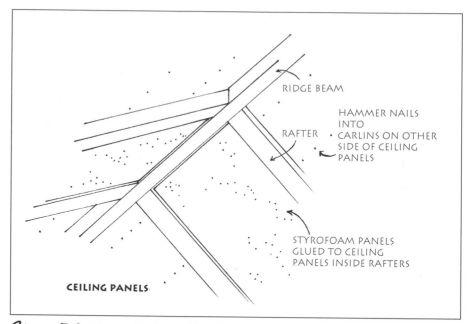

RIDGE BEAM

HAMMER NAILS INTO CARLINS ON OTHER SIDE OF CEILING PANELS

RAFTER

STYROFOAM PANELS GLUED TO CEILING PANELS INSIDE RAFTERS

CEILING PANELS

Figure 7-2. **Alternatively, add insulating ceiling panels on the inside, between the rafters.**

the whole roof and covers the uppermost ends of the corrugated metal. The endcapping runs down the edges of the metal at each end of the roof, the upper end of the corrugated iron running *under* the ridgecapping, and seals this area against the weather. You'll need enough ridgecapping to run the entire length of your roof, and enough endcapping to cover each of the four ends (assuming a peaked roof).

You'll also need special nails, with barbed shanks and rubber gaskets (your dealer will have them). These keep out the rain, but *only* when the nails are driven into the *top* of the corrugation, not into the valley. Normally, you'll need a nail about every three or four corrugations, and always along an overlapping edge, where it secures both top and bottom sheets.

Before we get started, if you're using corrugated iron it's a good idea to give the edges a coat of metal primer to inhibit rust. Although the sheets are galvanized, over time moisture trapped beneath the overlap eventually will cause rust to attack the unprotected edges. Corrugated aluminum won't need this treatment.

Now, with materials in hand, and only light winds blowing, stand the sheets of metal, say one or two at a time, on the deck leaning against the roof edge, and then clamber up onto the roof. Pull a sheet up toward you and slide it up the length of the roof. Push it along until the edge is aligned with the edge of the roof (i.e., the first rafter), then tack it into place, using

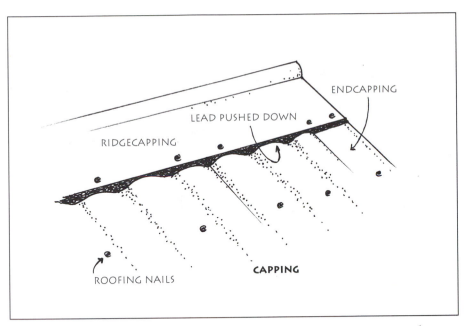

Figure 7-3. Ridgecapping covers the uppermost ends of the corrugated metal, sealing out the weather.

one of your gasketed nails somewhere in the middle of the sheet, into a middle purlin.

Bring up another sheet and slip it over—or under—the first, with 1½ corrugations covered by—or covering—the ones on the first sheet. Which way this works depends on which way you want the exposed edge of each sheet to face—North, South, East, or West. It is always preferable to have them facing the direction that bad weather does *not* come from. Driving rain will not penetrate an edge facing away from it.

If you start laying the roof from the bad-weather end, turn the sheet so that the edge rolling upward is also facing the bad-weather quadrant. The edge rolling downward will then be facing the lee quadrant, where you are. The next sheet brought up and laid down will be slid *underneath* the edge of the first one, so that the downward roll is into the valley of the second sheet. The second sheet is then tacked into place, somewhere in the middle, on the middle purlin. Go back to the first sheet, and when both sheets look to be fairly square, run a line of nails along the middle and bottom purlins. Remember not to nail into the valleys, and don't drive any nails into the extreme edge yet, or along the ridge-beam purlin.

Back to the first sheet. Lay the endcapping so that it fits comfortably on the edge, overlapping a few corrugations one way and the face of the end rafter the other way. When it all looks true, nail it down, still keeping the top purlin free. We won't nail into the top purlin until the ridgecapping—the final addition—goes on.

It should be easy from now on. The next sheet is brought up and put into place, the corrugations overlapping as they're supposed to, and it's nailed on—and so it goes, until finally, the endcapping at the far end is installed. The process is repeated on the other side of the roof, and there we have it: a new roof. That is, it will be when the ridgecapping is in place.

As the sheets of metal are aligned with an eye toward the direction of fierce weather, so too are the pieces of ridgecapping. Unfurl the lead seal along each edge of the ridgecapping, then start nailing, aiming to penetrate the capping piece, then the metal underneath, into the top purlin. When the whole thing's been nailed on, push the lead foil into each corrugation to seal everything against the weather. That's it. It's incredibly satisfying to stand under a roof you've just built. Especially if it's begun to rain.

WALLING

Out of interest, the good-old-days criteria for houseboat walls went along these lines:

- 1 × 8-inch shiplapped pine
- ¾ × 6-inch shiplapped cypress
- ¾ × 4-inch T&G pine or white cedar
- ½-inch sheets of Homosote wall boarding

The good old days notwithstanding, plywood is the best material to use for sheathing a houseboat, combining as it does light weight, low cost, great strength, easy application, and absolute weather seal. To capture the look of a period houseboat, ⅜-inch planks, perhaps with V-shaped edges, can be nailed on top of the plywood wall sheathing, but be sure to allow for the extra weight by using the time-honored method of loading that much weight aboard and seeing what happens. You may find you'd rather use that extra weight allowance to bring aboard more books.

Plywood wall sheathing is prepared much the same as sheets of roofing metal: A couple of coats of primer paint, either acrylic or enamel, are brushed thoroughly into the edges of each sheet of ply. The paint protects the laminations from absorbing water and delaminating. A builder conversant with the mixing and applications of marine resins would use them instead, but paint will be okay. Priming paint is best, but any will do—as long as it soaks in and is thoroughly done.

Begin sheathing by cutting a sheet of plywood to the height of the wall frame *plus* enough overlap to drop down into the scupper. This will prevent water from penetrating under the bottom plate, and tie the house and raft together to make an extremely strong, rigid structure. Use 1½-inch (5d) galvanized nails, and don't skimp on them, nailing at about 2- to 2½-inch intervals into all the members of the wall framing—the studs, noggins, sills, lintels, and top plates. These plywood plates are the strength of the houseboat.

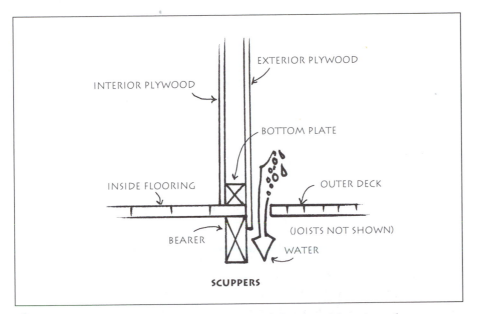

SCUPPERS

Figure 7-4. The plywood sheathing, cut so that it overlaps into the scupper, will prevent water from penetrating under the bottom plate and add strength to the house/deck joint. If the bottom plate is 2 inches thick and the deck is 1 inch thick, add another 5 or 6 inches of plywood.

If you don't plan to install an interior lining, but instead intend to leave the studs exposed, staple builder's paper to the studs and framework before nailing on the plywood. To eliminate the unsightliness of the builder's paper as seen inside, we could fill the gaps between the studs with softboard or similar, which would be effective insulation as well. However, skipping internal lining is not advisable in climates where the word "winter" has any meaning.

"Studs constitute the foundation of most exterior walls of houseboats, and oftentimes a very good result is obtained by leaving them exposed inside, staining them and filling the space between with some goods or stuff, the whole giving the effect of a panel," was Bill Atkin's opinion. I think he meant the internal cavity could be lined with, say, softboard covered in burlap. Alternatively, the 2-inch depth left by the studs could be used for shelving, but what can you put on a 2-inch shelf? A far better idea would be to pack as much insulation in there as we can get and cover it with a layer of plywood (with a 6-mil poly vapor barrier between ply and insulation; see Chapter 11). Insulation keeps out the heat of summer just as effectively as it keeps out the cold of winter. And the twin layers of ply enclosing the wall frames will give our houseboat enviable strength.

Start a'plying in one corner and proceed around the house, just as you did with the roof. If there is a hole for a window, hold the sheet of ply against the frame and mark the hole's shape from inside, on the back of the sheet, then lay the sheet down and cut out the hole. Hold it up again and nail it on. Don't worry about bringing the edges of the sheet exactly into line with the next one, or with the sill or window studs: 2- or 3-inch battens (possibly 4-inch if your building technique is really hopeless) will cover *all* joints.

If you work steadily around the frames, the whole thing will be enclosed relatively quickly. The result may look a little strange, but take heart: The worst is definitely over. The house structure is standing, the roof is on, the walls are up, and all that remains is a little fine-tuning.

Figure 7-5 shows two ways to deal with the top edges of the sheets of ply where they meet the rafters. The first method (a), with the ply notched to fit snugly between the protruding rafters, is tidy. Some people have trouble keeping things tidy, however, so in (b), the top edge of the ply finishes at the bottom of the rafters, leaving the top plate exposed. A batten, perhaps 5 or 6 inches wide, is then fitted and notched around the rafters. Either way, some notchin' gotta be done, but a thin batten can be worked much more easily than a long, awkward sheet of ply.

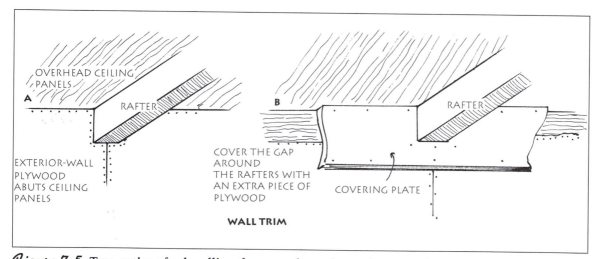

WALL TRIM

Figure 7-5. Two options for handling the area where plywood meets rafters. A separate plywood covering plate adds strength and places fewer demands on craftsmanship.

The first method is fractionally stronger, locking as it does the top and bottom plates together with a strong plywood gusset, but the second method will protect the top edge of the plywood from moisture, particularly if paint is spread along the edge beforehand. The batten will hide the joint—and the color of the reject paint that you've found no use for until now.

Windowing and Dooring

Did I say that the worst was over? I lied. We forgot the windows. It's worth having windows, of course. The views are unparalleled. Installing windows and building window frames are not the easiest of jobs, though, and you're left with an array of puzzling options as to how to proceed.

There was much to watch from our windows, too. The boats on the big river could be seen, often tying up their tows to double-trip up through the cut-offs. Many boats came into the Greenville lake, some of the largest ones. Frequent passers-by were two small boats towing sand and gravel from the sand digger we had passed on the way down. The boat we observed with most interest, however, was the Sandford E. Hutson, *a small old steamboat, side-wheel, with one stack. It came pounding down from Greenville in a cloud of steam, with a log barge and derrick, went out into the river and we never saw it again. This boat was a survival of the past. . . .*

Harlan Hubbard, *Shantyboat: A River Way of Life*. Lexington: The University Press of Kentucky. Copyright 1953 and 1981 by Harlan Hubbard.

A frame is a box that surrounds the window sash (the wooden bit that holds the glass) and it is to the frame that the sash is hinged. In the case of nonopening windows, the sash is nailed or screwed to the frame.

Avoid unframed windows as a first option; as a second, put them in the wall unframed. The third option is to frame the windows but leave them nonopening; the fourth is to get someone else to frame them. The fifth option is to bite the bullet and do it yourself. We'll do a version that avoids dovetailing joinery and all that hard stuff.

Assuming you want the windows mounted flush with the wall, measure the wall's total thickness: If it has 2-inch studs, ½-inch outer ply, and ¼-inch inner lining, we have a total wall thickness of 2 ¾ inches—the width of the 1-inch planking we'd use to make the window frame. If we don't

Figure 7-6. **Installing large windows will be worth the time and effort.**

mind having frames poking out of the wall, we'd use whatever width was convenient, like 1 × 3 or 1 × 4, with, respectively, ¼-inch and 1¼-inch protrusions. For the dogged planed timber enthusiasts, that'd mean a ¾-inch × 2½-inch plank would leave ¼ inch protruding from a wall that comprised 1½-inch studs, plywood of ½-inch external and ¼-inch internal, by the way.

To find the overall dimensions of the frame, use the formulas below. Let's say we have a window sash 18 inches wide by 42 inches high, we're using the 1-inch framing lumber mentioned above, and we want to fit the window between two studs. We'll take the horizontal dimension first:

A ½" gap on each side	=	1"
Frame width, 1" each side	=	2"
Sash width	=	18"
A little for luck	=	⅛"
Total		**21 ⅛"**

The extra ⅛ inch is to give the sash room to swing. Adding all that up, we'd cut the top piece of the 1-inch framing 21 ⅛ inches long. This is the first piece of our box.

Now measure the length of the sash and, using our example and the formula and measuring from the bottom, calculate the length of the frame members:

Sill to frame	Thickness of frame	Length of window sash	Allowance for sash
½"	1"	42"	⅛"

Figuring our example sash at 42 inches long, the frame sides will be 43 ⅝ inches; we need to cut two of them. These planks will be nailed to the top plank to form a sort of wooden Greek *pi*; the top plank goes *on top*: the bottom plank is fitted later, *between* the two side ones.

Measure ½ inch from each end of the top plank and mark it with a pencil. Then mark the frame thickness—in the example above, 1 inch. Nail the side planks to these marks, leaving an inner space equal to the sash width plus ⅛ inch (example, 21 ⅛ inches).

Measure down the side planks from the top piece a distance equal to the sash length plus ⅛ inch, and mark them. The bottom plank—which is the same as the inner space (example again, 21 ⅛ inches)—will then be nailed into place, with its outer edge angled down just a little to let rainwater run off. It's not easy to describe, but by referring to Figure 7-7, you'll see that the frame is a simple box, but a box with a unique way of going together. Once you've made a few, you'll be an expert at it.

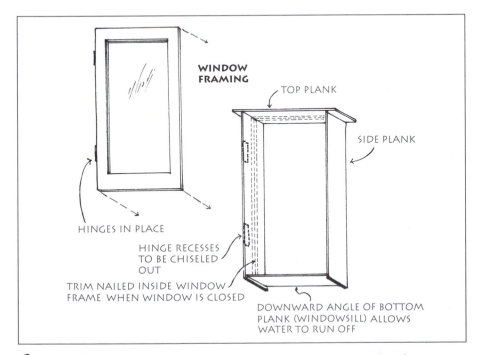

Figure 7-7. With the hinge areas recessed into the inside window frames, insert the framed window panel. Shim it in place with shingle scraps while you screw the hinges in place.

Finally, it's time to fit the hinges. Hold the sash in place in the frame and decide where you want them. (Hinges are mounted on the side of the window that swings out.) Mark their locations on the front of the sash, then pull the sash out of the frame. Next, lay each open hinge against the edge of the sash, against its mark, and carefully mark the outlines of the hinge leaves. You need to chisel out a sliver of wood equal to the hinge leaves' thickness from both the frame and the sash. Stand the sash on its opposite edge and gently tap the chisel into the pencilled outlines to a depth equal to the thickness of the hinge leaf. Now lay the sash flat and gently tap the chisel along the surface, inside the outlines, to gouge out (carefully) the recess.

Screw the hinge leaves to the sash, then lift the window into the window frame. Using the same technique, mark and chisel matching recesses on the inside of the frame, then screw the other hinge leaves into place. That wasn't so bad, was it?

It's easier to frame nonopening windows. Make the frame as before and drive some nails through, from the outer edge, into the window sash (use screws if you doubt your hammering abilities near all that glass).

Figure 7-8 shows how the now-framed windows are inserted into the holes in the wall. Each frame is lifted into place, and nails to hold the frame are driven through the studs from inside the house, into the sides of the frame. The nails are not driven home. In a sense, the frames balance in the holes and are held loosely by the nails. By levering the frame up and down and to and fro inside the hole, you can quickly set it square and true so that the sash opens and closes smoothly. A catch will eventually be put on the sash and frame to lock it.

Surplus, already framed windows that have come directly out of the walls of houses will have wider frames, usually 4 or 6 inches. They will protrude from the wall, but this need not be unattractive and helps to break up the wall's flat uniformity. A wide frame is shown in Figure 7-9, where 6-inch battens are tucked tightly up against the side of the frame and nailed into the wall, with narrower battens added on top, again tight against the frame, after mastic or silicone caulking has been smeared liberally into the corner created by the first batten. Another layer of caulking can be run along the joint for a truly weatherproof seal.

Battens are thin planks, of whatever size seems appropriate, measured, cut, and nailed along every plywood seam. Caulking or other waterproofing compound is smeared liberally on the inside of the batten when it is put up and nailed. The corner of the house has battens that overlap one another, just to make sure the seal is as tight as possible and to keep the weather outside where it belongs.

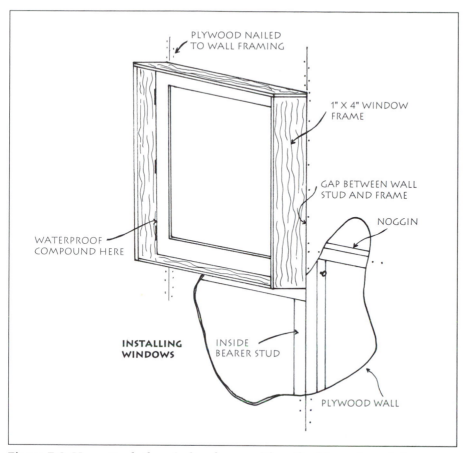

Figure 7-8. Now attach the window frame with nails, driven through from inside the house. Caulk the gaps between frame and studs.

Where window frames are custom-made for the walls, battens are nailed directly across the gaps, into the studs on one side and the face of the frame on the other. Again, don't spare the caulking.

FINISHING

Windows completed; now to the doors. Try to find doors in their frames, but if it's not possible—or you've made your own door out of a gorgeous slab of heart-red cedar or the like—then you'll have to make a frame pretty much like the window frames, but without the bottom sill piece. As mentioned in the last chapter, sometimes it's easier just to hang the door directly from the stud adjoining and eschew building a frame. Trim

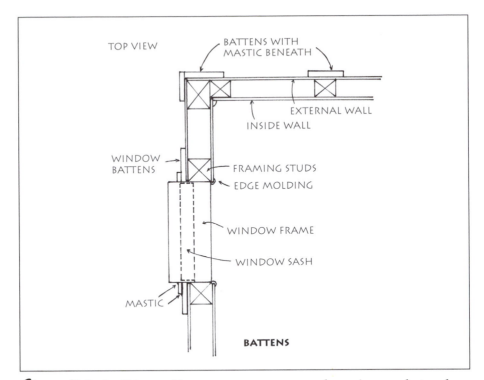

TOP VIEW

BATTENS WITH MASTIC BENEATH

EXTERNAL WALL

INSIDE WALL

WINDOW BATTENS

FRAMING STUDS

EDGE MOLDING

WINDOW FRAME

WINDOW SASH

MASTIC

BATTENS

Figure 7-9. **Caulking and battens at corners, around openings, and at each plywood joint help create a weatherproof seal.**

battens can then be added easily, and we've already got a doorstep: the bottom plate where the door goes.

When a latch is screwed or bolted to the door, the house stops being a construction site and becomes a secure home. Furniture can be brought aboard to sit in and sleep on; an oven can be installed for cooking. While the living standard may be little more than basic, it's a beginning.

Now let's leave linearity behind and loosen up a bit here. People do strange things with houseboats. They put odd-shaped bits of Plexiglas in the wall and call them windows; they hang bus doors out front instead of conventional wooden things from suburbia; they even mount backless china cabinets in a wall to make them into 180-degree windows instead of repositories for the untouchable china of dusty aunts.

Long, elegant windows can be turned sideways to make short, expansive ones. Plastic fishbowls can be screwed over round holes in the wall to make ogling portholes, and window sashes can be mounted in the roof to make skylights (and here is a place to be positively lavish with caulking). Doors can be cut in half to make Dutch barn doors, and automobile windows can be installed in walls to wind up and down electrically.

Frankly, you can do anything you damn-well please, if:

- you've got something to nail to and

- you squirt caulking anywhere there's a gap to make the whole thing weatherproof.

Cladding and Trimming

Moving in aside, there remains only the interior plywood cladding and the trim. The homeowner (for that's what you've become if you've gotten this far) could opt for the lovely effects of tongue-and-groove panelling or anything else you fancy and can afford. With a pragmatic nod to frugality, we'll carry on with ¼-inch plywood. It's about as thin as we can go; depending on the state of the budget, the builder's nervousness, and the amount of weight already built in, you could use ⅜-inch, ½-inch, or even thicker ply.

You'll need as many sheets as you used outside, but be sure that the joints don't fall directly on the same studs. Where the first sheet was applied outside, cut a sheet down the middle and start with half a sheet on the inside. This seemingly minor concession of staggering the joints will add to the great strength of your houseboat.

Before nailing up the inside plywood, stuff as much insulation as possible into the cavities between the framing pieces. This is also a good time to fit the plumbing hoses and the power cables, if you don't want them to be seen. Read through the next two chapters for details, but it's simply a matter of feeding the pipes and wires along the studs to their respective destinations, and predrilling holes in the wall panels through which the pipes and wires can be pulled to their ultimate destinations.

Figure 7-10 shows the three basic types: half-round trims any two adjoining edges on a flat surface; quarter-round is tacked into corners; cove molding, or scotia, is used like quarter-round, usually between ceiling and wall; L-moldings and flat moldings cover edges and corners or projecting edges.

Shower boxes can be lined with plywood impregnated with epoxy marine resin, but it is easier to buy specially formulated panels, like Seratone or Formica, that positively reject water. The panels, like ply, are available only in modular sizes and can be installed by following the instructions.

What follows next is the application of varnish or paint, each within the dictates of whim or fancy. As there are so many possibilities, potentials, and pitfalls in home decorating, we won't digress: Any paint merchant worth his salt would be happy to discuss your ideas.

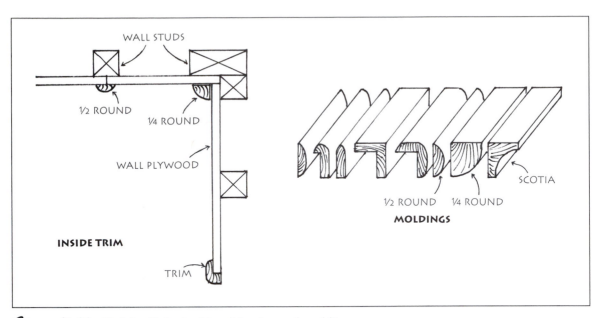

Figure 7-10. **Finish off the inside with trim and molding.**

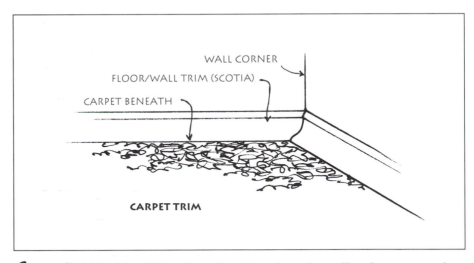

Figure 7-11. **Add molding along the edge where the wall and carpet or other flooring meet, too.**

Flooring

Meanwhile, down at toe level, it's time to think of comfort. Foam or felt underlayment can be dragged aboard and laid down, with carpeting laid over that. (Old reject carpets can be used instead of underlay.) The more layers of carpet, the softer the tread, and the less draft up the trouser leg. Floor trim, called baseboard or scotia, can then be added along the bottom edges to really tidy the whole room.

A floor can be left bare, too—sanded smooth and varnished, or just waxed—but because of rising dampness, only if it's a second floor laid over the raft decking, with a layer of plastic or builder's paper sandwiched between.

Celebrating

Well, it's celebration time. You're halfway through the book and two-thirds of the way through building the house—and the best part is yet to come. It's time to pass around the beer and pull the cork from a bottle of champagne. You've done a lot of work by now, and are entitled to invite a few friends over to toast the beginning of a beautiful relationship.

Important Diseases and Injuries of the Head

The following conditions are of such frequent occurrence that their symptoms and treatment should be clearly understood and remembered.

Intoxication

Cause.—Excess in drink.

Symptoms.—Odour of liquor in breath, insensibility usually not complete, patient can usually be roused, no stertorous breathing, pupils of equal size, and usually dilated (large), cornea sensitive to touch, temperature of body 2 degrees to 3 degrees below normal, pulse soft and frequent, no difference between sides of body, both being equally helpless.

Treatments.—Emetics; cold water applied to head; warmth to surface of body and extremities.

Admiral Sir Frederick Bedford, *The Sailor's Pocket Book: A Collection of Practical Rules, Notes, and Tables, for the Use of The Royal Navy, The Mercantile Marine, and Yacht Squadrons.* Portsmouth: Griffin & Co., 1898.

Figure 7-12. The interior of *Tsunami* under construction—exposed rafter beams can be effective. The windows are recessed into 6-inch-thick walls.

Your houseboat can now be lived in, and it's time to quit the apartment or the tent or the camper in which you've suffered so long. There remain a few refinements yet to install, but not everyone on this planet has plumbing in their home, nor electricity. Water can be brought aboard in a jerry-can, and candles can light the way to the sink, at least until you've completed the final stages of building your new floating home.

CHAPTER EIGHT
Water Inside, Too

For the bachelor the houseboat is a moveable home, where he can repay any obligations by entertaining his friends on board.

There is nothing complicated about plumbing. Water is collected at one end of the system and comes out another; what we do with it in between keeps plumbers amused and their bankers fat and happy. This business of plumbing is where we begin our journey down the road of self-sufficiency, which we shall pursue right through to the end of the book.

Water is something we must have—for drinking, cooking, making cups of java, washing dishes, cleaning our teeth, or standing in a shower. Seawater can be used for cooking, being already lightly garnished with salt. It can also be used for washing dishes (especially if you use—no plug intended—Joy dishwashing detergent, which rinses free in salt water), but obviously we're also going to need fresh water. And since many houseboaters are moored in fresh water already, let me amend that to read, *clean* fresh water. Who would dare today to follow this advice written in 1935 in *How to Build 20 Boats*: "A shallow well dug 6 to 10 feet from the river bank will nearly always yield good water and a tank could be mounted on the roof with a hand pump and length of hose to pump it full." Not unless I was a hundred miles from the nearest factory, buddy.

RUNNING IN

Fortunately, the planet takes care of our freshwater needs, and has for millennia. Water vapor in clouds precipitates and falls on our heads (unless we're standing under umbrellas) and on the roof, where it runs down into gutters. The gutters (use rust-free PVC gutters installed per the manufacturer's instructions) run along the eaves of the roof and convey rainwater to downpipes that lead to storage tanks.

A simple system would follow the layout shown in Figures 8-1 and 8-2. The 60-gallon drums we've used for flotation work well for water storage, too. They should be black, or painted that color, to shield the water from daylight and prevent the growth of microorganisms. If you need more than one barrel for water storage (heavy users, infrequent rains), they can be hooked together in series, with fittings at the bottom of each barrel and a single line fed indoors. Alternatively, a hose can be thrown into a full barrel and swapped to another when it's empty. This is a good way to keep an eye on how much water you're actually using.

You may find—actually you will find—that visitors unused to life afloat can run tanks dry very quickly. On goes the tap, and precious water runs obliviously down the sink and overboard. Landbound visitors have to be reminded that every drop is Gaia-given and not to be squandered.

Marine shops sell small devices that can be installed inside a water tank to indicate how much water is left. A lower-tech option is to go on deck, lift the lid, and look in.

Marine shops also can supply hand pumps, mounted on the basin or sink, that draw water from the tanks through tubing. An alternative, which leaves both hands free to juggle the soap, is a floor-mounted, foot-operated pump. Other than a bucket of water and a dipper, this is the least sophisticated system.

Figure 8-3 indicates the next step, a gravity-fed system where the water is periodically pumped up to a header tank mounted on the roof. The pump can be either electric or manual, but if it is the former, make sure that it is capable of pumping to the height of the tank. This inherent pumping height limitation is known as a pump's *head*.

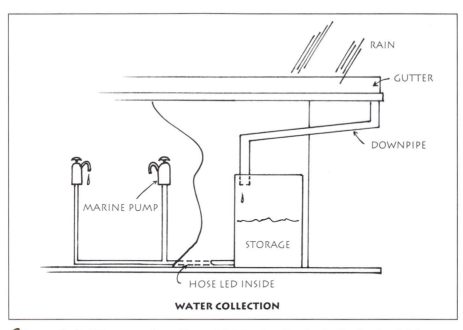

RAIN

GUTTER

DOWNPIPE

MARINE PUMP

STORAGE

HOSE LED INSIDE

WATER COLLECTION

Figure 8-1. Water can be collected fairly simply. An inch of rain yields roughly one gallon per square foot of roof.

Figure 8-2. Here's the system shown in Figure 8-1; it's easy to install and relatively unobtrusive.

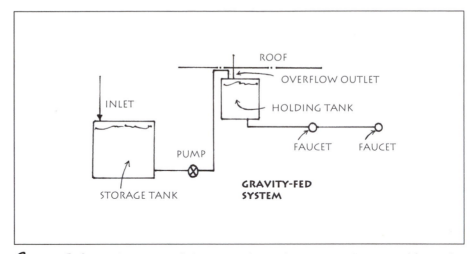

Figure 8-3. In the gravity-fed system shown here, water is pumped from the main storage tank to a smaller holding tank mounted on the roof.

The header tank is normally sited on the roof (in frost-free climates or seasonally occupied houseboats), over an end wall or bulkhead. You'll need this extra support to carry the weight of the water, since a 55-gallon (44 Imperial gallons) tank weighs about 440 pounds—a lot of weight to be concentrated in one place.

It would simplify things greatly if the header tank could be mounted just beneath the roof gutters, yet still above the faucets. Unfortunately this is usually impractical. Gravity is a function of height; the higher the tank, the greater the water pressure at the faucet. Because it runs from the faucet slowly, low water pressure will conserve water, and so gravity-feed is ideal for unsophisticated systems. For more sophisticated systems, appliances like hot-water caliphonts (on-demand water heaters) will not operate at all on low pressure.

To bring the plumbing to another level of convenience—pressurized water and on-demand hot showers—you'll need electrical power and an impeller pump (also available at marine stores, or from recreational vehicle suppliers). An impeller pump will give you the kind of water pressure you're used to ashore. Although it may sound complex, a pressurized water system eliminates the need for mounting a heavy header tank up high, just where you don't want extra weight in a floating home. In addition, because the height from tank to faucet is less, it can use a less sophisticated and less expensive pump than might be used to lift water to a header tank. A representative system, complete with pressure switch (so the pump comes on automatically) and accumulator tank (to even out the pressure and reduce pump cycling) is shown in Figure 8-4.

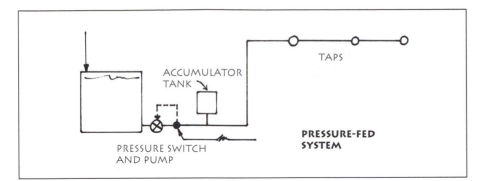

Figure 8-4. **A step up the technology scale is a pressure-fed system, providing pressurized water and on-demand hot showers. Its primary disadvantages are prodigious use of electricity—and water.**

The Ins and Outs of Plumbing

The cheapest way to install plumbing is to use hose—ordinary, everyday, garden-variety hose assembled with the standard range of garden fittings, connectors, Y-valves, and the like. Where the hose terminates at conventional plumbing fittings, like taps, the connections are made as follows: Purchase standard polybutylene connectors and carefully hacksaw across the aluminum ring, leaving the interior plastic nozzle fully exposed. Slip the hose ends over the nozzle, and tighten with hose clamps. Wrap Teflon plumbers' tape around the conventional tap thread and screw on the connector, as in the figure showing the underside of a hand basin. When the plumbing has been in use for a while, go back and retighten the hose clamps—especially with hot-water hoses, where heat causes things to expand a bit.

The lengths of hose are laid out from fitting to fitting, say, from tap to junction to appliance, then cut to the right length. If the hose is to run out of sight, inside the walls, it can be routed through the studs, either by chiselling a nick from the face, or by drilling a neat hole through each stud and laying the hose in place. Naturally, the builder will do his best to avoid driving a wall-panel nail into the hose.

Polybutylene pipe can be used instead of hose if the builder doesn't mind the extra expense. In that case, the pipe is laid to length between each fitting, like the hose, and cut to length. Connections are made by sliding the appropriate connectors over the ends of each pipe (each brand of polybutylene pipe seems to use its own connectors; follow the manufacturer's instructions). Although relatively flexible, PB, particularly in larger diameters (say ¾ inch) is unhappy about being bent sharply, and connectors

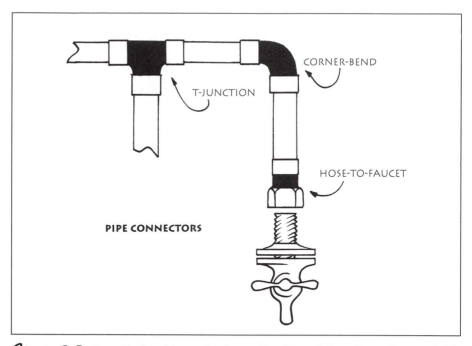

Figure 8-5. **Install plumbing using hose, flexible polybutylene pipe, or rigid PVC pipe and plastic pipe connectors.**

will be required for corners, as well as straight-line, T-junction, and pipe-to-tap connectors.

Another option is CPVC (chlorinated polyvinyl chloride)—the off-white plastic tubing sold in home-improvement stores. CPVC is assembled by gluing the joints with a special solvent. Because it should not be bent, you'll have to be extremely accurate with your measurements and planning. PB allows for more imprecision, while garden hose is totally forgiving.

Whichever system you use, make sure that *all* of the connectors have been clamped tightly before nailing up any inside wall panels. The easiest way to test this is to turn on the pump. If there's a loose connector, there'll be a squirt of water. It's better to find out now rather than later.

When all the pipes or hose are in place (as well as the wiring, if so desired), the inside wall panels are nailed on. Observe where the pipes (and wires) are and ensure that nails aren't driven through any. Don't laugh—it's been done. Holes are drilled in the wall panels where taps, shower-mixer (and electric sockets), etc., will be mounted, and the pipes or hose left to protrude until the final fitting of sinks and basins.

The galley sink or hand basin can be marvels of hand-sculpted hardwood, or they can be demolition-surplus bargains. The latter is usually the case, but the plumbing techniques pertain to any level of quality the homeowner can afford.

Standard sinks and basins are settled in place atop a custom-built box made of 2 × 2 framework. The box is then panelled with ply, like the walls, with the option of adding cupboard doors beneath.

RUNNING OUT

The bottom of the sink, shower, or hand basin—where the plug hole exits—will need a plastic adapter screwed onto it. This connects to a length of PVC pipe long enough to reach down through a hole in the floorboards, where it then exits overboard or is funnelled to a holding tank. Marine life has no objection to this graywater, which contains moderate amounts of soap, fat, dirt, and other biodegradable goodies from the food-preparation and people-preparation areas. It's all food. Naturally, if local marine regulations prohibit any discharge at all, all pipes will go to the holding tank. There is no question *whatsoever* that the pipe from a toilet, which carries *blackwater* containing, uh, fecal matter, will go to a holding tank.

In the United States, Coast Guard regulations are quite explicit about what can and cannot be dumped overboard. Inside the 3-mile limit—which includes lakes, rivers, bays, and sounds—it is illegal to dump plastic (biodegradable or otherwise), paper, crockery, rags, glass, metal, food, or dunnage. It is permissible to dump dishwater, graywater, and fresh fish parts—if you've been lucky enough to catch any. Again, local regulations often restrict this to zero discharge. It is *never* permissible to dump water contaminated with human waste. There are a number of ways of dealing with this.

Portable Toilets

Caravans and small boats often use chemical toilets. Most are about the size of a suitcase and separate into two halves, the upper containing fresh water or seawater, and the lower sewage. When in use, a lever is pulled to flush the waste into the lower half of the toilet, where a previously added chemical attacks the sewage, breaking it down and neutralizing the nasties. Periodically, the lower half must be emptied, either down a hole in the ground or into a public toilet. Be forewarned: This is not exactly an aesthetic experience, but it is a humbling one.

Formalin is used in most of the commercially available toilet chemicals like Liquid-Gold, which essentially paralyzes the pathogens. The commercial chemicals remain active for a long time. Household bleach can be used instead, and although it has to be added daily because it evaporates (about a spoonful after use, or a cup a day), it is cheaper and has no over-powering odor. Chlorine, the active ingredient, kills pathogens.

Although portable toilets are inexpensive and certainly easy to install, they're really only a temporary solution to a long-term problem: what to do with our waste.

Holding Tanks

Holding tanks, categorized by the U.S. Coast Guard as Marine Sanitation Devices (MSD, for short) Type III, are nil-discharge systems; that is, waste does not go overboard but is retained and pumped out at an approved facility. Unlike portable chemical toilets, holding tanks built into boats are not portable; the boat itself must be taken wherever facilities exist to pump out the tank. The availability of such facilities in your area, and the portability of your houseboat, may be the determining factor in whether or not you'll go this route.

Holding tanks must be of reasonable size; browsing through any marine supply shop will give an indication of what size you'll need. It may be larger than you think. The tank must be large enough to contain both the waste and the water flushed through the toilet bowl. As a rule of thumb, a 60-gallon tank will be nearly full after a couple of months when used by one person for toilet waste only.

If we already have 44- or 60-gallon flotation drums beneath the house, it can be very convenient to sacrifice one of them to a needy cause. Figure 8-6 shows an end barrel used as a holding tank. Not shown are the lengths of chain that would have to be wrapped around the barrel to secure it in its pocket beneath the raft. After all, when it begins to fill up with you-know-what, it will have considerably less buoyancy than when filled only with air. We don't want it to sink.

The PVC pipe (no smaller than 1½ inches in diameter) from the toilet is led from the toilet discharge through the floor, along the nearest bearer, and into either a hole cut in the end of the barrel or, if the fit is tight, into the old bunghole. (This stuff doesn't bend at all; pipe is cut to length and fitted together by gluing on appropriate angle-pieces, available as standard plumbing fittings.) A vent air-pipe (no smaller than ¾ inch in diameter) must be fitted to prevent back-pressure, and can be installed either somewhere along the PVC pipe, like the long vertical pipe in Figure 8-7, or through another hole in the side of the holding tank barrel. In Figure 8-7, the vent pipe is attached at the toilet exit and runs vertically up the back wall. With a holding tank in place, it is an easy matter to extend to the tank the pipes from galley sink, hand basin, or shower, if necessary.

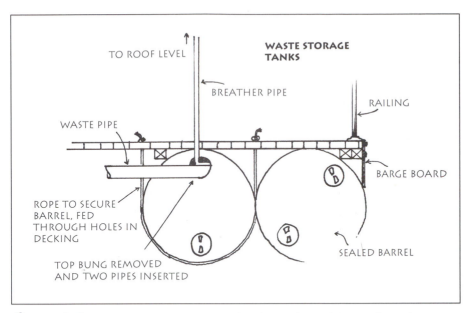

Figure 8-6. A waste-storage system that fits right under your houseboat. You can find pump-out facilities at most marinas. *Do not* straight-pipe it into the water.

Figure 8-7. A long, vertical pipe provides an essential air vent, while waste is discharged into the storage barrels beneath the boat. The vent pipe would be more efficient if it cleared the roof ridge by 18 inches or so.

Wastewater from basin, shower, or sink may be food for marine life, but sewage definitely is not. Untreated sewage (maybe even treated sewage) simply *cannot* be allowed to go overboard, and why should it? There are so many other disposal options available for boats that simply to bucket and chuck it, whether from dinghy, cruiser, yacht, or houseboat, must be considered, at the least, environmental vandalism.

Toilet Training

There are various inventive ways to deal with the natural by-product of our bodies; the simplest—should the houseboat be moored adjacent to friendly land—being to dig a fairly deep hole in the ground, erect a hut over it, and then (over time) allow it to fill with reconstituted meals. Whether you call it a long drop, chic sale, or plain old outhouse, this system is recommended for use in environmentally sensitive areas by, among others, sanitation departments in Canada, Australia, New Zealand, and various states.

This is the same old system familiar to farmers around the world. Cats do it, ants do it, and African kings do it. However, just letting waste disappear down a hole is in itself wasteful. Every day more than 150 million tons of human waste are flushed into rivers and oceans around the world. Curiously, this "waste" contains the same fertilizing elements—nitrogen, phosphorus, and potassium—that chemical companies produce and sell to farmers. We can do this ourselves with a neat device called a composting toilet.

Composting

Composting toilets convert bad stuff into good stuff, which is then sprinkled on gardens to make them grow. It's as simple as that—no holding tank, no pumping out, no discharge of noxious chemicals. Small versions are available for installation in boats, including houseboats. The Canadian-built Sun-Mar NE, for example, designed for continuous use by up to three people, is only 2 feet 8 inches long and just under 2 feet wide. It provides a benign environment where microorganisms grow, aerobically decomposing—or composting—the excrement, loo paper, and kitchen scraps (and peat moss, a cup per person per day). The water vapor from the waste evaporates up a flue. What we're left with is plain old-fashioned humus, rich in nitrogen, potassium, phosphorous, and micronutrients—the same stuff we sprinkle on strawberry plants in the garden: No chemicals, no sludge, no pollution, just plant food.

Chemicals

If this kind of indoor organic gardening is just not your cup of manure, new technology offers complete treatment/discharge systems that can process waste chemically before being pumped overboard. There is no need to depend on pumpout stations ashore; the system on board becomes the houseboat's own mini-sewage plant.

The Coast Guard categorizes this type of system, too. Type I MSDs, for boats less than 65 feet long, must remove visible solids and, by mixing the effluent with chemicals such as chlorine or formaldehyde, reduce the coliform bacteria content to 1,000 parts per 100 milliliters (about one-twentieth of a pint). The wastewater then may be discharged overboard outside of no-discharge zones (check local regulations). Type II MSDs, required for boats over 65 feet long, must be even more efficient, reducing the coliform level to 200 parts per 100 milliliters before going overboard.

The Sealand SAN-X1 and SAN-X2, for example, signal when the tank is full, at which time the houseboater throws a switch that injects formaldehyde into the tank, cranks up a macerator, pumps the treated effluent overboard, then adds more chemical to the tank. A normal cycle runs for about 20 minutes, drawing 8 amps.

An alternative, the Lectra/San, doesn't require any chemical additives. It kicks electricity through the seawater used for flushing and carrying the waste (drawing 45 amps for 2 minutes of operation, equal to 1½ amp-hours), creating sodium chlorine ions that bond loosely with water atoms, creating chlorine. The chlorine kills the pathogens and treats the waste, which can be pumped overboard. The chlorine then evaporates. House-boats moored in freshwater areas can use fresh water in their systems and throw in some salt.

Another system, the Microphor, doesn't need electricity. The waste is trapped in redwood chips, which organically treat it, producing carbon dioxide and wastewater, which are then passed through a chlorination area to kill the bacteria. The treated waste then drains overboard.

Yet another system uses an LPG-fired furnace (one popular brand is the aptly named Destroilet) literally to cremate the remains of your last meal. These incinerating systems leave behind little but ash, but are not exactly fuel efficient. One must weigh the inconvenience of buying and bringing aboard large tanks of propane gas with the inconvenience of finding a place to dump large tanks of waste.

As you may expect, treatment systems like these are expensive and of dubious benefit to the environment. Although they're legal, I'll leave the decision about their use to your own sense of ethics.

Flushing Your Cares Away

Meanwhile, back in the powder room, an extensive range of toilet bowls and systems is available to convey homemade effluent to the holding tank or other treatment device (excluding composting toilets and waste incinerators, of course). The most common in the marine environment is the manual toilet—a bowl with an attached, hand-operated pump to flush water through the system. To keep the hand pump primed, that is, with water inside to help the pump do its start-up, the inlet pipe that draws in fresh water or seawater should rise at least 12 inches above the base of the bowl. Periodically, a minute amount of hydraulic or brake fluid can be added to the water in the bowl to keep the pump plunger's washers soft and pliable.

A manual toilet can be upgraded to provide no-hands operation; just purchase the appropriate adapter kit to add an electric pump.

Manual vacuum toilets operate on a slightly different principle. As the bulk of the sewage consists of previously uncontaminated water brought into the system solely to move the waste, we can greatly extend the capacity of the holding tank, thus prolonging the periods between pump-outs, by eliminating the need for water. After use, a vacuum is pumped up inside the bowl—with the lid shut and sealed, not being sat on. With the flick of a lever, the waste is discharged and the seal is broken, ready for the next user.

An electric vacuum toilet is built in three stages: bowl, accumulator, and pump. The pump is switched on to build up a vacuum within the accumulator, which can take about half a minute. It's something to listen to while contemplating the decor of the room. When contemplation is finished, a small amount of water is added to the bowl, a lever depressed, and the bowl contents are exposed to the vacuum in the accumulator. Like waste jettisoned by a manned satellite, it is immediately blown apart in the vacuum, reputedly travelling at 20 feet per second down the pipe to the holding tank.

These marine toilets are elegant but also (naturally) expensive. An equally elegant but more economical toilet can be adapted from surplus stock intended for use ashore. A house-type toilet with cistern and bowl, of either china or plastic, is installed in the houseboat, and a pump, with a pressure switch, mounted below it. The pump draws water from whatever is floating the houseboat and feeds the cistern. If the pump is an impeller, i.e., a pushing type, mount it on the floor; if it's a suction-type pump, keep it close to the cistern inlet.

This is an inexpensive option, but there is a catch: House-type toilets use up to 5 gallons of water per flush, so your holding tank will fill up very quickly.

Care and Feeding of the Marine Toilet

The failure of a toilet and its attendant plumbing can be irritating, at best. It's usually caused by a blockage of some sort, so using plenty of water (where it's freely available) to move the waste along, and again plenty to flush the bowl, will help prevent that. Waste is very reluctant to move of its own accord.

With the old adage "an ounce of prevention is worth a pound of cure" in mind, be prepared to remove and inspect the pipes occasionally—particularly if you're pumping seawater through them. The salt that inevitably accumulates needs to be scraped out. In certain areas, marine life will colonize the inlet pipes. New England seawater is home to zillions of baby mussels looking for a sheltered place to live—like inside your inlet pipes. Many areas of the Great Lakes, despite being fresh water, are similarly afflicted by a recent immigrant, the zebra mussel.

Flushing water need not come from river, lake, or sea, and in some cases—where the houseboat is allowed to settle between tides—it can't be; there's nothing out there but sand or mud. Fresh water from the storage barrels could be used, but what a waste. We can, however, recycle washing-up and shower water. This water will contain residual detergent and grease that will keep the toilet system cleaned and lubricated. A smaller, ancillary holding tank is installed somewhere to collect the graywater from the sink, basin, or shower waste pipes; that water is then pumped into the toilet bowl whenever needed, to be discharged finally into the main holding tank. An overflow pipe must be connected between the two tanks.

Another alternative is to collect graywater from the shower by not installing an overboard drain for it at all. In its place, a shower sump pump is installed (any marine shop can supply one) in the shower base, and the water is pumped up to a header tank, where it gravity-feeds to a toilet cistern below.

RUNNING HOT

On a houseboat, a shower with *hot* water that cascades down one's back and washes away soap, grime, and fatigue is not a luxury, it's an essential. The problem is how to turn cold water into hot.

No Fuel

In the sky is a nonstop nuclear fission reactor that will be more than happy to heat water for us. We're probably all familiar with the surprisingly hot water that comes from a hose left lying on the lawn. Similarly, a coil of black piping left lying in the sun on the roof becomes a rudimentary solar heater, rapidly heating the water inside it. A jerry-can painted black is equally effective. Both hose and can should be protected from the cooling effects of the wind. (A wide array of books is available about solar water heating; the reader is encouraged to check the library.)

Ascending the scale of sophistication and efficiency, an economical panel can be made by enclosing the black hose beneath a window sash. Aluminum foil, used by builders to insulate houses, is laid beneath the hose to reflect sunlight back, and the ends of the pipe are led out through two holes cut into the sash frame. The longer the length of hose (black polyethylene pipe is readily and inexpensively available from builder's suppliers), the more hot water you'll have.

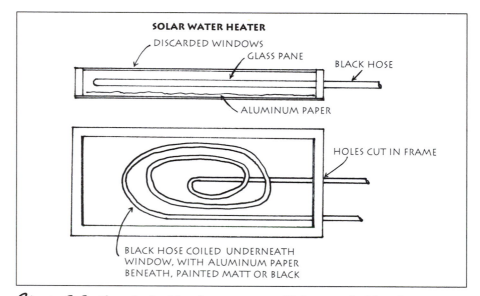

Figure 8-8. **If you're looking for an energy-efficient, no-fuel heating system, a solar water heater may be the answer. Besides, it's the perfect way to recycle one—or several—old windows: the longer the hose, the longer (and hotter) the shower.**

There would be little point in heating water if it could not be stored. Showers are at their most enjoyable first thing in the morning and in the evening, while washing-up water is required at odd times throughout the day. The sun is indifferent to our human needs and habits, thus the need to store the hot water so benevolently generated. This simply means supplying an insulated tank and allowing the water to find its way there via its natural tendency to convect. Convection currents are caused by differing temperatures in different locations of the same body of water.

Hot water naturally rises, and cold water naturally sinks. If we can coax the cold water into the solar heater and the hot water into storage, we set up a slowly circulating, perpetually warming system.

Any storage container will do, whether a barrel or a copper tank or a properly emptied beer keg. To prevent the heat from radiating out, the storage tank is well wrapped in insulation—the more the better. Figure 8-9 shows a representative system, where cold water moves from the bottom of the tank and through the heater before returning of its own volition to the top of the tank. We tap into the top entry to run a hose to the hot-water faucets; the cold-water faucets are fed from the bottom of the tank.

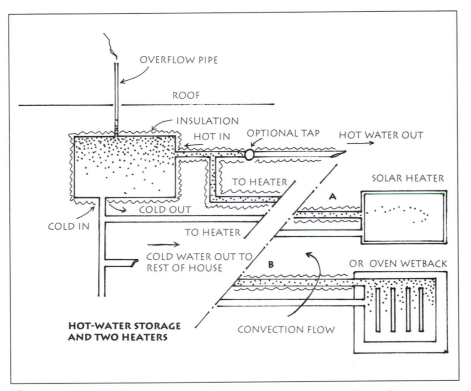

Figure 8-9. This system allows hot water to be heated, with a solar water heater or an oven wetback, and then stored for use later on.

A venting pipe from the top of the tank is essential. It may be fitted anywhere along the hot-water intake line, but must reach higher than the highest level of water stored. Water expands when heated and finds its own level; if the exit were lower than other parts of the system, it would quickly overflow.

Correct installation of the storage tank means that it should be no more than 2½ feet from the heater, and pipes should be straight or gently curved—not bent into hard angles. Turning a pipe 90 degrees has the same effect as reducing the diameter of the pipe by one-half.

Old Fuels

Another form of heating, shown in Figure 8-9, is an *oven wetback*, a loop of pipe within the firebox of a standard wood- or coal-burning stove. Water is convected through the pipe, heated in the stove, and scurries back to storage. Wetbacks are extremely efficient, and boiling water is quickly generated. Consequently, this is not a job for the amateur; no one but a plumber should install a wetback in a firebox that does not already have one. Water-filled tubes inside a firebox are the driving force behind steam engines. The water pressure generated inside a faulty contraption could be intense. The explosion would be spectacular and lethal.

Figure 8-10 shows a complete system that includes a bottled-gas hot-water caliphont, or on-demand water heater. The solar panel heats water in the summer, the wetback in the wood-burning oven heats it in the

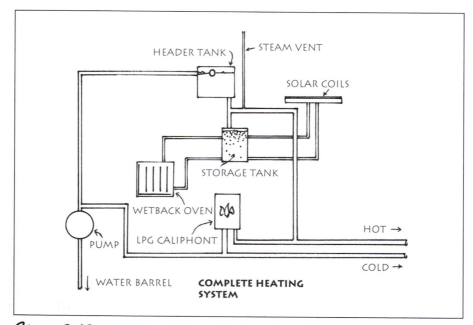

Figure 8-10. **Combining solar, wetback, and LPG heating, this system works on days when neither solar nor oven-heated water is available—just switch on the gas burner.**

winter, and in the event of sunless days (and when the fire is out), the caliphont kicks in and a hot shower is assured.

Caliphonts are very efficient—enough so that they can be installed as the sole water heater. As they are only turned on when hot water is required, they use a minimal amount of gas, especially if the pilot light is not left burning, but relit as occasion demands. (Caliphonts without pilot lights that have piezoelectric ignition are also available.) The water temperature at the tap can be varied from mildly warm to very hot, not only by adjusting the level of gas flame but also by adjusting the speed at which water flows through the machine.

Caliphonts require reasonable water pressure; most shut down if it drops below about 5 psi, so ensure that the water pump is hefty and close to the heater; that is, within 6 feet or set up according to manufacturer's instructions. A gravity-fed system generally will not support a caliphont.

Caliphonts have much to recommend the initial investment. They compensate for the sudden drop in the bank balance by affording savings in other areas—and by the sudden elevation of the comfort quotient. If you have gas aboard—whether CNG or LPG—for lights or a cooker, you needn't supply a separate gas bottle for each appliance. You can simply insert a T-junction in the gas line to divert gas to the caliphont. However, two gas bottles, one for each appliance, does mean that should one bottle run out in midshower—or when cooking a roast with guests due—there will always be a spare to swap over.

Showers

If you've managed to build a houseboat, you'll find building a shower easy work. Basically, a commercially molded shower base is laid on the floor and measured for size and the drain hole pencilled and cut out. Four battens are then nailed to the floor, in a square, to support the base edges. As with a sink, a plastic adapter is screwed onto the bottom and a short length of PVC pipe fitted to lead into the drainage system. The base is laid down with the pipe exiting through the floor, then beams at least ½ inch higher than the supported edges are nailed to the floor around it.

A second set of planks is then laid on top of the first four, overlapping the edges. If the bottom beams are, say, 2 × 4s on edge, the second set might be 2 × 3s laid flat, to allow a 1-inch overlap. A box-like frame, built from the same material as the second set of planks, is then erected directly on top of the planks. When the shower panels are nailed up, the condensation and spray that runs down the panel will drip cleanly from the edge onto the shower base; the overlap prevents the water from creeping along cracks and up inside the woodwork by means of capillary action. For extra

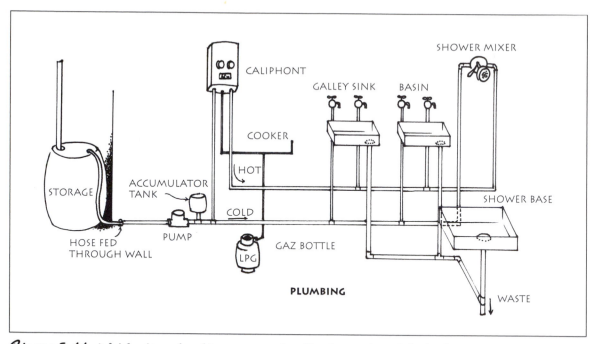

Figure 8-11. A fairly ritzy plumbing system. A collection tank, at left, feeds to a pump and pressure switch; the pump switches on automatically when it senses a drop in pressure. The accumulator tank, a small container with one hose leading into it, absorbs fluctuations in the pump supply and guarantees a smooth flow of water. Even though suppliers of systems will argue that the accumulator is essential, it isn't. The hose we use for plumbing is flexible, and over a length has many of the attributes of an accumulator.

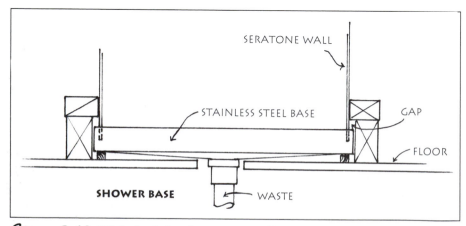

Figure 8-12. With the help of a commercially molded base, a shower can be installed relatively easily.

insurance, caulking compound can also be squeezed along the planks, under the panels, before nailing. Normal quarter-round trim can be nailed into the corner edges inside the newly created shower compartment, but caulking compound must be run down the edges first.

The shower panels could be a waterproof material like Seratone or Melanine, or you could use ordinary plywood, in which case soak the edges in paint (like the bottom edges of the house's exterior wall panels), nail them into place, add the trim and caulking, and splash paint about inside the compartment with abandon. Applied liberally, paint is surprisingly effective at sealing plywood.

A more efficient sealer is epoxy resin, available as a two-part mix. After the two parts are mixed together, the builder has a short time in which to brush the mix onto the panels before the resin cures, after which the hardened resin will resist water with alacrity. Typical marine resins are available from WEST System or System Three and at any marine supply shop.

Washers

If trudging along, laundry under arm, to a local laundromat is impractical, and there are no nearby washing-machine–equipped friends to visit once a week, despair not. The devices shown in Figure 8-13 may be just the answer to a houseboater's or houseboatress's prayers. In the first device, the soiled linen and a little soap are tossed into the tumbler. If the day is windless, the handle (shown as a dotted line) is enthusiastically cranked.

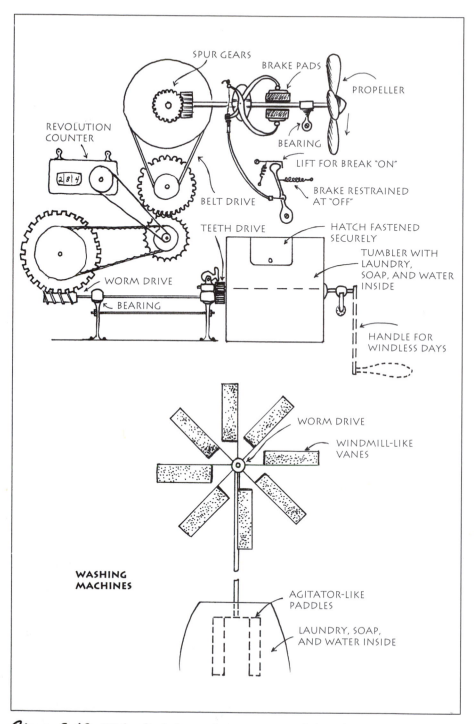

Figure 8-13. With a little ingenuity you can wash laundry no matter where you are. This Rube Goldbergian setup really works.

Alternatively, a treadle, converted from an expired sewing machine, can be used. If a wind is blowing, however, the brake pads—liberated from a bicycle—beside the wind propeller are released. The second device turns not the tumbler, but paddles inside it. Small, manually operated tumblers are available for yachts and so would be fine for houseboats. Small, 12-volt washing machines are also available from alternative energy supply outlets, such as Real Goods Trading Company (966 Mazoni Street, Ukiah, California 95482).

Mankind has managed to survive well into the twentieth century—with mostly clean clothing—without access to computerized washing machines. With a little ingenuity the houseboat owner need not become a character in a *National Geographic* photograph, pummeling clothes along riverbanks for an authentic stone-washed look. It's all part of the challenge of meeting one's own requirements.

CHAPTER NINE

Sparks

The perfect artificial light is electricity, but that may be put aside with hardly any comment, as it is rarely practicable on any but the largest and most expensive houseboats.

～～～～～～～～～～～～～～～～～～～～

The quotation above, made back when electricity was still generated by large steam engines—or the newfangled but unreliable gasoline-powered generator—has been rendered obsolete by discoveries made in the last few decades in the field of small-scale power generation. This is where we leave behind the monthly power bills and turn our backs on centralized power-generating stations of doubtful morality, like nuclear reactors or oil- and coal-fired power plants. If we can't take care of our own needs, then, like adults, we must compromise or learn to do without. By being personally responsible for producing the energy we consume, we leave the natural environment in peace. In fact, the natural elements—wind, sea, and sun—provide us with that energy free of charge.

Like plumbing, there's nothing complicated about the type of simple electrical circuit found aboard a houseboat. Reduced to its essentials, power is collected at one end and comes out the other. Once we understand the basic rules of electricity, we can do what we like with it. We'll need to digest a few technical terms first, but their meaning will become clear as we progress:

- *Voltage*, or *volts*, measures potential electrical force.

- *Amperes*, or *amps*, measure the rate of flow of electricity—the current.

- *Watts* measure power—work that is actually being accomplished.

- *Amp-hours (Ah)* and *watt-hours* are those units multiplied by time.

Extending the analogy with water in a gravity-fed system may help to advance our understanding. Imagine our storage tank as the battery, water pressure as the voltage, and the amount of water flowing through the system as the current, or amperage. A paddlewheel inserted in the system will, if rigged up to drive fan blades, consume power and perform work—watts.

In the case of electricity, however, it isn't gravity that pulls current from the battery; rather, it's the difference in electrical potential—the voltage—between the battery's two terminals. A return line pulls free electrons—current flow—from one end of the battery (the positive terminal) and back to the other (the negative terminal). Along the way it spins the motor in the electric fan, consuming power and producing work (and cooling you off)—watts. When the tank, I mean battery, is empty, we fill it up again with homemade electricity.

Electricity is employed to such an extent in several vessels now afloat, that a short account of its more important uses has been thought advisable.

In the Royal Navy it has been applied with advantage to so many purposes, that the increase of wires, instruments, batteries, bells, etc., on board a modern ironclad has become somewhat startling to those who are unacquainted with the scientific principles on which they depend.

Admiral Sir Frederick Bedford, *The Sailor's Pocket Book: A Collection of Practical Rules, Notes, and Tables, for the Use of The Royal Navy, The Mercantile Marine, and Yacht Squadrons.* Portsmouth: Griffin & Co., 1898.

If all this seems confusing at first, take heart: Electricity has always seemed a magical force. Obviously this can't be a definitive treatise. It will, however, get you by. If you are consumed with curiosity and want to know more, read some of the books listed under Suggested Reading.

One more thing to remember: If you know two of the values in an electrical circuit, you can easily find the third. And since we'll be dealing with a 12-volt system on our houseboat, that particular value will remain a constant. Remember this:

- Watts equal amps times volts.
- Amps equal watts divided by volts.

STORING

A battery stores electricity. Like the water tank, the greater the storage capacity, the less frequently you'll need to refill it. The greater the number of appliances you turn on, the greater the drain. The battery must have enough capacity to withstand being completely flattened on occasion by your appliances. It happens, even if we try to avoid it. Ashore, a light left on accidently won't worry the national grid one bit; on a houseboat, the buck stops at the onboard power company . . . and its battery.

All batteries are not created equal, however. Other than as a temporary measure, the average automobile battery is of little use as a storage tank for our home-generated electricity. Auto batteries generally are rated at about 55 Ah; theoretically, they can provide 1 amp for 55 hours. But these batteries aren't designed to supply small amounts of current over long periods; they're meant to deliver a hefty charge to a starter motor very briefly—remember how quickly you can flatten a battery when the car won't start—and then be recharged rapidly by the car's alternator.

The average truck battery may have a capacity of 200 Ah; a starting battery for huge marine diesel engines may have a capacity three times that. Still, these batteries are designed to supply large but infrequent bursts of power and do not fare well if drained slowly of juice. Most automobile batteries can survive only about 20 complete discharges, or cycles, before succumbing.

Deep Cycle

Other batteries are specifically designed to withstand such treatment and can be flattened a great many times without harm. These *deep-cycle batteries* are the kind we want for our houseboat. Whether intended for marine use or to power golf carts or mine vehicles, deep-cycle batteries are meant to be cycled continuously, charged and discharged as much as you like, within reason. The best deep-cycle batteries, if discharged to 80 percent of capacity, are rated for about 1,500 cycles; at 50 percent capacity, at least double that. If that still doesn't sound like much, in average use they may last 5 to 10 years. But in average use, 50 percent capacity should be considered the *maximum* they should be discharged.

Most deep-cycle batteries are of conventional lead-acid construction. That is, lead plates are immersed in electrolyte, a dilute solution of sulfuric acid. Lead-acid batteries are relatively cheap, well-proven, and easy to maintain, but they're not perfect neighbors aboard a houseboat. Among other bad habits, they can spill their highly corrosive battery acid, with occasionally dangerous and always inconvenient results. And during charging, lead-acid batteries emit a fair quantity of hydrogen gas—the stuff that filled the *Hindenberg*. Consequently, these sloppy, explosive-gas–spewing things must be contained in a leak-proof, vapor-tight enclosure, which must in turn be vented to the outdoors. (If you're in a cold climate, they shouldn't actually be outdoors. Batteries lose about half their capacity as the thermometer moves toward zero. Moreover, they also lose capacity—from 1 percent to as much as 3 percent per day—when left to their own devices. This is called, appropriately enough, self-discharge.)

An alternative is a *gel-cell*—a deep-cycle battery, like the Stowaway ST-154 or the Prevailer 110A, that is completely sealed and has a jelly-like electrolyte packed between its plates. Thus a gel-cell battery can be stored inside, outside, upside down, or even have a hole hammered in one of its casings, and present no hazard. They are much less affected by extremes of heat or cold. They don't produce acidic vapor during charging. They can be discharged to 100 percent of capacity and rapidly recharged a month later—something that will finish off even the best of lead-acid batteries. And when left to their own devices, they don't engage in the injurious pastime of self-discharge.

Gel-cells aren't perfect, though; they cost two to three times more than comparable-capacity lead-acid batteries. Despite advertising claims of a long, trouble-free life, at least some of them have suffered unexplained and premature deaths (although Prevailers, and probably by now other brands, carry five-year warranties). Even the best of them have rated lifespans half that of the best lead-acid deep-cycle batteries (such as a Surrette). And unlike abused lead-acid batteries, which often can be resuscitated by an infusion of fresh electrolyte and a good stiff charge, when a gel-cell is dead, it's dead.

Whether you choose the new gel-cells or the traditional lead-acid batteries, there is no justification for purchasing less than the best. It's like using steel barrels for flotation: The expense is only delayed, and the money spent meantime is lost. The battery is the heart of the houseboat's power system; there are no such things as kerosene- or LPG-powered microwaves or TVs. Living on a houseboat in the style that predated Messieurs Edison, Marconi, and Sanyo sounds romantic, but such a lifestyle demands severe compromises that few today would accept. We've been conditioned to accept as normal certain creature comforts—and indeed, why deny ourselves? Especially if we can have them without damaging the environment or hiring others to damage it for us.

Increasing Storage Capacity

With our plumbing system, the larger the water tank, the more water we can store. If we want to luxuriate in water, we could muscle aboard the biggest tank we could find. But that's not really a practical solution. One gigantic water tank, aside from being frightfully expensive, hard to find, and not really space-efficient, is actually dangerous: If something happens to that one tank, or the water in it, you have no water—all your eggs are in one basket. Compare that with using a series of cheap, readily available, easily handled 60-gallon drums. If one starts to leak, you've got others to rely on.

The same holds true for batteries. If you conclude that your dependence on electrically driven modern inconveniences will require a storage capacity of 300 Ah, it doesn't necessarily follow that you should go out and buy one 300-Ah battery. For one thing, a 300-Ah battery weighs roughly 225 pounds—not exactly the sort of thing you'd want to wrestle aboard—and costs around $500 US. For another, if one cell of this monstrosity goes bad (cells do fail on occasion), the whole thing becomes just so much toxic waste.

It's a far better idea to buy two 150-Ah 12-volt batteries—or even four 85-Ah batteries—and hook them together in parallel. With this system, each battery weighs about 100 or 60 pounds, respectively, and costs roughly $150 or $75 US. We've spent less, lifted less, and if one of them suffers a premature demise, it can be easily and economically replaced without interrupting service.

Another popular alternative is to wire together in series (negative to positive, positive to negative) two 6-volt batteries (often the popular and widely available 220-Ah 6-volt golf-cart batteries). When wired in series, the amp-hour capacity remains the same, but the voltage is the sum of the battery voltage in the system: Two 6-volt 220-Ah batteries equals a 12-volt, 220-Ah supply.

When batteries are wired in parallel, the voltage stays the same, but the amp-hour capacity increases by the sum of the total capacities: two 12-volt

220-Ah batteries equals one 12-volt, 440-Ah supply. However, when batteries are connected in parallel, one dead cell in one battery can flatten the rest of the cells in the system. Fortunately there's a way around that, and I'll get into the specifics of wiring multiple batteries later on, but first we have some math to do.

DRAINING

To figure the size of our electrical storage tank, we need to know the demand. By making a list of all the electrical gadgets we intend to use, figuring the current they draw multiplied by the time they'll be turned on, then adding everything together, we can find our daily current use. These figures will be an average—an estimated average at that—but they'll do for setting up a system. And don't worry if you can't foresee every electrical appliance you'll ever use: Your storage and recharging system can be improved any time as the need arises.

Although some boats, mostly large ones, use 24- or 32-volt systems (which are more efficient, for reasons that needn't trouble us), we'll assume that, like most everyone else, you'll be installing a 12-volt system. Most appliances available for the boat and recreational vehicle trade are manufactured for 12 volts.

In actual fact, all "12-volt" systems are actually relying on the battery, in good condition and fully charged, to have 12.6 volts tucked away in it. The number 12 is a working standard, a polite fiction if you like, with which we do our sums. This little bit of knowledge has but one use: measuring a battery's state of charge. If a voltmeter (if you don't have a voltmeter or a multimeter, and you plan to install and maintain your own electrical system, run, don't walk, to the nearest electronics store and buy one—preferably a digital unit) connected across the terminals reads 12.6 volts or more, it's in the prime of health. If it reads 12 volts, it wants charging; it's actually at only 25 percent of full charge.

Most batteries are considered "flat" when down to about 60 percent of their capacity. At this stage, a digital multimeter connected across the terminals will read 11.5 volts. There is power in there—but not much. The actual voltage delivered to the system may be as little as 9 volts. If the nearly flat battery is connected to, say, a 12-volt light bulb, the feeble current barely lights it, and because the light bulb demands more current to compensate for the "missing" volts, the battery's end is further hastened. Moreover, some appliances can be ruined by being fed low voltage. With all this in mind, it's worthwhile to figure your loads accurately.

What's Watt

Many appliances are rated in watts, so dividing by the voltage (which we know is 12) we can find the amperage. For example, a 12-watt bulb draws 2.5 amps. Here's a sample electrical system for a modest houseboat:

Appliance	Amps ×	Hours =	Amp-hours
TV set, B&W	1.50	6.0	9.0
Stereo set	0.25	6.0	1.5
Video player	3.00	1.5	4.5
Water pump	5.00	1.0	5.0
Filament bulb	2.50	1.0	2.5
Fluorescent 1	0.50	4.0	2.0
Fluorescent 2	0.50	4.0	2.0
Total			**26.5 Amp-hours**

The total, 26.5 Ah, is a fairly hefty daily demand. In actual use, presumably the TV and the stereo would not be on at the same time, nor would all the lights. Nonetheless, it demonstrates a point about our electrical system that we must consider at all times: *What is taken out must be returned.*

Now, to err on the side of safety, let's increase the daily estimate to 30 Ah. And, since we'll be generating our electricity with sunlight or wind, and we might logically expect it to be sunless or windless for five days, we multiply our 30 Ah daily drain by five: We need 150 Ah of capacity. But batteries aren't 100 percent efficient, and repeatedly discharging them below 50 percent of capacity dramatically shortens their life, so we just double that 150-Ah battery and find that our sample houseboat needs roughly 300 Ah of storage capacity.

This isn't a perfect calculation, either, however. Using a 300-Ah battery (or a bank of batteries totaling 300 Ah), our daily draw represents 10 percent of the total stored. Remember, we can draw up to 40 percent of capacity before the battery is functionally flat. That is not to say that 40 percent would equal four days' worth of electricity at 10 percent per day. On the second day, there might be only 12.2 volts left in the battery, which, if not recharged, would mean an increase in the current needed to sustain the total power demand. Drawn on a graph, the load on the battery would curve dramatically upward and the demand would become exponentially greater. As voltage continued to drop, current drain would increase—exactly as if we had to keep turning the tap to maintain the flow of water.

This brings up another point: *To maximize capacity, minimize use.* Note in the above example that standard filament-type light bulbs, better known as incandescents, are hopelessly inefficient compared with fluorescents of equal brightness (more about lighting in the next chapter).

Browsing through any marine or recreational vehicle shop will show the builder just how extensive a range of electrical gadgets is available for the houseboat—everything from refrigerator/freezers and ice-cube makers to electric hair dryers and microwave ovens. The demands for power that these "energy-saving" devices can create may give a builder pause to wonder. How necessary is it to have a color TV demanding 5 amps, or a blockbuster stereo that needs 20 watts just to warm its tubes?

In other words, money spent on the most efficient appliances will save your spending money on bigger batteries. And unnecessary appliances foregone equal even more money and capacity saved.

There must be a certain foregoing of very cherished household customs obtaining on land, which must not be expected on the water. Meals cannot very well be so elaborate. Rather early rising will be the rule, as it is on board a yacht; and there cannot be much entertaining, because for houseboat life a minimum of servants is essential. Servants are a difficulty always, as they hate not to have all their usual apparatus round them.

PRODUCING

We know what we want to take out. Now, how to put it back? There have been many and varied attempts at solving the battery recharging demands of mariners (and explorers, astronauts, and submariners too, for that matter), including tidal generators that move with the waves and propeller-driven generators towed behind yachts, but two generators are especially suited to houseboats for their simplicity and convenience: the photovoltaic generator and the wind generator.

Photovoltaic Generators

Commonly known as a solar panel, a photovoltaic generator is an array of photosensitive silicon cells that converts sunlight into direct-current electricity. The principle was discovered when a transistor, which had been left in a clear casing instead of the conventional dark one, began to generate small amounts of current in the daytime completely of its own accord.

Figure 9-1.
If the climate is right, solar panels may be the best way to create efficient, maintenance-free energy.

If the sun consumes billions of tons of hydrogen every day to fuel life on Earth, generating a small amount of power from it to run our houseboat seems reasonable enough. As long as there's light to see them by, solar panels will be quietly generating current. They will work underwater and in the light of a bright moon, although with sharply reduced output.

A primary advantage is that solar panels are completely maintenance-free. Panels have nothing to wear away. They don't need greasing or oiling or filling with fossil fuel, and for the most part they don't need clip-on gadgets bought separately to control their performance.

With the typical 14.5-volt panel often recommended for use on small systems, it is impossible to overcharge the battery, as the panel feeding it is self-regulating—that is, as the pressure (voltage) increases in the battery, the panel stops pumping so much in. Unfortunately, these low-voltage, self-regulating panels are unable consistently to charge a battery completely—especially so at high temperatures, when their output may drop well below the 14.5 volts the battery wants to see. Consistent undercharging of batteries is a major but little-known factor in bringing about their early demise.

With higher-voltage panels, which typically produce 16 to 17.5 volts, charge controllers (a $50 to $100 item) are recommended to taper the charge and prevent the panels from overcharging the battery (when the battery reaches approximately 80 percent of charge, the controller gradually reduces the voltage to approximately 13.8 volts). However, one or two 16-volt panels—a typical setup for a houseboat—can get by without a charge controller provided the panel's (or series of panels) rated output is equal to about 0.5 percent or less of the amp-hour capacity of the battery it's charging.

Angling
Despite the fact that solar panels are at their best when facing the sun at right angles, far too many are mounted flat. A solar panel so mounted may be as much as 50 percent less efficient than one mounted at right angles to the sun. Compounding the loss, a panel's efficiency also decreases with heat, by as much as 50 percent in truly hot climates. A panel left lying on a hot tin roof would be more efficient if permanently mounted, with a gap left behind for cooling air to breeze through. Even more efficient would be the open-air bracket shown in Figure 9-2, which not only allows air to circulate, but allows the panel to be angled for the seasonal declination of the sun and swivelled to follow its daily course.

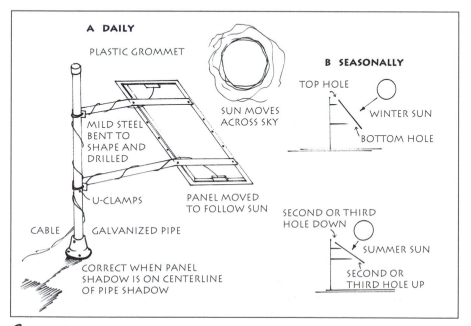

Figure 9-2. Open-air brackets allow you to angle solar panels according to the season and time of day.

Briefly, the bracket is in two parts, a short top leg and a longer bottom leg. Both are cut and bent from mild steel and drilled according to the pipe, U-clamps, and panel width. The bracket with attached solar panel is then clamped to the vertical pipe in such a way as to place the panel at right angles to the sun at midday. Now we can track the sun and markedly improve our panel's efficiency—as much as 50 percent.

As summer approaches, the sun rises higher in the southern sky in the Northern Hemisphere and conversely in the Southern Hemisphere. Because the change is slow, we need alter the setting only once each season. To find the optimum seasonal setting for the solar panel, you need to know the sun's angle from the horizon at noon. Anyone who can use a sextant will tell you this; so too will an astronomer or an astrologer. We can find it ourselves, though, by trial and error.

Place the panel roughly square to the sun, with perhaps the top bracket bolted in place, then stand a builder's set-square or a child's drawing triangle on the panel. As long as the uppermost point is throwing a shadow, the panel is not square. Move the panel until the shadow disappears, and you'll find a true 90-degree angle to the sun. Now bolt the bottom bracket in place and you're set for the season.

That leaves the second variable, the sun's steady daily movement from east to west. To track this, the panel is simply swiveled about the pipe. Loosen the nuts on the clamps just enough to allow the bracket to swivel around, but not so much that they will no longer hold everything in place. A little WD-40 or grease helps. Obviously the panel can't be monitored every minute of the day, but if the houseboater happens to be home and quite naturally wanders out on deck every couple of hours, it only takes a moment to move the panel. If no one is at home, the panel can be left at the midday position. You'll lose a bit of efficiency, but if you're not home, you're probably not using much power.

Sizing

Solar panel output can vary from 4 watts to 60 watts (.27 amp to 4 amps for a 14.5-volt panel), but we shouldn't accept the ratings at face value; clouds have been known to cross the face of the sun, and of course wet or overcast days cut into their output. To allow for this we should reckon on about 70 percent of rated performance. We should also allow for about five hours of sun a day, again figuring an annual average (your neighborhood meteorologist can supply you with the actual figures for your area).

Back to our example houseboat, with 30-Ah daily demand, in an area with five hours sunlight daily. Here's the calculation:

Amp-hour (30) X 100 ÷ 70 ÷ hours of sunlight = panel output
    42.8   5   = 8.571 amps

We need 8.571 amps of panel output to satisfy our needs.

Since panels commonly are rated in watts, and voltage varies from brand to brand, (usually either 14.5 or 16), we find our wattage (remember?) by another calculation:

Amps   X   panel voltage =   panel wattage
8.571A X   16V   =   137.14 watts

Therefore, to supply the example's current demand, we'll need (rounding off) two 60-watt panels—which should supply all the power we'd ever need. (Like batteries, panels can be wired together to increase output.)

Solar panels aren't inexpensive, though, and large arrays of them can take up a lot of space. If you are tempted to buy those two panels (which might cost more than $600), try making do with just one. You may be surprised to find you don't need the other after all—especially if you reduce your electrical demand during sunless weather. That's the killer—those rainy, windswept days. Of course, there's another option to take advantage of that.

Wind Generators

A wind generator operates as long as there's wind and couldn't care less if the sun is shining. Readers living in cloudy, windy climates, like Maine or Oregon, may find a wind generator of more use than solar panels. There's always wind where water meets land; it's part of this planet's natural breathing cycle. As the sea breeze begins to blow, the electricity begins to flow—if there's a wind generator there to catch it.

Wind generators supply power when demand is most acute. On beautiful, sunny days, folks aren't home—they're at the beach, promenading, visiting, walking the dog. The stereo isn't playing, the TV isn't on, and the power demands are minimal. But in winter, when wind and rain and sleet and even snow set in, the houseboater is snug inside, watching a ball game or reading, popping popcorn, pulling a beer from the ice on deck. To support this sybaritic lifestyle, electric current is needed. With no sun to excite the electrons in the solar panel, up on the roof the wind generator is cranking merrily over.

A fairly typical wind generator delivers 1.25 amps with a 10 m.p.h. wind speed, while at 20 m.p.h., output is a respectable 3.75 amps. Using the deliberately hefty example of 30 Ah per day, this generator would cope adequately, given average wind speeds:

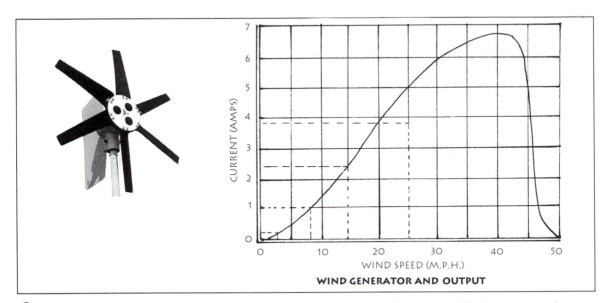

WIND GENERATOR AND OUTPUT

Figure 9-3. Depending on where you live, a wind generator may be a more efficient source of energy than solar panels. Ideally, you can hedge your bets with one of each.

MPH	Hours	Current	=	Amp-hours
20	6	3.75		22.5
15	4	2		8
8	4	1		4
4	10	0.25		2.5
Total				37 Amp-hours

The blades on the types of wind generator we're interested in are usually about 3 to 5 feet in diameter, so the wind generator is best mounted on a pole high enough to be well clear of people's heads, preferably bolted to the barge board at the end of the roof. This puts it up in clear, undisturbed air, well above roof edges and house corners where the wind can tumble and swirl in confused eddies.

In areas where light winds are the norm, pressure on the blades can be increased by mounting a wind generator at the end of a tapering tunnel.

Like the down-draught in a carburetor, the tunnel acts as a venturi—funneling air into an ever-diminishing volume to raise its pressure, and thus the speed of the blades.

Wind generators have to contend with heavy winds, too. Well-designed models flip themselves aside, out of harm's way, when winds build beyond a predetermined level—45 m.p.h. in the illustrated example (Figure 9-3). Notice the sudden drop of output, tapering to zero at 50 m.p.h. One of these types, a New Zealand-made Furlmatic, was left unattended in Antarctica for two years; when someone got back down that way and reexamined it, it was ticking over perfectly.

It seems clear that, given the prevailing conditions of sun and cloudless sky alternating with wind and rain, there is a place on the ultimate self-sufficient houseboat for both generators, solar and wind—once again diversifying our energy eggs among several baskets.

Found Alternatives

Of course, they cost money. But the tinkerer can find suitable alternatives for charging batteries that need not be expensive at all. The author, living on a houseboat for the first time and as broke as the long-suffering church mouse, was given an antique lawnmower engine. The city dump yielded an automobile generator, and when the engine and generator were mounted on a board and connected by a belt, a generating plant resulted—a totally ugly and noisy generator, true, but it did its job. To keep the batteries charged, it needed to run about 10 minutes a day. In the struggle for human achievement, it wasn't a giant step for mankind, more of a stumble for one bloke, but it was a start.

For those interested, Figure 9-5 shows the wiring diagram for a home-made generator. The motor, generator, and voltage regulator (also from an automobile) have been connected to a common wire. The negative lead goes to the battery, while the positive battery lead goes to B on the regulator. The small terminal on the back of the generator, the dynamo winding, goes to the D terminal of the regulator; the larger generator terminal, the field, leads to a switch, thence to the F.

In use, the switch was flicked off until the little 1½-h.p. motor had been pull-started (which, like most two-stroke engines, was never without tribulation); when it was warmed up, the switch was flicked on, the engine revs dropped as the generator started to work, and current was produced.

An automobile alternator, the modern equivalent of a generator, produces something like 60 to 80 amps. Unlike generators, they always produce current, even at the slowest idle. They also don't need complex wiring, with the load and current being controlled by diodes inside the

Figure 9-4.
**If you're
resourceful,
you can build
a homemade
generator from
junkyard parts,
as the author
has done.**

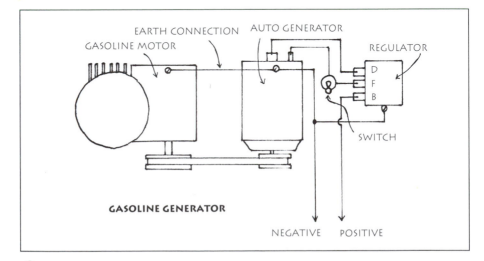

EARTH CONNECTION   AUTO GENERATOR

GASOLINE MOTOR

REGULATOR

D
F
B

SWITCH

GASOLINE GENERATOR

NEGATIVE   POSITIVE

Figure 9-5. **This wiring diagram gives you the basics for constructing a
gasoline generator similar to the one shown in Figure 9-4.**

alternator housing. You may find an alternator even more suitable as a homebuilt generating plant.

Trusting in the premise that, if a propeller can pull a machine with a person strapped inside it off the ground, then it sure ought to be able to drive a homemade wind generator, some dedicated experimenters have built a very efficient generating plant: A three-bladed propeller from an ultralight airplane was connected via a pulley and belt to an alternator, the whole thing set facing into the wind. It was very successful.

An alternator could be mounted inside the houseboat, up against the roof's ridge beam, with a shaft protruding through the end wall to a propeller or windvanes. This would keep the alternator and its sensitive electrical connections sheltered from the weather. To adapt the system for prevailing local winds, two windvanes move more sedately than three or more when the angle at which they're twisted is the same. In recent experiments, large windvanes have been built along the lines of the small toy windmills with which children delight in running through fields. The spinning bit was cut from a small square sheet of plastic, with each segment folded over to meet at the center.

The reader will be encouraged to pursue these lines of enquiry. Who knows? Just as a humble transistor in an unpainted case opened the door to a new solar-based technology, perhaps a humble houseboater, mucking about with an old alternator and bits of tin, might unlock a new era in our understanding of atmospheric dynamics.

High Voltage

It is possible to buy inverters that turn the 12 volts DC (direct current) from our batteries into either 120 or 240 volts AC (alternating current—what we have in our homes ashore) to drive standard household appliances. Possible, yes, but the current drain is phenomenal. A sturdy bank of batteries and a healthy generator are needed to cope. Not that anyone addicted to household appliances need despair. Generators, either gasoline or diesel, are available that happily crank out such voltages. Modern ones are relatively silent in their operation, and can be mounted on a back deck to power chandeliers, washing machines, freezers, vacuum cleaners, computers, or an entire workshop if necessary. They only need fuel and oil levels topped up—and a healthy infusion of cash at purchase (and refueling) time. They do conflict with our vision of environmentally responsible power generation, however, and they introduce added complication.

If a high-voltage generator is installed (or if the houseboat is intended for main supply facilities at a marina), it is imperative that you understand that you *must not pump* such voltages into the houseboat's 12-volt wiring circuits—unless you're fond of pyrotechnics. The houseboat will need to be wired for both levels of voltage, and each socket and insert suitably labeled; better yet, use a completely different plug and socket configuration so there is no possibility of plugging your 12-volt radio into your 120-volt outlet. Unless you have absolutely no doubts about your knowledge and skill, have the high-voltage wiring installed by a registered tradesman. Unlike the comparatively benign 12-volt circuits we've been playing with until now, high voltages kill.

WIRING

Wiring for a houseboat need not be complex. In the simple system shown in Figure 9-6, two wires enter the house from the generator and are led to the battery. The battery then supplies the appliances: two bulbs, a fluorescent light, two sockets (for radio and TV), another bulb, etc. Every appliance has a positive (marked P or +) side and a negative (N or -) side. We always connect positive sides to positive sides and negative sides to negative sides (with one exception, which I'll explain in a bit).

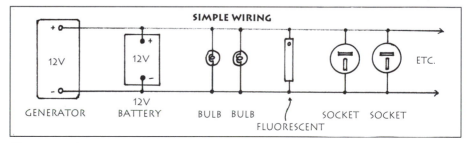

Figure 9-6. The basics—this system would service a few light bulbs, a fluorescent light, radio, TV, etc.

The appliances in the example are all wired in parallel, that is, each appliance is fed by a circuit branching off the main—positive to positive, negative to negative. This parallel circuit ensures a constant voltage at each appliance irrespective of how many are switched on—and also means that turning off one doesn't plunge off every other one as well, like old-fashioned Christmas tree lights.

The opposite of parallel wiring is series wiring, where all the components are lined up along one wire. The state of one component determines the state of every other down the line—an ideal situation for a switch. Apart from metering instruments like an ammeter (measures amps), only switches are wired in series, with that one exception I mentioned: Often, two 6-volt batteries are wired in series (positive to negative, negative to positive) to produce 12 volts.

There are drawbacks to this rudimentary circuit, however. If every appliance were to be switched on, apart from instantly blowing the 5-amp fuse, the total current drain would require fairly hefty (and very expensive) cables to carry it all. Also, over long lengths the resistance of the wires themselves absorbs some of the pressure of the electricity, causing a voltage drop, which in turn demands even heavier cable. After all, think about how an electric heater works: A great deal of current is forced through small-diameter wire, which then heats red-hot—not the sort of thing you want going on behind your wall paneling.

An alternative is shown in Figure 9-7 (which details a circuit diagram, or schematic), suitable for a small houseboat with modest power requirements. Instead of packing all the appliances onto one circuit, or loop, the loads have been distributed between two circuits. You'll notice that just as each appliance is paralleled, so too are the two loops. You'll also notice that the lights are grouped together, as are the appliance sockets. What we have here is a separation of the various loads: The heavier loads go on one loop, the lighter loads on another. Each of those loops is protected by a fuse: a 5-amp fuse for the lightly loaded loop, a 10-amp fuse for the other.

A fuse (which is always inserted in the hot, or positive wire) is designed to blow out if the current exceeds its rated capacity. It might be shorted wiring in the walls, a defective appliance, or whatever—if there's an overload, the fuse blows and shuts down current in the circuit.

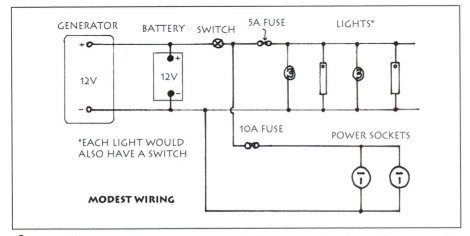

Figure 9-7. This system, which is divided into two circuits, each protected by its own fuse, would be adequate for a small houseboat with moderate power demands.

This is the principle that determines how to draw the circuits for any houseboat, as well as automobiles, airplanes, tanks, computers, radio stations—whatever: Divide up the total load into separate, paralleled loops, each loop responsible for certain amounts of current. Allocate fuse ratings for each loop, from, say, 5 amps for lights and 10 amps for appliances, to 15 amps for pumps. The fuse amperage should equal the total amperage load of all appliances on the loop: Three 5-amp appliances equal a 15-amp fuse (although you can make allowances for appliances that will not be drawing power simultaneously).

Each loop is then further separated for different areas of the houseboat, so that lights on one side of the boat or in one room are separated from lights on the other side of the boat or another room. Ditto for appliances, pumps, etc.

In Figure 9-8, specific areas of the houseboat have been identified, and different load demands in each area separated. On the left side of the house there are two lights protected by a 5-amp fuse, as well as two power sockets protected by a 10-amp fuse. The right side of the house has two separate loops as well. The water pump has been given its own loop and probably warrants a 15-amp fuse. Breaking things down into these three categories of current drain—light, medium, and heavy—will suffice for our needs.

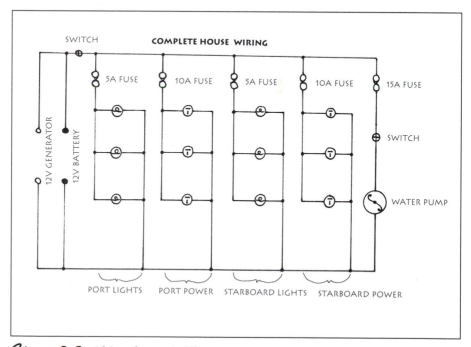

Figure 9-8. This schematic illustrates a more sophisticated system that separates appliances according to current drain.

Wire Gauge

We now need to know what size wiring to install for the loops. For houseboat use, where the gentle rocking of waves translates into enough vibration to damage solid copper wire (never use aluminum wire) over time, use only flex, or multistranded wire. And since 12-volt wires must make a complete circuit from battery to device and back to battery, which means running two wires, you might as well buy two-wire cable, often called twinflex. Use tables 9-1 and 9-2 to size the wires for your system.

We can now allocate specific wiring gauges to specific loops. You'll have to figure out your own custom requirements, but it won't be hard: All you need to know is the current demands of each appliance you'll be installing and the total run from battery to load and back to battery (twice the run from battery to appliance). If, say, a TV using 5 amps, a radio using 0.25 amp, and a stereo using 1 amp were on one loop, the total load on the circuit would be 6.25 amps. Assuming it is 5 feet from power source to devices (or a 10-foot run out and back), you could use 18-gauge wire. To be on the safe side, however, you should use 14-gauge.

The following, if installed by default, will be more than adequate for the average small houseboat. One solar panel or wind generator, with, say, a maximum output of 6 amps, would be comfortably equipped with cable rated at 12 amps—12-gauge twinflex. The internal wiring, at a minimum, might be 14-gauge twinflex for light current, 12-gauge twinflex for medium current, and 10-gauge for heavy current.

Total current on circuit in amps	Length of conductor from source to device and back to source in feet									
	10	15	20	25	30	40	50	60	70	80
5	18	16	14	12	12	10	10	10	8	8
10	14	12	10	10	10	8	6	6	6	6
15	12	10	10	8	8	6	6	6	4	4
20	10	10	8	6	6	6	4	4	2	2
25	10	8	6	6	4	4	2	2	2	1
30	10	8	6	6	4	4	2	2	1	1
40	8	6	6	4	4	2	2	1	1	0
50	6	6	4	4	2	2	1	0	2/0	3/0

[Wire sizes in American Wire Gauge (AWG); for European conductor sizes, use Table 9-2.]

Table 9-1. **Conductor size for 3 percent voltage drop.**

Conductor Size in AWG	European Equivalent (diameter in mm)
18	1.024
16	1.290
14	1.630
12	2.050
10	2.590
8	3.260
6	4.110
4	5.190
2	6.540
1	7.350
1/0	8.250
2/0	9.270
3/0	10.400

Table 9-2. **AWG conductor sizes and their European equivalents.**

Junctions

Like the plumbing pipes, the flex will be fed around the studs of the houseboat walls before the inside panelling is installed. If joints are needed along the lengths of flex, use the plastic connectors shown in Figure 9-9. We will not be alarmed by Admiral Sir Frederick Bedford's warning in *The Sailor's Pocket Book*, written before the advent of plastic: "Making Junctions.—the importance of making good junctions in insulated wires cannot be overstated; everything depends on them; making junctions is an art which cannot be taught on paper, anyone wishing to learn them, must obtain an instructor and acquire the knowledge by practical methods."

Don't just twist wires together to make a joint. Over time, corrosion will weaken it, and resistance will increase; appliances on the far end of the boat will no longer work. The ultimate in long-lasting connections is a soldered joint shielded with insulating tape or heat-shrink tubing. Soldering, however, is a bit of an art; for our purposes, plastic crimp-on connectors will suffice. Be sure to use the appropriate-size connector for the wire you're using, and cover the joint with electrical tape or heat-shrink tubing.

Twinflex usually is color coded to allow you to keep your polarities straight (if you're using individual wires, buy separate colors). By convention, in the United States the hot wire is red or orange, and the return

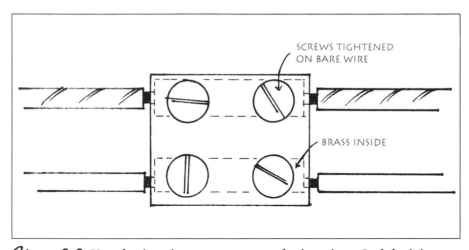

Figure 9-9. Use plastic, crimp-on connectors for junctions. Seal the joints with heat-shrink tubing or silicone.

wire black or white. If your creative urges dictate a different color scheme, be sure to follow it throughout, or you'll never be able to unscramble the results. Thus, at each connection ensure that the red (or striped, or pink, or whatever) is connected to the positive (+) side. At each connection, the red (or striped, or pink, or whatever) side connects only to the next red (or striped, or pink, or whatever) section. Likewise, the negative (-) wire only connects to the black (or green, or puce, or whatever).

As each series of wires is put in place, leading back to the battery (or better yet the fuseboard, which we'll come to shortly), wrap some masking tape around each length of wire and write down just what it feeds—i.e., "Left-hand side, lights"—to prevent being suddenly overwhelmed by a profusion of unknown wires acting like demented spaghetti. Label them, and you'll know what each wire is and where it's supposed to go.

Polarities

When all the flex has been laid, and the wall panels are in place, with flex poking out of holes in the wall, we're ready to install wall sockets and light fittings. The polarities, that is the respective positive or negative orientation of the wires, are not important for incandescent light fittings, so simply screw either wire into either terminal behind each fitting.

Polarity is important for fluorescent lights, however, and for the wall sockets that will drive such appliances as radios and TVs. Incorrect polarity can seriously damage transistors and chips inside electronic things, so even if you've allocated the red or striped or pink or whatever side of the flex correctly and faithfully ensured its continuity, it pays to double-check.

At the battery end of all the wires, clip the ones that are supposed to be negative to the negative terminal of the battery, and the ones that are supposed to be positive to the positive terminal of the battery. Now go around to all the wall sockets and push the prongs of a multimeter, set to read voltage, into each socket. By convention, the left side of a two-prong socket is positive; thus the meter's positive prong (it's red) goes to the left. If the meter gives a positive reading, all is well. If the needle flicks down below zero (or if a digital meter gives a minus reading), then the polarity is reversed in the socket; simply remove it from the wall and swap the wires.

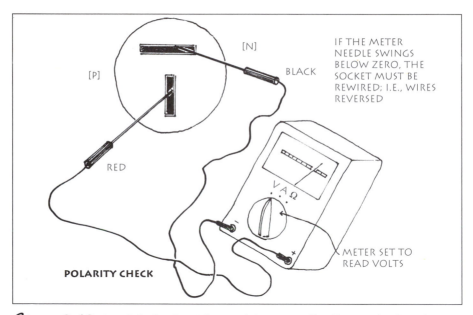

Figure 9-10. **A quick check with a multimeter will tell you whether the polarity is reversed.**

As I've mentioned, a multimeter is indispensable for houseboaters producing their own power: Among other things, it can be used to check the health of the batteries. But you may want to monitor more closely the current being generated by the solar panel or wind generator, as well as the current being drained by appliances. Automobile ammeters are good for this, as they show both a charge side and an opposing discharge side. Certainly on overcast, windless days, the hesitant needle in the charge area is a good reminder that very little power is going into the system. We find ourselves automatically respecting the state of the battery by cutting back on power usage. The behavior of the homeowner becomes conditional on the behavior of the sun or the wind—a symbiotic relationship as old as mankind.

A wiring diagram for meter installation is shown in Figure 9-11. Note that the ammeter is wired in series, or fitted along the length of the positive wire. The voltmeter is fitted in parallel, from negative to positive. An ammeter put across the battery would blow up. The voltmeter, incidentally, should have a switch to turn it off; otherwise, it would constantly be pulling current, like a light bulb or any other load.

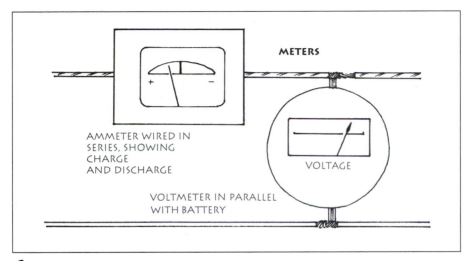

Figure 9-11. **Installing ammeters and voltmeters.**

Fuseboards

A good place to mount the two meters that monitor the electrical system is on a fuseboard—essentially an attempt to centralize and tidy up the controls and switches that govern the wires leading to and from the battery. The fuseboard is the control room of the electrical system.

While at first glance the fuseboard is a daunting and bewildering array, it actually makes order out of chaos by organizing the confusion of wires poking out of the wall into a neat, linear set of connections on the back of the board. This makes later troubleshooting extremely easy, provides a professional-looking installation, and, by packing all the controls into one place, lets the houseboater know in a glance what's happening in the system.

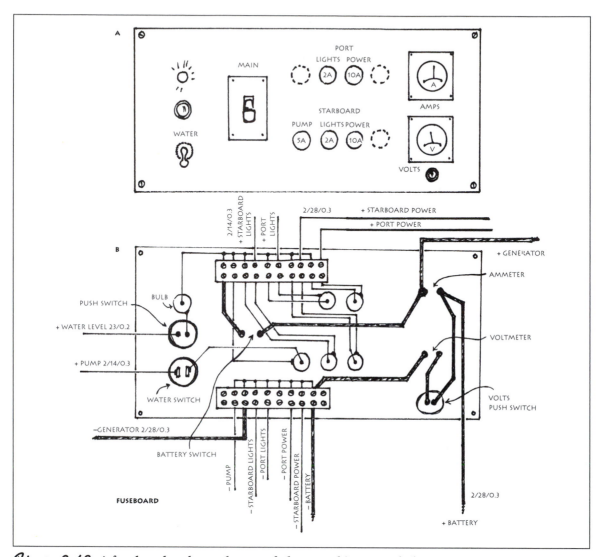

Figure 9-12. **A fuseboard makes order out of chaos, and it's a good place to mount your ammeter and voltmeter.**

This fuseboard, with a few extra things added for convenience, would be used in wiring the sample circuit shown in Figure 9-8. Looking at the top part of the drawing, which represents the front of the board, there are two meters on the right-hand side, the ammeter (top) and the voltmeter (bottom). The push switch for the voltmeter is below it. Fuses for the houseboat's left and right sides are next, with space left for fuses (the dotted lines) that may be installed at a later date, just in case the houseboater discovers that he can't live a moment longer without, say, a 12-volt electric blanket.

The main switch will cut off all circuits from the battery, apart from the generator, and would be used if the houseboat were left unattended. On the right-hand side, the bottom switch controls the water pump and allows it to be shut off if the plumbing needs repairs. Above is a push switch and a bulb connected to a standard marine-store tank-level sensor; push the switch and the light indicates water to spare or water bare.

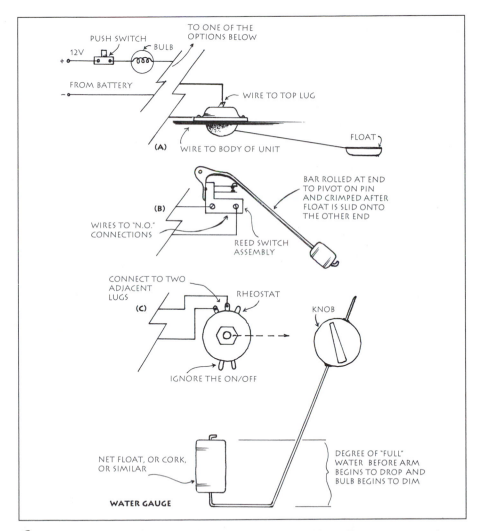

Figure 9-13. A water gauge will alert you to your dwindling water supply *before* you get soaped up. In part (c), if the bulb grows brighter as the arm drops, move the wires to the two adjacent lugs; alternatively, let the brightness indicate caution in water use.

Now, looking at the back of the board, trace along each wire with a pencil, and the layout will become clear. The positive (+) battery lead (red by convention), bottom right, goes to the ammeter and also to the voltmeter switch. After going through the ammeter, it leads away to the positive generator, thence to the main switch. The other side of the switch feeds a long, plastic-covered connector strip that distributes power to the individual circuits.

On the other side of that main feed are short connecting wires that join up Numbers 2, 3, 5, 7, and 9. The electricity continues through the wires, on the opposite side again, to the fuses and then back to numbers 4, 6, 8, and 10. We'll call this part of the board the positive (+) supply strip, because it's from those four slots on the strip that the appropriate wires feed out through the houseboat to supply various appliances. As indicated, the fuse governing "port power 10A" leads to the port side (left side facing forward; starboard is right side facing forward) of the houseboat and to the appliance wall sockets; the maximum rating is 10 amps.

The other side of the port power flex, the negative (-) side (black by convention), is led to the bottom negative supply strip, as is every other negative lead from the battery, generator, utilities, etc. This negative terminal is called a *common* rail, and in conventional house-wiring would be a long strip of copper with screws along it for securing each negative wire.

The short connecting wires on the top of the positive supply strip are pre-fuse power supplies. The four individual wires coming from the top have been routed through the fuses below them. There is no reason to combine the facets of this positive power side all on one strip—it's just the way it got drawn. The wires into and from numbers 4, 6, 8, and 10 could just as easily have been taken to another plastic strip. Your choice.

To boil a fuseboard down to its essentials, we feed power from the battery, via the meters and the main switch, to the positive supply strip, to be taken from there anywhere the builder cares to go. The negative returns all come back to the common rail, thence to the battery's negative terminal—everything in one neat package.

Wiring Multiple Batteries

Earlier we mentioned stacking up several batteries to increase storage capacity. It is possible, of course, just to wire two 12-volt batteries together in parallel—positive to positive, negative to negative—but it is a better idea to isolate one from the other in case one decides to have a breakdown.

If wired together in parallel, a battery that is deteriorating will, vampire-like, suck energy from a healthy battery and bring them both to collapse.

Both batteries could be ruined in the process, and there is also a risk of fire from overheated wires.

Diodes

The solution is to fit some diodes, devices that allow current to flow only in one direction. They are shown in circuit diagrams as arrowheads with a bar. The current flows only in the direction of the arrow.

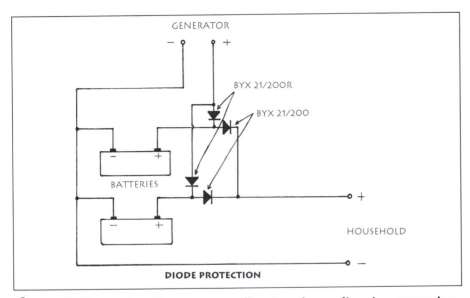

Figure 9-14. Diodes allow current to flow in only one direction, protecting batteries from accidental discharge.

The batteries' negative sides are connected as usual to every other negative wire in the system. On the positive side, however, the current must flow through a diode (a BYX 21/200 or its equivalent will work; check marine stores or recreational vehicle shops) before entering the positive household supply. The current cannot go from one battery across to the other battery because, although the first diode is set to pass current flowing in that direction, the other battery's diode is set to block current flowing in that direction.

So far, so good; the current can only go out into the system and not to the other battery. Now, to make sure that current can get into the batteries from the generator, another pair of diodes, this time reverse-blockage diodes, like the BYX 21/200R, are fitted behind the first pair. These diodes pass current from the generator but prevent it from flowing back. A solar panel, for instance, may dissipate current at night when it isn't charging.

Although this sounds confusing, the current flows will become clear if the reader traces along each wire, stopping where a bar appears to block the path, but continuing where there's an arrowhead—a bit like a child's maze. Current flows only in the direction of the arrowhead.

Heatsinks

Diodes generate heat—nothing that we'd notice with a fingertip, but enough to scramble the diodes—so they are mounted on aluminum bars, called heatsinks, that dissipate heat from the diodes. (Note that although diodes aren't hot as in warm, they are hot as in electrical. Shorting out the heatsink to ground is the same thing as shorting out the battery terminals.) Although storebought heatsinks are inexpensive and easily found, aluminum moldings with heat-dissipating fins (used in the construction of doors, ranchsliders, and windows) may be used.

In the system shown (Figure 9-15), two moldings, one per battery, were each drilled with holes for the diodes, and a third hole for attachment to the battery terminal. Each molding carried a BYX21/200 and a BYX21/200R diode; these can handle the current from a solar panel but are too small for the massive outputs of automobile alternators. Diodes should have a capacity equal to the maximum amperage produced by the charging system.

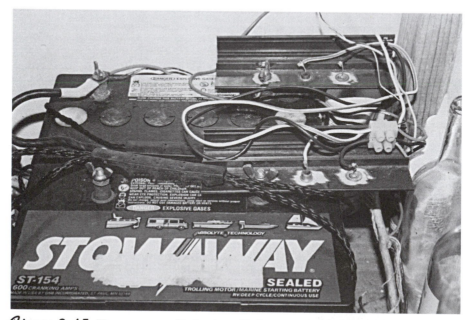

Figure 9-15. Here you see diodes installed on a two-battery system; the diodes are mounted on homemade heatsinks made from aluminum door track.

Any electrical or electronic shop will make up two heatsinks with correct-size diodes. Good batteries are expensive and merit this low-cost protection.

Plugging In

Because many appliances used aboard a houseboat are intended for the recreational vehicle trade, they are likely to come wired with adaptors intended to be used with automobile cigarette-lighter sockets. For use aboard, however, these should be replaced with household plugs (to plug into our wall sockets), and it is important to retain the correct polarity.

Usually, the manufacturers follow the convention that a red wire, or a red stripe on another color, is the positive wire. Just cut off the old adaptor and screw the positive wire into the P terminal of the new plug, the negative wire to the N terminal. Sometimes the wire lead has a small plug at the other end, where it enters the appliance, or a small diagram may be printed or molded on the appliance.

If the wires are the same color, and there are no diagrams either on the appliance or in its handbook, take a small screwdriver and pull off the back (or bottom or whatever). Carefully trace the wires that lead from where the power is fed in: The color that goes to the switch is the positive wire; the negative wire will lead directly to the circuit board.

If there are no plug-in points and an appliance is battery operated, like a portable radio, as long as it's 10 or 12 volts, we can adapt it to life aboard. Remove the panel where the batteries are normally inserted and find the polarities of the two springs that press against the batteries. Peel back the insulation from a piece of flex; wrap a negative wire around the negative spring, and a positive around the positive spring. Plug the other end of the flex into the wall, and that's it. No more queuing up for D-cells at the supermarket.

If the appliance draws less than 10 volts, say 3 volts for a small calculator or 6 volts for a mast-mounted strobe light, you can find a *transformer* (a device to convert one voltage to another) at a radio fix-it shop or electronic handyman's store. Order one with 12-volt DC *primary* (input), and whatever DC voltage output (the *secondary*) you require. Wire the transformer with the primary leads fed to the wall socket and the secondary wires to the appliance (noting carefully the polarities). The incurable tinkerer would look for nonworking marine equipment, like a depthsounder or a radio, intended for use on a 12-volt system. In pulling it apart, the transformers inside can be salvaged for just such adult playtime.

Electrical playtime is a good way to understand electricity (as is studying the books recommended in Suggested Reading). The more you understand about it, the more you'll be able to do with it. If you're in doubt, by all means call an electrician, or even have one come aboard and do the job. But however the builder chooses to proceed, whether in the care and control of a professional or stumbling into the dark of his own ignorance (which, after all, is slowly dissipating), then wotthehell? As long as there is forward movement—what matter the means? Electricity inside the houseboat is something that we have supplied (or at least we've attempted to supply) ourselves.

DANGER FROM WITHOUT

Outside the houseboat lurks a less benevolent form of electricity. Whenever two dissimilar metals are in conjunction with moving water, say, in any city plumbing supply, an electrical current will travel through the water and etch one of the metals away. This phenomenon is known as *electrolysis*—the steady generation of a small amount of current in the water surrounding the houseboat. Metals corrode according to a strict hierarchy of *nobility*—with magnesium and zinc being least noble and platinum being most noble. If steel and bronze are together, for instance, the steel will be corroded away—steel is less noble than bronze.

Boats, particularly boats with electrical circuits aboard, are prime targets for the predations of electrolysis. We must attempt to overcome the etching of metals both by insulating them from one another with plastic or nylon and by sacrificing the least noble metal on behalf of the others. The sacrificial victim is a block of zinc, called an *anode*, bolted to the hull and connected to the negative terminal of the battery by a heavy-gauge wire. As the zinc slowly corrodes away, the other metals are protected. Periodically, when only 40 percent of the block is left, it is replaced.

Plastic drums will not need protection, but steel barrels, pontoons, ferrocement hulls, or the like definitely will. Fortunately, anodes are inexpensive and easily found in a marine store.

TUNING IN

And so we come to the last item, that of keeping in touch with the outside world. It is within the realm of the now defunct god of communications, Mercury, that the twentieth-century houseboater can feel as though he has never left dry land. Television is instantly available, VHF and cellular telephones enable quick phone calls to office or mate, while fax machines and laptop computers enable a houseboater to conduct business right from the lounge.

We'll look briefly at TV, and a little longer at VHF, as these are the two items of most interest to the cost-conscious builder. Readers interested in the latter toys will find manufacturers and retailers more than willing to help explain their workings.

TV

Television sets that can't pull in a signal with rabbit ears can be beefed up with an outside antenna. There's no need to buy a multi-element antenna, when often the coaxial antenna cable alone can do the same job. The rods on a complex house antenna are there basically to bounce the signal to one receiving rod, thereby amplifying the signal. What we do is fool the TV into believing we've bought an expensive antenna. Take a length of twin-wire TV antenna lead-in cable, split the insulation for about 3 feet, and spread it in a straight line from one part of the boat to another—crucified, in a sense, over 6 feet, with the rest of the cable dropping from the center and leading to the TV. (You can do the same thing with coax cable by stripping off 3 feet of insulation and running the braided shield in one direction and the insulated core wire in the other.) Reception with this type of antenna, called a dipole if you're interested, is strongest broad-on to the length, and weakest off the ends. If reception persists in being terrible, chop most of the two lengths off and connect the cable to a marine TV antenna.

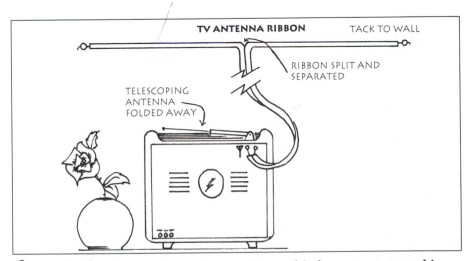

Figure 9-16. There's no need to invest in a multi-element antenna—this homemade TV antenna will do the job if you're not too far from the station.

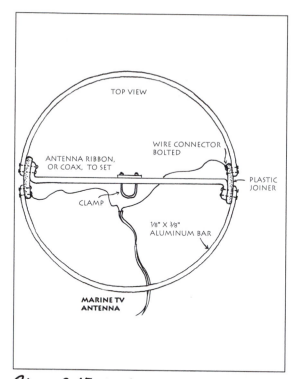

Figure 9-17. An alternative is a marine antenna, tuned to TV wavelengths. Storebought antennas are expensive, but it's easy to roll your own with plastic pipe and twin-lead.

Figure 9-18. A marine TV antenna up and operating.

Marine antennas are circular plastic frames, with two outer terminals and a length of ribbon inside that is "tuned" to TV wavelengths, just as the ribbon was tuned when we bared 3 feet of it. The circular shape makes these antennas nondirectional, unlike our homemade dipole. Since boats move around at anchor without regard to the location of shoreside TV stations, that's a real benefit in marginal reception areas.

VHF

We all know what TV stands for, but VHF may not be so well known. It means Very High Frequency radio—a handy communications system that connects the houseboater with all manner of things, including talking to the Coast Guard, receiving weather bulletins, issuing Mayday calls when in genuine distress, talking to other boats, and making telephone calls through shoreside radio operators who will connect you into the telephone system (for a fee).

VHF antennas should be as high as possible. Unlike shortwave radios, which bounce signals from Earth to ionosphere and back, like skipping a stone on water, VHF communication is by line of sight. The higher the antenna, the greater its range.

Like most antennas, a VHF antenna is basically a tuned length of wire. They are not expensive to buy, but the inveterate tinkerer may make his own by adapting the base of a gutter-mounted automobile radio antenna. The old length of antenna is cut down to about 2½ feet long, but unless you are absolutely sure of what you're doing, it should be measured and cut by a radio serviceman. (Too short or too long, and your homebrew antenna could damage your radio's output transistors, as can attempting to operate the transmitter with no antenna at all. The wrong-size antenna can also generate harmonics—unwelcome multiples of the radio's frequency—that will get you in trouble with the authorities.) The inside wire of a length of coaxial cable is then soldered to the antenna terminal, and the outer sheathing wire of the cable soldered to the base. The base is then screwed to the roof which, if made of metal, will act as a ground plane to reflect signals to and from the antenna.

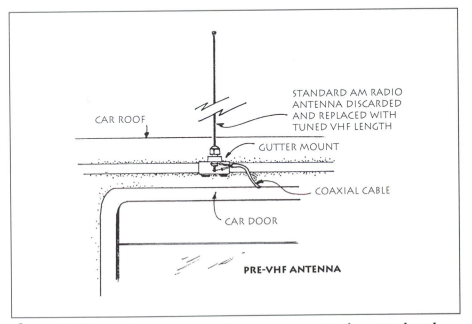

Figure 9-19. An old gutter-mounted car antenna, cut to the proper length (check with a radio shop) will serve as the VHF antenna of a resourceful houseboater. The higher the antenna is installed, the greater its range.

If the antenna is attached to a wooden base, lay some aluminum tape (the kind of tape that panelbeaters use to repair cars, found in most service stations) along the wood first, in the form of a cross, then position the antenna at the center. The tape, even if painted over, will still work as a ground plane.

A VHF operator's license is necessary to transmit. In some countries a short test is given before the issuing of a license, but the test is designed to ensure that the applicant knows what the radio service is and not to fail him or her. Most countries require an application only, after which a personal call-sign will be allocated.

The twentieth century has brought us all these wonderful gadgets, and if we can control them, so much the better. Unlike gadgets ashore, we have to support each of them personally, with our own onboard energy systems (who was it who coined the ultimate deceptive phrase, "energy-saving device"?). If we aren't prepared to support them, then perhaps we don't need them after all.

CHAPTER TEN
• • • • • • • • • • • •

Let There Be Light

Next *in point of desirability is acetylene gas, and today this system has been perfected to such an extent that it is safe and reliable. It gives a very good and steady light and all odors are eliminated.*

Oil lamps give an excellent light, but they are a great care, besides being greasy and of a strong odor. In most cases they will have to be used, but much caution should be exercised in handling them. In selecting gas and oil fixtures, buy only the best grade in the simplest designs.

〜〜〜〜〜〜〜〜〜〜〜〜〜〜〜〜〜〜

This chapter is being written under the illumination of various devices—and with only a little eye strain. At the moment, an 8-watt fluorescent tube lights the shadows in a far corner. Next to the typewriter, two candles are burning. Candles give off a natural, golden-hued light, formed from the controlled combustion of oxygen in the surrounding air. Who knows?: Maybe burning up surplus oxygen in the candle flame will keep it from going round rusting things.

STRIKE A MATCH

Candles whisk us back to the balmy days of childhood when anything was possible; when pirates gloated over their treasure in caves, candle wax dripping on their shoes, with no one telling them not to make a mess. Wee Willie Winkie tiptoed his way up a flight of stairs, a candle lighting his way, although we were never told what he and his lady got up to.

Candles illuminate with, no surprise, one candlepower. Their output can be increased by standing them in front of mirrors or polished reflectors. Houseboat owners who aspire toward greater self-sufficiency can make their own candles, either from paraffin wax mixed with crystalline wax, or from beeswax. (Check out the library for how-to books on the subject.)

OIL'S WELL

Oil lamps that burn with a natural flame, like candles, are also extremely soothing. The lighting method of choice between the age of candles and the age of electricity, paraffin or kerosene lamps are regular visitors to campgrounds around the world. Tents glow, and dark forms loom across the walls as the inhabitants move about. Such lanterns have a very useful place aboard a houseboat.

Wick-type kerosene lanterns, like that in Figure 10-1, use very little fuel, but that fuel must be the best obtainable. Yellow-tinted kerosene is not pure. It'll smoke, and it'll stink. Clear #1 kerosene will burn much cleaner.

Kerosene lights are easily maintained. To keep the light burning cleanly, the wick should be cleaned of ash periodically by carefully trimming the top with scissors to leave a reasonably even, clean new edge. Kerosene is an oil, and like all oils, any that gets spilled finds its way into everything. Use a funnel (preferably a filter funnel) when filling the reservoir. The fastidious will carry out the operation outdoors on a metal tray.

The next breed of kerosene lamp operates with the kerosene under pressure, and the light is far more radiant. The old-fashioned English Tilley produces a light almost as intense as a 100-watt bulb; the 500-candlepower Chinese Anchor is half again as bright. Either one is bright enough to illuminate any small houseboat, but one thing it won't be is romantic. Industrial-strength lights of this sort are for when you're already married and the kids want to do their homework.

These types of lanterns work by pressurizing the fuel (again, use only the best-quality, well-filtered kerosene) in the tank with the hand pump/ filler plug. The pressurized fuel is sprayed up the central column—the quantity controlled by careful adjustment of the upper knob, which moves a very fine needle into a jet—whereupon the fuel is atomized in the generator, as the top of the column is known. This atomized fuel enters the mantle—a sack of special mesh fabric—where it is ignited to glow with a brilliant white light.

Handled with caution these lanterns are perfectly safe and very efficient. All fuel-burning lanterns produce water vapor, however—about the same quantity as the amount of fuel originally in the lantern's reservoir. Excess

KEROSENE LAMP

Figure 10-1. **A kerosene lamp provided illumination for writing this book.**

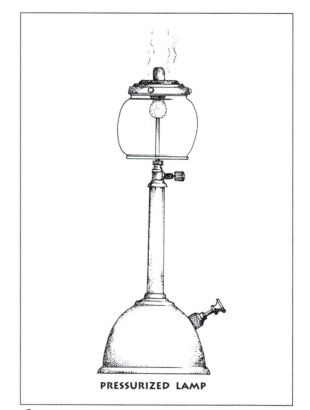

PRESSURIZED LAMP

Figure 10-2. **A pressurized lamp with a single mantle.**

humidity can become a problem aboard a houseboat, and I'll have more to say about that in the next chapter.

PUSH A BUTTON

The acetylene gas from houseboating's early days has been replaced with two modern options, LPG and CNG (liquid propane gas and compressed natural gas). Gas lamps are quiet, effective, and generally safe. The lamps usually are permanently bracketed to a wall, and a gas line leads to wherever the bottle happens to be, usually adjacent to the galley. Gas lamps vary in size and capability but start at around 200 candlepower. There are always drawbacks, however: Gas lamps can be expensive to operate compared with other forms of lighting. On the other hand, they are brighter than electric lights, help provide heat on cold winter evenings (or, unfortunately, on hot summer evenings), and they are readily available.

The benighted houseboater will never need to hunt through his pockets in the dark for matches to light any of the new-generation gas lamps: With the push of a button, a piezoelectric crystal bumps a spark across the face of a small vent, ignites the gas, and lights the way to bed.

Portable gas lamps, the small "Gaz" things sold to campers, are completely useless for houseboats. The mantle and glass surround, similar to that used for permanently mounted gas lamps, screws onto a gas canister that is thrown away after use. Nonrecyclable products like this are an insult to the planet any time, but the cost and limited life make them unacceptable for other than casual users.

FLICK A SWITCH

Electric light is the epitome of convenience. With a flick of the wrist, we are provided with clean, trouble-free, smokeless light. Candles may be romantic and kerosene may be economical, but after staggering about looking for a match and finding you've run out, it's very soothing to reach out and flick a switch, whereupon all will be revealed.

As mentioned in the last chapter, filament-type bulbs are inefficient energy wasters. Only 40 percent of the energy they radiate is light; the rest is in the form of heat. The true nature of incandescents gets worse, though: Only about 3 percent of the energy they consume is ever translated into visible light. That's a lot of charging and recharging of your expensive batteries, all to little purpose. A houseboater operating his own power company has to be a little more responsible.

The popularity of incandescents is related to their economy and their pleasant yellowish hue, akin to that of our old friend, the humble candle. We could install one, perhaps, as emergency lighting, but there's a much better choice—if we can just get past the sterility of its color.

The fluorescent tube—sickly greenish cast notwithstanding—produces the same amount of light as a comparably sized incandescent bulb while consuming one-fifth the power. Fluorescents operate by passing an electric charge through an inert gas to excite its electrons into violent motion, causing them to fluoresce, or emit light. Once excited, the gas needs only a low current to maintain its glowing state. When a fluorescent is switched on, a starter jolts the gas with a blast of high current, but then relaxes and passes only a low current drain to keep the light going.

Fluorescent tubes designed to more closely approximate natural light are available. So are compact fluorescents, which work in the same sockets and have a color very close to that of standard screw-in incandescents. If you have the old-style tubes and can't bring yourself to throw them out until they expire of natural causes, you can always light a candle or two.

A mirror behind any light will help immensely in aiming light where it's needed. There seems small advantage in illuminating the wall behind a lamp fitting when a small mirror will bounce all the light issuing from the lamp out into the room.

ON THE MOVE

Traditional marine lighting must include what are known as navigation lights, which must be used whenever a houseboat (or any vessel) is moved at night. The International Regulations for Preventing Collisions at Sea (COLREGS) require specific lights of specific colors mounted in specific locations for specific sizes of vessels. These lights are required for a power-driven vessel between 12 meters and 20 meters long:

- One white light high up in the forward part of the boat, visible for at least 3 miles, aimed forward over an arc of 225 degrees.

- One red light on the port side, not less than 3 feet below the white one, visible for at least 1 mile, aimed from dead-ahead, and back 22½ degrees.

- One green light on the starboard side, not less than 3 feet below the white one, visible for at least 1 mile, aimed from dead-ahead, and back 22½ degrees.

- One white light at the stern, visible for at least 2 miles, and shielded, to be unseen from the sides or forward.

The idea behind all this uniformity is to allow other boats approaching in the middle of the night to tell where you are, and where you're going to be, by the pattern of lights and how they change. If the upper white light and a red one below it were visible, they'd know they were approaching your port side. If the red slid backward, revealing a green, they'd know they were heading across your path.

No one wants to collide with a houseboat, so in the interests of common sense, legal jurisprudence, and continued insurance coverage, all these navigation lights should be fitted to a houseboat on the move.

There is also merit in mounting around the houseboat a number of reflectors, the circles of plastic attached to trailers, trucks, and bicycles that glow in headlights. Most vessels traveling at night will shine at least a flashlight in the direction of another vessel—and you'll glow with a forest of red or amber pinpoints. This also makes it easier to find your way when rowing home late at night from neighboring festivities.

When traveling at night, a red-shielded flashlight should be used for reading a chart, finding the coffee cup, or checking the oil-pressure gauge. A red light will not destroy night vision, whereas a full 10 minutes of acclimatization would be required for regaining night vision should a bright light be turned on.

AT REST

Finally, when a houseboat is sitting quietly on its mooring or at anchor, it should show a mooring or riding light (exceptions are made for designated anchorage areas in some harbors; check with the harbormaster). Houseboats are big things to bump into in the night, so other boats should be warned. While the owner is still up, reading a newspaper or watching TV, light will be pouring from the windows, and the houseboat would be hard to miss. However, when it's time for bed and the house is plunged into darkness, it's only common sense to flick on an anchor light. The regulations call for a single white light, mounted as high as possible and visible from 2 miles away, covering the full 360 degrees of the horizon.

Inside the house, the family sleeps safely on.

One of the greatest charms of life on a houseboat is its complete freedom and independence. If the owner so wills, he can cut himself and his family off from civilization as completely as does the hunter and angler who plunges into the deep woods and travels afar, simply to avoid the crowd and be alone with nature. The disciple of houseboating has many advantages over the man who seeks the woods and mountains. A comfortable habitation with a tight roof and a dry bed is always at hand.

CHAPTER ELEVEN

Keeping it Comfy

A boat which is at the same time a summer home
would please many a man who may have enjoyed
boating, canoeing, sailing or fishing in his youth, but
who, when he has the care and responsibilities of a
family, does not see his way clear to enjoy his old
pastime. To such a man a houseboat will appeal.

~~~~~~~~~~~~~~~~~~~~~~~~~~~~~

Sitting in an armchair in the middle of winter, warmed only by the
meager heat of a kerosene lantern clamped between your knees and the dog
draped across your feet, can seriously dampen enthusiasm for life aboard
a houseboat. It does not have to be like that.

180

RISING DAMP

Humidity is a measurement that Dr. Albert Einstein would have relished. It has no meaning or value in itself, but can only be understood relative to a point that is itself relative: Humidity is a percentage of water saturation relative to air temperature.

A theoretical 100 percent humidity, or 100 percent saturation of water, is part of an equation that says how much water *could* be in the air—at a certain temperature—and then compares it, as a percentage, with how much is *actually* there. The same quantity of water may be present in two different rooms, but if they are at different temperatures, the relative humidities will be different. The warm room will have low humidity, while the cold one will have high humidity—same water content, different temperature, and thus different relativity.

As temperatures drop, the ensuing increase in relative humidity may lead to a precipitation of the water. It doesn't actually rain inside, with little gray clouds hovering over a favorite armchair; instead, moisture condenses on windows, walls, and ceilings—just as on the inside of your auto's windshield. This excess moisture leads to rot, mildew, and ill health. In the words of the health inspectors, "rising damp, buddy, is what we're looking for."

Air Combat

Good air flow will combat mildew. The tiny spores aspiring to colonize damp spots of a houseboat abhor moving air. To forestall their colonial aspirations, open windows, open ventilator panels, and fit ducts that funnel air into cupboards and out-of-the-way stowage areas. During the day, a houseboat can be thoroughly aired; at night, heat from a fire or a vented heater will keep humidity to an acceptable level. Lack of heating and ventilation causes unattended boats and houses to smell musty.

Water that condenses needs cold surfaces. That's why Styrofoam panels fitted between the ceiling rafters seem such a good idea. They totally insulate the houseboat's roof—where most of the heat is lost—and virtually eliminate moisture flows along the ceiling and into the walls.

Chemical Warfare

Introducing moving air usually costs nothing, but it isn't always practical. In these cases, there are two chemical methods of combating excessive dampness. In the first, a small plastic pot with several small drain holes (as in an indoor plant holder) is suspended above another, larger pot. A liberal quantity of calcium chloride crystals (used in swimming pools) is poured into the upper pot, and the whole contraption left in any room at risk, like a bathroom, bedroom, or clothing locker. Calcium chloride is hygroscopic and will slowly absorb atmospheric water. Wrapped in a molecular embrace, it will drip down into the lower collecting pot, unable to collect on ceilings, clothes, or lungs.

The second method requires silica gel, available from the neighborhood pharmacy. Unlike calcium chloride, silica gel can be reused. A small quantity is poured into an open container and left wherever thought necessary. As they absorb moisture, the silica crystals will slowly turn from bright blue to white or pink, at which time they'll need reactivating. Place them on a metal tray and put them in a 400-degree oven until they turn blue again; the moisture is driven out and up the flue.

Water vapor is everywhere and comes from many sources—teakettles, wet clothes, even breathing. Surprisingly, the biggest culprit often is a device that is supposed to be driving out moisture, the heater.

Portable paraffin or kerosene heaters may seem an economical way to heat a houseboat, but they have drawbacks. Although they're inexpensive to buy and operate and produce upward of 10,000 Btus (British thermal units), they produce a lot of humidity as well. Because of the nature of liquid-fuel combustion, a gallon of fuel will vent into the houseboat's atmosphere, in addition to various pollutants and toxic gases, a gallon of water vapor—not the sort of thing you want hanging around your living spaces. Any heaters used aboard should be vented to the outside.

KEEPING IT IN

It will be of small use for us to produce heat on board only to have it worm its way quickly outside through the wood and glass (conduction), or through open gaps (convection) around windows, doors, and joints. To ensure a warm, easily heated environment, it's important to fill every gap you can find: underneath doors with strips of carpet, around windows with sticky-backed foam rubber, around rafters with caulking compound or putty, even plugging the shower, sink, and hand-basin drains. Ventilators can be covered with flaps, perhaps backed with glued-on blocks of Styrofoam. Vent flaps can be swiveling, hinged, or on custom-fitted sliding tracks.

Relentlessly hunt down gaps, and there'll be no chilly reminders of a cold, wintry evening whistling in and up your trouser leg. Here's a simple test: On any cold night, when the fire's burning or the heater is hissing, walk around inside, putting your hand on as many parts of the walls,

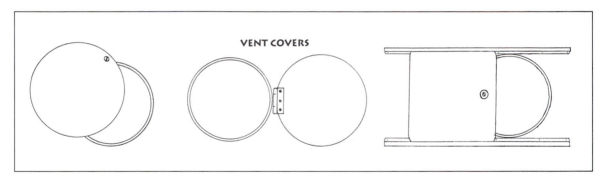

Figure 11-1. **Several options for vent flaps: swiveling, hinged, or on custom-fitted sliding tracks.**

ceiling, and floor as you can find. Areas that feel cold are, not surprisingly, losing heat.

Conversely, checking for heat loss could be done on a hot summer day—when there would be less of an air of desperation in your search for trouble spots—while friends are outside jumping into the water and then dripping their way all through the house. Any areas that feel exceptionally warm need extra insulation.

Insulating

Conduction is the steady transference of heat from warm to cool—like the handle of a frying pan, or more pertinently, through our thin plywood walls and thus to the great outdoors. To slow this drain on our heating bill, we install insulation—a material designed to trap air—a very poor conductor of heat—in zillions of tiny pockets. It might seem that one huge empty air space trapped inside the wall would be an efficient insulator. In practice, however, that air space would develop convective air currents (*convection* is the movement of heat energy from one place to another by moving molecules), and lose heat very quickly. An efficient insulator traps air in isolated air pockets; it is their isolation that slows the passage of heat.

Warm air rises; cold air falls. Figure 11-2 shows the extreme range of temperatures in a heated room. Hot air above the coal-range rises rapidly to the ceiling, displacing the cooler air there, which then begins to fall to the floor along the cooler wall, eventually being drawn back to the stove, where it is reheated and sent back on its journey—and on and on. Because the maximum amount of air movement is along the room's perimeter, it is warmer at the far wall than in the middle of the room.

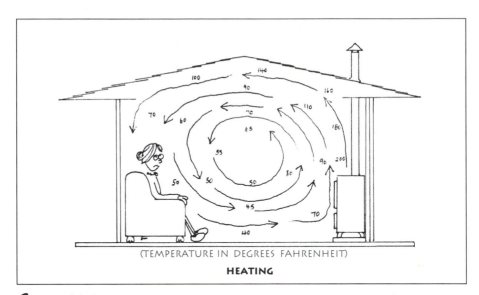

(TEMPERATURE IN DEGREES FAHRENHEIT)

HEATING

Figure 11-2. Temperatures fluctuate widely in a heated room. If you have sufficient headroom, a slow-turning ceiling fan can redistribute the heat.

Note that this illustration depicts a houseboat with insulation in the roof. If there were none, the warm ceiling air would lose much of its heat through the roof sheathing and out into space. Just as heat is trying to escape, the frigid cold outside is doing its damnedest to get in. The insulation that keeps heat, like a wayward daughter, shut inside the house, also keeps out the tang of winter, as if it were a hormonally addled adolescent intent on entry at any cost.

Ceiling insulation is a priority precisely because warm air rises. It's more important than wall insulation. Most land houses have several insulating layers beneath their roofs; for heat to escape, it has to find its way through bales of spun fiberglass insulation, often topped with softboard ceilings, as well as a wide expanse of trapped air between the insulation and the roof.

For a comfortable houseboat, insulation in the walls and ceiling is vital. The better the insulator, the less heat you'll lose. Hard Styrofoam, for instance, retains heat twice as well per inch as bead-board polystyrene (what disposable coffee cups are made of). It's also twice as expensive. Foil-covered polyisocyanurates, such as Koppers Insulation Board, are about 40 percent more effective than hard Styrofoam—and about 40 percent more expensive, too.

If you're on a budget, insulation need not be expensive. In a pinch, anything with minute air pockets will work as an insulator, for air is a very poor conductor of heat. Lateral thinking will provide all sorts of avenues for acquiring free insulation if money is tight: Old clothes or rags pushed into burlap sacks and squeezed into the wall frames; the stuffing from old furniture, like horsehair, kapok, or foam rubber; low-grade clips of sheep's wool, if you're in a rural area; cork, egg cartons, old blankets, corkboard, or softboard chunks, or Styrofoam packing material salvaged from electronics stores.

The Vapors

Although insulation is important—even crucial in many climates—it cannot perform well over time unless it is protected from dampness by a vapor barrier. Water vapor, ever present in homes (particularly floating homes), inevitably migrates through cracks in the inner wall surface. If the wall cavity is uninsulated, the water vapor condenses against the cold outer wall sheathing and evaporates (usually) harmlessly. In an insulated wall cavity, however, the water vapor condenses within the insulation itself. Over time, the insulation becomes soaked and unable to trap air, and thus no longer keeps in heat. Even worse, the sodden insulation creates exactly the kind of conditions enjoyed by mildew and other microscopic ne'er-do-wells. Sooner or later, the wall framing begins to rot.

This was precisely what happened after the energy crisis of the 1970s, when elderly uninsulated houses that had been kept cozy by 19-cent imported oil suddenly found their walls stuffed with insulation in an effort to retain the feeble heat of 50-cent-or-better oil. The houses were warm for a few years, but gradually grew less so.

Their owners noticed another phenomenon, too: The paint was peeling from the outside walls, as the pressure of water vapor trapped within the walls forced its way through the siding. In a few more years disturbed homeowners began removing rotten siding, and finding beneath it a mass of sodden insulation and often seriously rotten framework. What to do?

Scientists, of course, had the answer long before, but it was ignored all too often because it seemed so, well, *cheap*: A continuous barrier of 6-mil polyethylene between the inside wall surface and the insulation not only prevented water vapor from migrating into the insulation and making of it a holiday spa for microbes, but it also reduced or eliminated the other major source of heat loss in a house, infiltration.

For less than $20, a homeowner, floating or otherwise, can ensure not only his comfort, but a long life for his domicile as well. Simply staple 6-mil poly to the face of the studs after you've stuffed the wall cavities, but before you apply the inside wall paneling.

Insulating Windows

Insulation and vapor barriers are key forces in the battle against cold. But the real enemy—the part of the house that will undo your best attempts at keeping warm—is the windows. True, windows let in heat from the sun—an astonishing amount of heat (about which more later), but they let it out again just as fast.

That heat loss can be slashed in half with double-glazing—two layers of glass separated by dead air space, ideally around ½-inch. There is already a layer of glass in the window, so we simply measure the inside measurements and put in another pane, separated from the inner one by thin strips of wood. Make sure the inner pane is well sealed with silicone caulking, or you'll get condensation between the panes. Secure the outer pane in place by nailing on lengths of quarter-round trim.

This is a good time to recommend that some of the inner panes be panels of stained glass. The entire window doesn't have to be colored, of course; perhaps just a border or a small central motif set inside ordinary transparent glass—a little touch of class.

Thermal Drapes

We've insulated our walls and reduced heat loss to a minimum. We've double-glazed our windows, but we're still losing a lot of heat from them at night. Even a double-glazed window is an inefficient insulator compared with an insulated wall. In the Mediterranean, where extremes of heat and cold are common, folks leave window shutters open during the day to admit heat from the sun, then close the shutters at night to keep in the heat.

We can make insulating shutters for houseboats, too, but another and easier solution is to make a complete set of thermal drapes to pull across the windows at night. Thermal drapes prevent the warm air in the room from touching the cold slabs of glass, which will set up a convective loop that will neatly wick away your heat. There's nothing esoteric about making thermal drapes. The material can be found after a little rummaging through fabric stores and then sewn up on a sewing machine.

A thermal drape can also be pulled across the biggest hole in the wall— one that lets an entire roomful of warmth escape every time the drape is opened. Whenever a person enters or leaves a houseboat, he has to open a door. If there is an insulated space between the door and the hemisphere of frozen air on the other side, the interior will stay snug and cozy. We sacrifice a small area inside the house, but it protects the warmth farther inside—much like our zinc anode, sacrificed for the sake of other metals.

SOLAR HEAT

We've set up our houseboat to retain as much heat as possible; now to get something to retain. The most powerful heater imaginable is one we often forget, a fusion reactor that destroys four million tons of matter every second, and has been doing so for millions of years. We're talking about the sun, of course. We can capture a miniscule amount of this heat for ourselves, and the dog can go back to its basket.

While the visible light of the sun, the shortwave radiation, streaks through glass as if it weren't there, the longer wavelengths of heat have a little more difficulty. A large percentage of them get bounced around inside the room, heating up the air and any objects trapped within the thermal envelope. As all greenhouse builders—and your dog, too, if you've ever left him in the car with the windows rolled up—know, a glass-enclosed space is very quickly and easily heated by the sun, trapping up to 70 percent of the heat energy that comes through the windows. We can use this greenhouse effect, and a few other interesting bits of physics, to our advantage.

Although the sun will generate a great deal of heat during the day, warming the interior rapidly, that heat is quickly lost at night, even though the space may be well insulated. We've found ways to store water and electricity on our houseboat; why not store heat, too? White objects reflect the sun's rays and stay cool, while black objects absorb heat like a sponge.

The plywood sheets comprising the walls are very good at storing heat; why not paint them black? Ferrocement is even better, as are bricks and stone (although heavy). The best heat storer of them all, however, is water. A pound of water stores 1 Btu per degree Fahrenheit of heat rise—more than five times as much as a pound of brick. We're surrounded by water, of course, but it's outside the thermal envelope provided by our walls (although it acts as a massive heat-sink to moderate temperature swings—like floating around in a tepid hot-water bottle if the sun's been out). To store heat inside, set 1-gallon jugs of water in the sun, preferably in front of a black-painted wall. All night long they'll slowly give back the heat they absorbed during the day, as will the black-painted wall.

Installing as many windows as possible on the side of the house that faces the sun in winter, painting the sun-washed wall black, and leaving jugs of water lying around or stacked neatly in shelves seems small effort to get all that free energy from the big space heater in the sky.

It isn't always cold, however. In the summer, the sun will stream in and heat all those black-painted surfaces just as effectively as in the winter, just when we need the opposite effect. But because of the mobile nature of our houseboat, there's a way around this (other than the obvious one of dumping the water in the jugs over the side). If we were to paint two walls white and the other two black, the house could be moored one way in summer and turned 180 degrees for the winter. The white summer walls would create a cooling Mediterranean villa atmosphere, while the black winter walls would be reminiscent of a warm and cozy Montana log cabin. The days of turning could become half-yearly celebrations, timed for the rites of spring and autumn. There'd be no need to sacrifice virgins or anything, but a little bootleg liquor might profitably be imbibed.

Shades can be erected over the windows to keep the sun off and the house cool. In summer, the sun will track more directly overhead, so shades may not be necessary: A roof overhang need project just enough to throw shadows across the windows in summer. As the sun's angle declines in the race toward winter, the shadows will move, every day, higher up the wall. The houseboat, like a sundial, will be attuned to the seasons.

ARTIFICIAL HEAT

Having done our best to accumulate and save naturally occurring heat, there still will be times—sometimes for months—when artificial heating is essential. To understand the relative merits of different heaters, we first need to know how much heat the houseboat will require. An invisible entity in itself, heat is measured by what it does, which is to increase the temperatures of things. The standard measurement of heat is the *British thermal unit* (or Btu for short): the amount of heat that will lift the temperature of 1 pound of water by 1 degree Fahrenheit (remember our water jugs). The output of heaters is rated in Btus.

As we're not heating a pound of water, but a houseboat's interior, we must do a little figuring. First we need to find the houseboat's inside volume by multiplying length times height times width. Now we need to think about where we are. Obviously, the amount of heat needed to warm a houseboat of equal volume in, say, Mobile, Alabama, would be different from the amount needed in Juneau, Alaska.

There are various scientific ways of finding out exactly the difference between the two climates, based on annual degree-days and various obtuse calculations. Fortunately, we can use a convenient rule of thumb, called the *seasonal factor*. This ranges from 10 to 20 Btus per cubic foot, with reasonably warm climates meriting a mellow 10 Btus, and the chilly areas a brisk 20. Let's say that we have a small houseboat, around 700 cubic feet, to rattle around in. In Alabama, that houseboat will require $700 \times 10 = 7,000$ Btus. For an *equivalent warmth*, the houseboat in Alaska would require $700 \times 20 = 14,000$ Btus. We know what size heater to buy (err on the side of too large; most heaters are more efficient running at half-throttle); now we need to decide how to fuel it.

Kerosene

Although their output in Btus is small, kerosene or paraffin lanterns do actually help warm small houseboats. Their pressurized cousins, which generate more light, also generate more heat—1,000 Btus or more. As we've seen, however, in addition to heat all liquid-fuel–burning lanterns and heaters add a great deal of undesirable moisture and pollutants (carbon monoxide being a particularly nasty one) to the air, in addition to consuming oxygen.

Vented kerosene heaters, which range from 6,000 to as much as 30,000 Btus, send their moisture and pollution up the flue. They are simple to operate, and the fuel is cheap and easy to find. In use, the flame should be blue with a white top. If it's yellow, then it's consuming too much oxygen, usually caused by a cracked mica window or an improperly sealed chimney. To keep them at their best, keep the circular wick clean, just as we trim the wick of a lantern.

Diesel

Diesel fuel is relatively inexpensive and widely available, too. Diesel heaters are particularly popular in the Pacific Northwest and aboard working fishboats everywhere. For mobile houseboats equipped with a diesel engine, a diesel heater would be an appropriate choice, as the fuel would already be on board. Diesel heaters need more cleaning than kerosene heaters, but can deliver a comfortable 20,000 Btus or more. Diesel fuel must be kept scrupulously clear of both dirt and water condensation by using filters and water traps.

Gas

One of the most popular and trouble-free ways to fuel a heater on board is with bottled gas, either CNG or LPG. CNG, Compressed Natural Gas (called SAFGAS in California), is lighter than air and thus safer in enclosed spaces. Where available, it's less expensive and contains more energy per pound than the more widely available LPG; unfortunately, outlets for refilling bottles can be hard to find. Make sure there's a local source before going the CNG route. (Also note that CNG and LPG appliances are *not* interchangeable. The pressure settings and gas apertures are completely different.)

LPG, often mistakenly called Low Pressure Gas, actually is Liquefied Petroleum Gas, and the liquid is stored at high pressure—200 to 250 psi. It's also heavier than air, and thus must be handled with respect. More on that in a moment.

LPG, which can be either butane or propane depending on the season and locale, vaporizes into a gas as the pressure drops when leaving the bottle. The pressure is regulated by, no surprise, the regulator, which screws into the top of the bottle. From there the gas is delivered through (hopefully) leak-proof tubing to the various appliances, where it combines with oxygen and is ignited.

The oxygen that a heater consumes is the same air that a warm, comfortable, and possibly sleeping houseboater breathes, so ventilation is vital in any room where a heater is burning. (A particularly energy-efficient way to provide this is with a small pipe with a shut-off valve run in from the outside directly to the heater's air intake.) Some heaters are equipped with an oxygen-depletion switch that, should oxygen content drop, blocks the flow of gas and turns the heater off.

The insidious danger with gas is that it is invisible; you don't know it's there until you strike a match. If it should find a weak connection or a minute hole in a hose, it may seep into the room, roll along the floor (remember, it's heavier than air), and accumulate at the lowest point, a potentially explosive mixture.

The best protection for a houseboater uninterested in unscheduled immolation is to leave the gas bottle outside, where leaking gas can waft away. Also, periodically check thoroughly along the lines for leaks. This is done, *not* by holding a match to the joints, but by brushing along them with a soapy solution, much as bicycle tubes are checked for leaks. If there is a leak anywhere, bubbles will appear. Hose-clamps should be tight, as should hose-to-appliance connectors.

In Figure 11-3, we see a gas bottle left outside with its own kennel, a theft-proof container that has been lined with Styrofoam insulation. Because the pressurized gas causes the bottles to become very cold, this small storage area will be cooled, a good place to leave drinks.

If a gas bottle must come inside, then drill holes in the floorboards around it; any leaking gas can then seep out and be dissipated by drafts and wind under the houseboat. After use, the gas should be turned off not only at the appliance, but also at the gas bottle itself. Then it can't leak. It is a sad fact that people regularly blow up their boats, their trailer-homes, and themselves with leaking gas.

Unless they're specifically designed for it, gas bottles should never be used on their sides. They should stand vertically, regulator at the top. If they are tipped horizontally, then the liquid, which is even more flammable

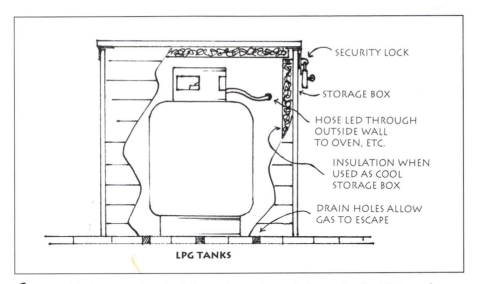

SECURITY LOCK

STORAGE BOX

HOSE LED THROUGH
OUTSIDE WALL
TO OVEN, ETC.

INSULATION WHEN
USED AS COOL
STORAGE BOX

DRAIN HOLES ALLOW
GAS TO ESCAPE

LPG TANKS

Figure 11-3. **A gas bottle, left outdoors, is a safe bet. Lined with Styrofoam, the protective kennel also provides cold storage, since the pressurized LPG acts as a refrigerant.**

than the gas, could be released. They can be carried, and stored, at any angle, when empty, of course.

Gauges are available to indicate how much gas a cylinder contains, but if you don't have one, you can weigh the bottle on a bathroom scale (after having weighed it whilst empty, to give you a benchmark). You can also pour boiling water down the side of the bottle. It'll condense where the liquid petroleum is, and evaporate above it, leaving a clearly discernible tide mark.

Gas appliances—everything from heaters through lights to refrigerators—are relatively trouble-free. If it doesn't work, usually you're either out of gas, or the supply tube is blocked. These can be cleared with a good blow through them—not by mouth, which will introduce water, but with a bicycle or car tire pump. If this doesn't work and you have plenty of gas, you need a new regulator.

Catalytic Propane

Perhaps human beings have to see flames to feel warm. Or is it, as with candles, a little more primeval? Regardless, if open flames on board make the houseboater nervous, there are flameless heaters available, called catalytic propane heaters, which produce heat from a chemical reaction. Propane gas mixed with air is fed to platinum, which produces heat—no flame, no fire risk. Like any other liquid-fuel–burning appliance, catalytic heaters produce water vapor, and therefore humidity, and should be vented. They are quiet and economical: A top-of-the-line model, the CAT, uses 1 pound of propane in 4 hours at 6,000 Btus. Models are available ranging range from 3,000 to 9,000 Btus.

Solid Fuel

Solid fuels, like wood, coal, coke, carbonettes, briquettes, etc., supply great quantities of heat (a pound of dry wood contains roughly 8,600 Btus), but to extract it requires work. Solid fuels have to be collected and stacked—in the case of wood chopped and split—then brought inside for the rituals of setting the kindling and cleaning the grate. Then some way must be found to dispose of the inevitable ashes. But how wonderful is a fire? How long is a piece of string? Like candles, solid-fuel fires warm the very cockles of the heart.

Old-fashioned potbelly stoves very efficiently pump heat into a houseboat. It may be snowing outside, but the family within can pretend they're at a beach, sitting in bathing costumes on a checkered cloth on the floor, and pass sandwiches and sunglasses around.

Some river people complain of the dreary confinement of winter, but we find it a season of special delight. The mere joy of being sheltered is magnified by our closeness to the elements: rain on the roof directly overhead, snow sifting on our faces asleep, the swaying and rolling of the boat, the wild and muddy world without. Our fires have the directness of campfires kindled in riverbank driftpiles for warmth on a winter walk. In bad weather, one can sit by the fire indoors without compunction, and not feel that he should be stirring about outside. It is then that we reap the harvest of winter, painting, writing, reading, making music.

Harlan Hubbard, *Shantyboat: A River Way of Life*. Lexington: The University Press of Kentucky. Copyright 1953 and 1981 by Harlan Hubbard.

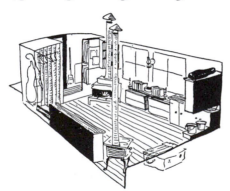

Potbellies (which I'm using generically to describe solid-fuel burners) come in all shapes and sizes, from tiny ones only 6 inches around to squat models, 3 feet across. There are single-burners and double-burners and ones with wetbacks that heat water. Most any of them will heat the average houseboat with economy and charm.

The secret of using limited space efficiently, however, is to have as many objects as possible performing multiple functions. If the houseboat builder opts instead for a wood- or coal-burning range (chip-ovens, to some), then while the house is being heated, a roast might also be simmering or bread baking. Chip-ovens have yet another attraction. No one in the suburbs wants them, and they can be had for a token price or even for free. In some areas, however, they've become retro-chic and thus overpriced. Look around for decidedly non-chic areas if you're afflicted with this problem.

Installation

Installing solid-fuel heaters is simple and low tech, but avoid being persuaded into recessing one into a wall. Not only is there an extra wall to build, which must be lined with fireproof material, but an incredible amount of heat whistles straight up the chimney. A potbelly that is freestanding, away from the wall, is far more effective and much safer.

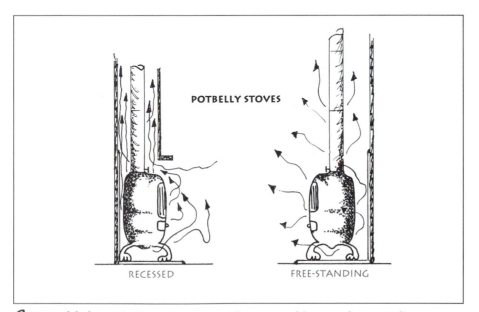

POTBELLY STOVES

RECESSED

FREE-STANDING

Figure 11-4. Potbelly stoves are good sources of heat. A free-standing stove is more efficient and safer than one recessed into a wall.

Solid-fuel heaters get much hotter than most liquid-fueled units; the surrounding area must be well protected. The best fireproof insulation can be any of a range of proprietary materials (Rockwall, Heatshield), again usually supplied in the modular size of 4 × 8 feet. We need to use the insulation behind and beneath the heater, and, if it's against a corner wall, beside it. For an average-size firebox, a rule of thumb is to install the stove no closer than 3 feet from a wall.

Flues

Solid-fuel burners produce copious quantities of extremely hot gases, which obviously must be exhausted to the outside through a properly installed flue. Figure 11-5a shows a proper flue exiting the ceiling through a hole cut in the plywood, with metal flashing slid up the flue and nailed into place, and roof flashing slid down over the outside of the flue to seal the hole against the weather. Note the Rockwall segments that line the hole, completely covering any exposed timber. The same principle is applied to the hole cut in a wall. Rockwall, or its equivalent, protects the wooden beams of the house from the heat of the flue. Note also that any Styrofoam, or other plastic insulations that are equally flammable, must be extremely well protected from the flue's heat.

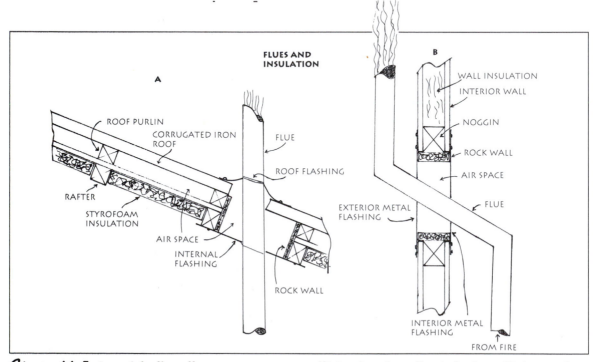

Figure 11-5. A straight flue allows gases to escape efficiently; a bent flue is far less efficient and tends to accumulate highly flammable creosote in the elbows. Keep hot pipes well away from walls.

The top of the flue that protrudes through the roof has a cap slid over it to keep rain from pouring in, but still allow smoke to billow out. The flue should extend higher than the uppermost ridge to prevent wind eddies from forming, which may blow back down the flue and fill the room with smoke. For a flue to draw properly, it must go up into undisturbed air.

A proper draw is necessary on any heater—solid fuel or otherwise—but solid-fuel heaters are particularly touchy about poorly drawing flues. One trap to avoid (Figure 11-5b) is forcing a flue to bend. Every time it bends, the diameter is effectively halved. A flue with two bends might draw only a quarter as well as a straight pipe. Such a contraption may look Kentucky-chic, but if it takes "a danged hour to git rid of the smoke ever' time the danged fire's a-lit," who needs it?

Flues should be cleaned at least once a year. There's no need to send an orphan up the pipe armed with brushes. If you're prepared to tolerate cleaning up the lounge afterward, you can climb on the roof, drop a chain down the pipe, and jiggle it about to dislodge the soot and creosote (a highly flammable gook distilled from incompletely burned wood). A far easier way to keep a flue clean is to buy one of the proprietary chemicals (Chimney Sweep and others) that are occasionally sprinkled on the embers last thing at night. The burning chemical unseats the soot and makes the yearly cleaning much easier.

Because flues do generate such enormous heat, wetback piping can be wrapped around them or inserted into the firebox itself, as mentioned in Chapter 8. Unlike most other things aboard, however, this job must be done by an expert.

VOLUNTEER FIRE DEPARTMENT

Any form of fire aboard a houseboat is dangerous. Fire fighters find it difficult to run across water with their hoses. Unless a houseboater can get a fire under control and extinguished by himself, all that will be left of his dreams and possessions will be charred embers.

Since we're surrounded by it afloat, a bucket of water may seem appropriate to throw on a fire—and in some cases it is—but if the fire is the typical liquid fuel or cooking-fat fire, water won't extinguish it, but will spread it around. Throwing sand on fires is an option, but it will do little for a liquid-fuel fire; besides, it's hard to imagine throwing a bucket of sand inside a paraffin heater.

A far better choice is to keep aboard several good fire extinguishers. Carbon dioxide (CO_2) fire extinguishers smother flames by depriving them of oxygen. The extinguisher is pointed at the flames and the trigger pulled to direct the high-pressure cloud of gaseous CO_2 at the base of the fire.

Figure 11-6. While this dining room looks quite sumptuous, replete with an elegant fireplace, our potbelly stove is a much better source of heat.

They are wonderful to have aboard, but won't smother CNG or LPG fires. For them, the only extinguisher is the unpronounceable Bromo-chlorodifluoromethane, known as BCF, or Halon. It smothers all flames, so there should be at least one aboard.

Fire extinguishers should be mounted handy to trouble spots, but not where you would have to reach across flames to grab them. The bottles shouldn't be hung on the wall and ignored: Check them annually to ensure that they're full and have pressure.

There is no security like taking care. A little time and money invested in preparing for emergencies beats the hell out of having to build another home.

CHAPTER TWELVE

Voyaging the Alimentary Canal

*M*odern oil stoves are most convenient and service-
able for the kitchen, and do not heat up the rooms.
When necessary the cook or man-of-all-work can sleep
in a folding cot in this room.

~~~~~~

This chapter will take a look at the subject dear to just about every
houseboater's heart—or to be accurate, every houseboater's stomach. We
won't digress into recipes for freshly caught fish, but we will examine the
devices we use to cook them.

COOKING IN THE SUN

There's no reason why a houseboater who is collecting electricity and heating his house from the rays of the sun can't also cook his nosh with the same free energy. Solar food cookers work by reflecting and focusing the rays of the sun on a container of food. There's nothing new about it. Back in 1878, a punkawallah in Bombay wrote to *Scientific American* describing a solar cooker that he'd built, easily capable of cooking the meat and vege rations of the seven soldiers in his command. It was an eight-sided, cone-shaped affair, lined with mirrors, that concentrated the heat.

Another solar cooker, of similar shape, is being manufactured today in the United States and is reputedly capable of cooking up to 15 pounds of food at temperatures of up to 500 degrees Fahrenheit. Most of the alternative-energy-type places (such as Real Goods in Ukiah, California) seem to carry them.

The most intense heat of the day is around lunch time, so all meals could be cooked at that time and stored for reheating later. At the least there would be a saving in fuel. The trouble is, this would be inconvenient for people who work away from home. Cooking with the sun needn't mean skipping home from work at 10 and heading back to work at 2, though: Solar cooking heat can be stored. You may have to skip home at about 11 for an hour, but you should do that for your mental health anyway.

The meal is placed in the solar cooker and left only until it reaches 212 degrees Fahrenheit, water's boiling point, to kill any evil-intentioned

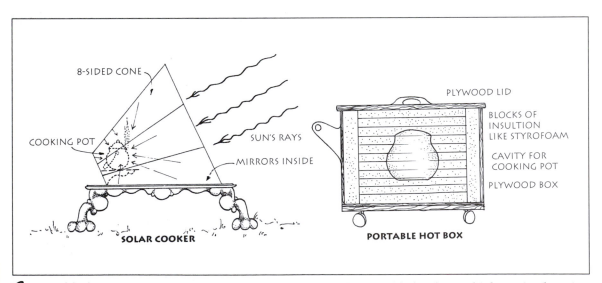

Figure 12-1. **Two options for the chef—solar cooker and a portable hot box, which retains heat in food brought to the boil; the food then cooks long and slowly—ideal for stew.**

bacteria that might be lurking about. The food is then transferred to an insulated container, such as a vacuum jar or a box lined with Styrofoam with a recess cut to accommodate the cooking crock. The partially cooked food is then left to continue cooking—stewing in its own heat. Depending on the initial heat and what you're cooking, this second cooking period might range from two to five hours.

Another system, first described in a 1923 edition of *Science and Invention* and later taken up and refined by the Smithsonian Institute, exposes to the sun a panel filled with engine oil. Just as in a solar water heater, the oil is heated, and by natural convection will circulate into an insulated storage tank. In the evening, or whenever cooking time arrives, the oil is allowed to convect through an oven above the storage tank; the heat is released into the food. The mechanically inclined may want to experiment with this system.

ARTIFICIAL COOKING

In reverting to conventional cookers, we accept the unpleasant reality of having to buy fuel. What we gain is that great twentieth-century necessity: instant gratification. In truth, the instant availability of nourishing food irrespective of the state of the sun appeals to anyone living in cold or cloudy climates.

Gas

The most common cooker found in caravans, trailer-homes, recreational vehicles, boats, and tents is the versatile LPG or CNG range. The gas (discussed in the last chapter) is convenient, easy to use, clean, and reasonably safe. Most gas cookers are fitted with an automatic shut-off valve that will close down the burner if the gas gets blown out. This occurs rarely, however, because a gas flame is so intense. This intense flame also means that water may be boiled, soup heated, chops stewed, or steak sizzled very quickly.

Gas cookers vary from simple one-burner elements to highly complex twin-level ovens with broilers and multiple burners, sort of culinary Cadillacs. As you would expect, prices vary widely, and for some reason, items bought from marine stores are generally more expensive than those found in general hardware stores. Be sure to shop around before dragging out your wallet.

If a wood-burning oven is aboard, the average person won't need a gas oven, too; a gas oven uses a lot of gas, and it's not that cheap to refill a bottle. Instead, he'd opt for a couple of burners, with maybe a grill compartment underneath for toast or Oysters Kilpatrick. A vast array of interesting and fulsome meals can be cooked on two burners, not just eggs and beans. The wood oven can always be fired up to cook complicated dishes requiring the services of an oven.

A pressure cooker is a very useful device to have aboard. Because they cook under pressure, they use less flame and thus less fuel—an important consideration when it must be lugged aboard.

Speaking of toast, the toaster in Figure 12-2 is a great addition to a humble one-burner setup and certainly beats holding a slice of bread over a flame. The fold-up oven in Figure 12-3 is also handy. A concertina-like arrangement often used by campers, it can be stored flat; when bread is to be baked or a haunch of meat roasted, it is opened out and left above the burner.

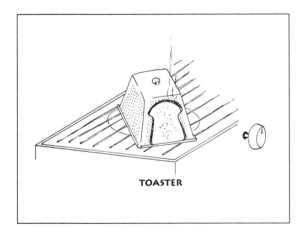

TOASTER

Figure 12-2. **Toast made easy on a stovetop.**

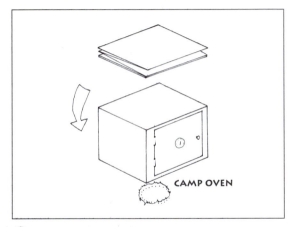

CAMP OVEN

Figure 12-3. **A convenient, easy-to-store camp oven works well atop any gas burner.**

Since so many land homes are equipped with gas ranges, managing the fire should be second nature. This seems rarely the case, however. A gas flame should be blue, with a touch of yellow at the top, and should begin at the element itself, with no gap. If the flame has a lot of yellow, then too much air is being mixed with the gas. If there is almost no yellow and it is hard to ignite, the flame is starving for air.

Adjustment of the air intake is straightforward. Some cookers include knobs that control this air mix, but if yours is less streamlined, look for a gap between the gas nozzle and the burner element. There will be either a locknutted screw or a sliding tube for the adjustment.

Let's say the flame needs more air; there's a gap between it and the element, and it's too blue. If a screw, slacken the locknut, turn the screw out a little, and try the flame. If it's not better, try bringing out the screw a little more. When the flame's right, tighten the nut again. If there is a sliding tube, move it back slightly to increase the air hole. If the flames are too yellow and easy to blow out, reverse the directions above.

Liquid Fuels

Paraffin or kerosene stoves are usually designed to burn pressurized vapor, just as pressurized lanterns and heaters do. The burner is preheated with meths in the priming cup (a popular alternative is to preheat the burner with a portable propane torch), then the element knob is turned on to release the vapor. Kerosene, like meths, is not cheap, and only clean fuel will burn well.

Kerosene/paraffin isn't the ideal cooking fuel. Even if it's scrupulously clean and highly refined, some people find that the often nauseating smell permeates their food. And because kerosene burns at a constant temperature, food can't be simmered; the flame has to be damped down by dropping an asbestos pad over it and replacing the pot. Because of the nature of pressurized fuel, some kerosene cookers have very small fuel reservoirs. To have to shut everything down in the middle of preparation, refill the cooker, pressurize it again, relight the meths, then pick up where we left off, can be annoying to say the least.

Even less impressive, though often recommended for marine use, are alcohol (or meths) cookers. They are expensive to operate, the flame has a low temperature, and fuel will drip out and go everywhere if the flame blows out, which it does all too often. Who needs it? Alcohol burners are on a par with the small Gaz burners that go through their expensive disposable cartridges at a prodigious rate.

Diesel-fuel ovens are an option, especially if there's an engine aboard and tanks of fuel doing nothing. They do not need preheating and are reasonably clean and efficient. They do need to be vented, though, either with a flue or, for some models, an extractor fan. They give off an alarming quantity of heat—as much as most solid-fuel burners—which may make them undesirable as primary cookers in warm climates.

Solid Fuels

Chip ovens or solid-fuel cookstoves are hard to beat as backup cookers, allied with an appropriate supplemental cooker burning something more instantaneous. For full-time use, of course, they are intensely energy and fuel consuming. Who would feed a firebox its hourly ration of wood just to boil a kettle for a cup of tea? Especially in the warmer months.

Figure 12-4. **A spacious kitchen aboard** *Hone,* **with a sink, refrigerator, and chip oven.**

A wood-burning stove's oven relies on the adjacent firebox and the hot gases directed around it to heat the thick cast-iron walls. These walls rapidly disperse heat in all directions inside the oven so that roasts or bread will be more or less uniformly cooked. When the oven reaches cooking temperature, only a sporadic topping up with fuel is required. Like candles and open-flame heat, there's an indefinable something about food cooked in a wood oven.

REFRIGERATION

While on the absorbing subject of food, but at the other end of the thermometer, just how essential is the ubiquitous refrigerator? Human beings have always cooked their food (well, almost always), but they haven't always had refrigerators. Anyone accustomed to buying food in 40-pound blocks and storing it at home in cavernous freezers will probably find life on an average houseboat more than a little different. Sure, suitable refrigerators in all shapes and sizes are available that burn LPG or CNG, or that plug into 12-, 120-, or 230-volt systems, but before looking for the wallet or credit card, try an experiment: Live without one for a while. You may just find you can live without one.

Why would you want to? Because refrigerators and freezers are major power consumers. A couple of examples from a recent catalogue promise that the "flawless" propane model uses only 1½ gallons of gas a week, while the electric model needs 84 Ah a day—three times what our sample houseboat back in Chapter 9 uses for everything else combined.

There's actually no need to have a refrigerator at all, even if the beer's not cold and the butter has to live in a special dish so it doesn't melt everywhere. Wire meat safes, like granny used to hang under the eaves, are an excellent way to keep meats, eggs, and cheese. Hung in the shade in a windy area, the contents stay cool in all but the warmest climates.

If you have access ashore, a hole dug in the ground will keep food cool. Dig down about 3 feet and line the hole with a plastic rubbish sack. Make a wooden lid to go over the hole so no one falls in looking for extra rations at night.

As I mentioned in the last chapter, we made a very cool "cooler" after discovering that our LPG bottle is always cold. The bottle sits inside an insulated box (Figure 11-3) on deck with food stacked around it. Any insulating material will do, like polystyrene, insulated bats, or even blankets. The food is never chilled, simply cooler than outside temperatures.

Again, as granny would have done, you can keep perishables like milk in an icebox. Any well-insulated plywood or metal box will do; if there are no drain holes drilled in the bottom for melted ice to drip from, fit a raised platform atop the ice to keep the food packages out of the water.

Both the insulated LPG-cooled box and the icebox work much better if no empty spaces are left around the food. Pack the food closely, or, if the budget's a little stretched, with any insulating materials, such as liberated Styrofoam pellets. There has to be some use for the damn things.

FLOATING GARDENS

Finally, a word about the supposed disadvantage of houseboating for keen gardeners. Obviously, growing food for oneself can be difficult when there's no land off the back porch; difficult, but not impossible. The advent of hydroponic gardening has meant that with a simple arrangement of PVC piping, a very small electric pump, and a bottle of nutrients, anyone, anywhere, can grow most above-ground (as opposed to root) vegetables. The pipes are arranged, like a Roman viaduct, so that water flows slowly through them. Nutrients are added to the water supply and seedlings inserted in holes in the pipes. The roots are thus fed directly, without any need for soil—almost umbilically.

CHAPTER THIRTEEN

Whereto

For the artist the houseboat furnishes a moving studio that can always have northern exposure, beautiful surroundings, marine views or landscapes. The easel is safely placed on deck, and there are no limits to the background, most comfortable quarters to retire to, and no disagreeable thoughts at sundown that one must pack up one's traps and find one's way home in the dark.

More areas of the world are covered by water than by dirt and rocks and pebbles and sand. In fact, the area of hard stuff is quite insignificant compared with the area of oceans, rivers, lakes, canals, streams, and swamps—prime habitat for houseboaters anxious to leave behind a crowded world.

204

Oceans, of course, are the last place on Earth for any self-respecting houseboat. Ocean waves would quickly pound an average houseboat into matchsticks. Surfers might hang out there, but not houseboats. But even without the oceans, there's a lot of water left out there that will do just fine.

> **T**he houseboat, as a pleasure craft, has many advantages over any other style of vessel. The most important considerations are those of cost and danger, either of which, as compared with the like on the steam yacht, is infinitesimally small. Only the millionaire—and the multi-millionaire at that—can afford the extravagance of a well-appointed and properly manned steam yacht of any size, and in no other kind is it safe to venture out to open sea.

SITING

Houseboats can be designed to float in as little as 6 inches of water, so finding a suitable site should not be a problem. In fresh water, rivers, creeks, ponds, lakes, and swamps (yes, swamps) all play host to houseboats. In saltwater areas, the most popular sites are those where the tide's ebb leaves the houseboat sitting high and dry on mud, sand, or shingle. These may be right along sheltered areas of the coast, or up tidal rivers, creeks, or in bays. Simple houseboats are amphibious, sort of brain-dead creatures, happy to bob up and down on waves, and just as happy to sit still on terra firma between tides.

Ideal mooring sites vary depending on the houseboat owner's tastes. It's difficult to travel far along any road in most places, apart from perhaps Nevada or Central Australia, and not eventually stumble upon water. If the stuff's wet, you can generally put a houseboat in it.

Few houseboats could be called streamlined, by any stretch of the imagination. Most present a clear affront to the wind; sites with continuous high winds are best avoided. Equally undesirable are those sites subject to boisterous waves. Sections of the ocean protected by breakwaters or natural geography, and most inland waterways, are prime spots for houseboats. Observation of a good-looking spot will soon tell you whether it's suitable, and what weather it receives.

A call to the local weather office will tell you the direction and strength of prevailing winds. If the area is subject to fierce winter gales, is there a convenient, tree-covered hill between the snug cove you've found and

Figure 13-1. **A sheltered home for a coven of houseboats.**

those fearsome northwesterlies? Or is it wide open to the northwest, yet shielded from the gentle summer southerlies that blow mosquitoes and heat from the cove? Keep looking.

Look at the surrounding shoreline. Is it low and marshy, promising hordes of mosquitoes and wet, difficult access ashore? Or is it bounded by very steep banks or sand shoals. If it is, you'd be better off with the mosquitoes. Those banks are steep because waves crash into them, chewing off great hunks of shore and spreading it out into shoals.

It's not just the elements that are hazardous to houseboats: occasionally it's people. You'd think that with the advent of such low-cost, effective housing as houseboats, bells would be ringing from church towers, and politicians would be vying with one another to claim they thought of it first. It doesn't work that way, does it? Local authorities were just as worried in the past by these unorthodox forms of housing as you can imagine they are today—that is, once the gentry had abandoned them . . . it was okay until then.

If your houseboat will be the first on the block, it would be prudent to moor somewhere inconspicuous, on the fringes of the waterway. For something new and different, greater long-term success is assured when diplomacy and subtlety are employed rather than flashes of bravado and grandiose arrivals. As we examine where the new houseboat will go, let's remember that, because it's new, it's going to attract attention. If the attention can be kept to a minimum, then a certain acclimatization can take place.

Houseboats deserve rural settings. For most, it's infinitely more pleasurable to sit on the boat's porch and contemplate trees, sand, birds, and curious people sailing by than to contemplate the concrete pilings and automobile headlights of the standard city environment. Some, who may be wedded to an urban area by career or other circumstance, may find the rundown fringes of an urban waterfront an exciting and surprisingly secluded and inexpensive place to live.

Figure 13-2. The simple life.

Unlike the yachtsman, the houseboatman is not at the mercy of a crew. He is his own captain and his own navigator, and if needs be his own cook. He is the most independent man on the face of the waters. His staunch little houseboat can push in where the most seaworthy yacht could not, and would not, dare to venture.

For the more community minded, many urban areas offer specifically designed marinas that cater to liveaboards; for access to the city, just step ashore. For example, in Sausalito, Vancouver Harbor, or Canoe Pass Village, large houseboat communities dwell at marinas that pipe aboard telephone, power, water, even cable TV. Naturally, this convenience must be paid for with hard currency—usually much hard currency. And there are often restrictions imposed by community councils or marina owners that may prohibit, among other things, children under 14 years, pets, or the sale of a houseboat to anyone not approved of by The Committee.

One one of the many responses I received from houseboaters came from Henry Spruks.

Dear Mr. Conder,

Enclosed is a photo of my little 18' X 7' houseboat. Designed by William Atkin in the 1940s, she was built in 1985 by David Scarborough of Rock Hall Boats: cedar-planked, fiberglassed to the waterline, canvas-covered plywood deck, plywood house, powered by a 9.9 outboard.

I had her built as a week-end retreat, but before completion, I had a stroke. When I recovered enough to live alone, I moved to the St. Johns River in Florida and have lived aboard since 1987. (Beats living in a nursing home.)

For the person who wishes to live afloat alone *Retreat* is a most inexpensive means. Safely moored in some quiet bywater not too far from a shopping place, little *Retreat* offers much in the way of happiness and little in the way of complication and expense. (If you like the looks of *Retreat*, you'll find her plans at the back of this book.)

William Atkin and John Atkin,
"Herald of the Morning,"
MoToR BoatinG, 1947.

Some far more independent houseboaters prefer to be left alone and tie up in secluded bays or streams, forsaking the umbilical connection of their compatriots to rely on their own self-sufficiency. For houseboaters who wish it, in many parts of the world—even seemingly thickly settled ones— it is possible to be *truly* alone.

Others prefer a middle ground—a small water-borne community of like-minded individuals, but one less tightly controlled than the autocracy of an expensive urban marina.

The history of houseboats has, now and again, been associated with a certain amount of acrimony from local officialdom, or by the taxpayers who elected them. On the other hand, officials do exist who are capable of understanding that alternative ways of life *must* be explored if human beings are to remain a healthy species. Seek them out.

Neither houseboater nor City Hall—not by huffing'n'puffing nor bluff'n'bluster—can "own" any part of the area where the sea meets the land. It has to be shared.

> **T**here are few points of a sailor's education which require more attention than the study of that important movement of the waves, known as Tides. Although his numerous duties will not permit of an attempt at an investigation of the bewildering theories that surround the subject.

Admiral Sir Frederick Bedford, *The Sailor's Pocket Book: A Collection of Practical Rules, Notes, and Tables, for the Use of The Royal Navy, The Mercantile Marine, and Yacht Squadrons.* Portsmouth: Griffin & Co., 1898.

Tidal Areas

Tides are created by the complex, interrelated gravitational and centrifugal energies of the Earth, sun, and moon. These energies constantly pull and push the oceans (and the land, for that matter, although to a vastly lesser degree) of the world into an egg-shaped envelope of water through which the Earth revolves. As we stand on a beach that is moving inexorably into the enlarged lobe of that watery envelope, we note that the water level is rising—"the tide is coming in," we say. When we move past the peak, we say the tide is going out. But the water didn't go anywhere; it stayed in the same place. We just hurtled through it. We pass through the peaks—the flood—and troughs—the ebb—twice each lunar day—24 hours and 51 minutes.

Because the planetary bodies aren't static but ever moving through space, the floods and ebbs are themselves subject to floods and ebbs. When the sun and moon are in line and their gravities acting together, the Earth's bulge of water is increased, creating spring tides. When the sun and moon are at right angles, they exert less gravitational force, lowering the bulge's level and creating neap tides. These variations are themselves subject to further variations, as the distances between Earth and moon and sun increase or decrease with the seasonal tilt of the Earth and the elliptical orbits of the concerned parties.

All this pushing and pulling on the seas produces markedly different effects in different parts of the world, as local conditions—depth of sea, strength of wind, currents, barometric pressure, width and shape of channels—all get into the act. The planet's tides are anything but static. In winter along the east coast of Australia, the night tides can be 4 feet higher than the day tides. In the Rio de Plata, gales from the south may push tides an extra 8 feet higher. At Hastings, on the southern coast of

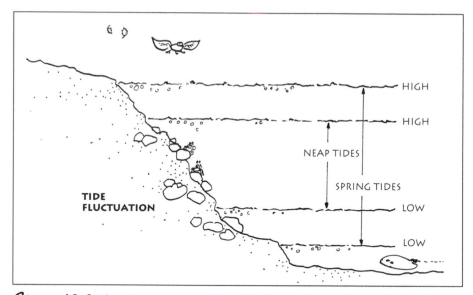

Figure 13-3. If you're unprepared for tide fluctuations, the results can be disastrous, as the owner of the houseboat in Figure 13-4 found out.

England, the greatest rise and fall of a spring tide is 24 feet, while along the northeast side of the Gulf of Mexico the tide's rise and fall is negligible.

If you're saying what's all this to do with me, note the houseboat in Figure 13-4. When an extreme low-pressure system passed overhead, inconveniently coincidental with a spring tide, the tide rose higher than normal. The houseboat, riding on a short chain, found its bow held down just enough to let water wash through the stern scuppers and into the bilges. The moral is simply to know what the sun and the moon and the tides and the winds and the barometric pressure and the geographic features are up to.

Don't despair at having to book computer time to figure all this out. Tide charts are freely available, in newspapers, boating magazines, or from marine stores that show the date, time, and height of the local tides, which is everything we need. The strength of the wind and the atmospheric conditions can be seen every day, out the window.

For those inclined toward salt water and the rhythm of the ebb and flood of the tide, the ideal is to find a spot where there is always some water, even at spring lows, and where a plank can be put ashore for ease of access. Perhaps by striking up an acquaintance with the owner of the adjoining land—or marrying his daughter—permission to build an informal jetty or dock could be secured. It need not be a permanent structure; it could be as simple as a series of barrel-supported planks leading across the wet tidal area.

Figure 13-4. **Her anchor line secured too tightly, this houseboat sank when a rising tide washed water over her bow.**

Houseboats may be moored in deep water, with access only by dinghy, or may be over an area that dries out between tides and hence are afloat only when the tide is full. Living with animals that need to go sniffing for a tree in the middle of the night is a good reason for mooring over tidal areas: When the tide's out, the bladder-full pooch or pussycat can look after itself, hopping down to the ground and walking ashore.

Non-tidal Areas

Freshwater houseboaters are spared (some would say deprived) having to align their lives and their houseboat's mooring arrangements with the daily ebb and flow of the tide. Yet water levels in many bodies of fresh water fluctuate just as much, although far less predictably, as many tidal areas. Failure to research local water level changes can leave your houseboat suspended between wind and water just as surely as ignoring the tide table. For example, in the manmade lakes of the southeastern U.S., water levels are drawn down weekly to control mosquito populations. In the winter, water levels are lowered to a predetermined depth to reduce ice damage and provide extra storage space to contain spring floods.

Ah, floods. There's a word to spark the freshwater houseboater's interest. In most moving bodies of fresh water, floods are a fact of life and must be dealt with. Look around the banks of your proposed houseboat site for debris cast up by high water. If a placid babbling brook enters the head of your chosen cove, consider that it might undergo a Jekyll and Hyde transformation after a cloudburst. Check the local newspaper for stories of local floods in years gone by. Talk with older residents whose years of experience may point out the ideal site. Learn as much as you can about your chosen body of water—go out in a small boat and drift around, letting the current take you where it will. Freshwater rivers and lakes have a rhythm and life of their own; you need only slow down to feel their pulse.

MOORING

In shallow water, to make a permanent mooring—permanent meaning it will take a little effort (certainly more than violent weather) to remove it—simply hammer an anchor's fluke down into the foreshore, then hammer a 1-inch water pipe through the anchor's stock. Alternatively, dig a hole in the sand or mud or shingle and drop in a tire, with a chain wrapped around it and shackled. When the hole is filled in and only the chain appears above ground, the holding power—suction—will be tremendous.

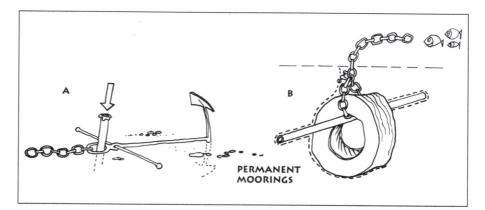

Figure 13-5. A 1-inch water pipe (a) conveniently secures an anchor. A length of pipe passed through a tire (b), buried in mud or sand, will increase holding power.

Mushroom anchors and large rocks that have settled into the mud act much like the buried tire. The deeper the anchors settle, the more the suction of the mud or sand will hold the houseboat. Lengths of heavy chain attached to the anchors also help by converting the pull on the mooring line from vertical to horizontal.

The working load limit (roughly half the actual breaking strength) of standard proof coil chain is roughly 4,500 pounds for ½-inch diameter chain, 3,500 for $\frac{7}{16}$-inch, and 2,650 for ⅜ -inch. If you can afford it, heavier is better, because the extra weight of the chain helps convert vertical into horizontal pull.

The chain need not reach all the way to the houseboat. Chain is more durable than rope, but it's also more expensive. If you're on a tight budget, buy only enough chain to provide about 10-foot lengths above ground. Tie rope to the ends of the chain, and lead the rope to the boat.

Unless you're on an extreme budget, use nylon rope, which is the strongest available. Moreover, it stretches under load, acting as a natural shock absorber. The approximate breaking strength of nylon rope (in tons) can be figured by squaring its circumference. For example, 2-inch circumference (⅝-inch diameter) nylon rope will hold approximately 4 tons before breaking. To be safe, though, figure normal working strain to be about half a given rope's breaking strain. Thus, if we have a 2-ton houseboat, 2-inch circumference rope will be about right. A 4-ton houseboat will want 2¾- or 3-inch circumference nylon rope.

Incidentally, even the best rope is no stronger than the knots you use to tie things together. The ultimate in strength is a well-worked eye splice, retaining almost 95 percent of the rope's rated strength. Next comes an anchor bend, at 76 percent, and a round turn and two half-hitches at 70 percent. The popular bowline retains only 60 percent of breaking strain, and the ubiquitous square knot—the only knot too many of us know—reduces breaking strength to around 40 percent of the rope's original capacity. Although it's a subject beyond the scope of this book, learn how to tie the right knots. (For some good books on knots and knotting, see Suggested Reading.)

Tires are versatile things. One slung over a bollard, with the mooring rope or chain fed back over it, will cushion the boat from any sudden gusts of wind. Alternatively, a mooring line can be shackled to a tire, which is then dropped over a bollard, the tire acting like a gigantic rubber band. This is surprisingly effective at reducing any shocks and jerks that winds or waves care to conjure; and tires, designed for 80-m.p.h. motoring, won't snap.

A very securely moored houseboat would have a mooring in the ground on each corner. However, if the houseboat is close enough to land to tie to some trees or to stakes driven obliquely into the ground (that is, facing away from the pull of the ropes), then so much the better—as long as the mooring lines don't impede strollers along the shore.

In tidal areas, you'll need to allow for extra rope to accommodate the rise and fall of the tides; the greater the rise and fall, the more rope you'll

Figure 13-6.
An old tire also
makes an
excellent
"spring" to
cushion the
pull on
mooring lines.

need. Once tensioned for the lowest possible tide, that is, for the farthest possible distance, they can be forgotten. Where mooring lines are tied tightly at high tide, the time of closest distance, there is no accommodating the movement of the tide. The ropes, bollards, boat, and trees it's tied to are all stressed. To increase the effective length of rope without moving the houseboat farther from shore, and to reduce its tendency to move about at its mooring, it's a good idea when setting out mooring lines to arrange them as shown in Figure 13-8.

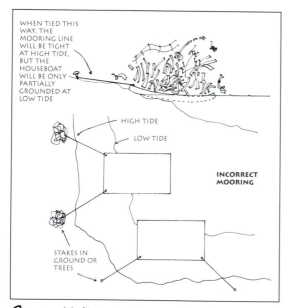

Figure 13-7. In both examples, the mooring lines are too short and too tight; when the tide goes out, the houseboat will be caught half-suspended, half-afloat.

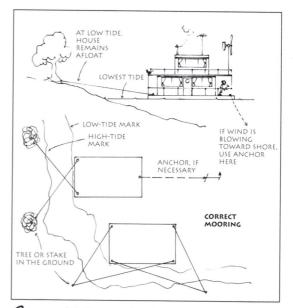

Figure 13-8. Mooring lines arranged in a sling are long enough to adjust to any tide but hold the houseboat securely in place.

Deep Water

Deep-water moorings require substantial weights if they are to be effective, particularly in holding something with the windage of a houseboat. Heaving a rock over the side won't do much. Railway wagon wheels, very large concrete blocks, huge slabs of granite, mushroom anchors, or old engine casings are generally used, with a set of chains leading up to the boat.

The recommended permanent mooring for a 40-foot motorboat with a 14-foot beam (which of course is infinitely more streamlined than a houseboat) in winds to 75 knots calls for a 500-pound mushroom anchor (or a 4,000-pound slab of granite), and a length of ½-inch-diameter chain equal to five times the water's depth at extreme high tide. For mixed rope and chain, the mooring line's length should be equal to seven times the water's depth at extreme high tide. With ½-inch proof coil chain selling for better than $2 U.S. per foot, you don't need to be a financial wizard to see that permanent moorings in deep water require deep pockets.

Moorings are prepared on a handy beach or foreshore by shackling the chain to the weight, then looping that chain over a plank suspended between two things that will float—often dinghies, small rafts, or a series of barrels. The theory is that the tide, as it rises, will lift the two floating objects, suspending the weight, free of the bottom, between them. The dinghies or rafts are then maneuvered out to where the mooring is to be, and the chain is released. Remember to tie a rope to the chain and a buoy marker to the rope. The buoy is left to bob about in the water until the houseboat appears next to it. The buoy is hauled aboard, and the rope slung over a bollard or hitching post.

In deep water, too, it's desirable to arrange mooring lines in a sling if the local weather can get nasty. The idea is that, as the wind blows and changes direction, the area of least resistance will automatically follow the veering wind. This sling will allow the houseboat to travel a full 360 degrees, so care should be taken that it won't hit anything in its travels.

To restrict it to a half-circle, a similar sling would be fitted to a second, rear mooring. There is actually no reason why a boat need swing 360 degrees. The 180-degree leeway of two moorings would still allow the boat—no matter which end is presented to the wind—to find the least resistance.

Deep-water moorings in official harbor areas will require permission from the harbor authorities. Generally, moorings must be constructed to the authority's requirements regarding weight, shackles, length and size of chain, and siting. Given this regulation, it is incomparably more convenient either to site the houseboat on the foreshore (between high and low tides), or to forgo permanent moorings in favor of anchoring.

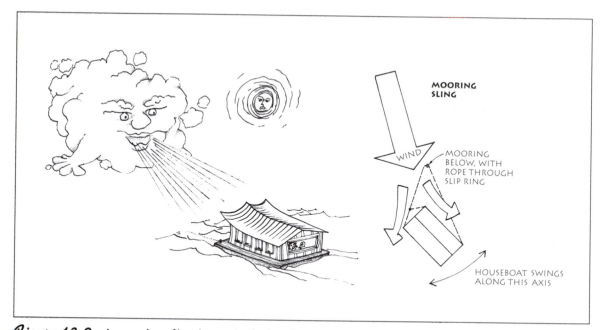

Figure 13-9. **A mooring sling is particularly effective in strong winds. The sling is led from the rear right (aft, starboard) corner of the deck, through a slip ring or a bowline knot, at the mooring end, and then back to the front left (forward, portside) corner of the deck.**

Anchoring

For the most part, one does not need permission to drop anchor, although that, too, is coming under the scrutiny of those whose life can't be complete unless they've found something new to regulate—most notably in South Florida. Anchors come in all shapes and sizes, but any of them must be heavy enough to do the job they're designed for: restrict the boat to a specific area on the water. There's almost an inverse law that the cheapest and most inefficient of anchors will fail when the most expensive possible launch or yacht is within striking distance. As a rule, it is good to economize on most things, but not with anchors and mooring lines. An anchor has to dig into the bottom, and dig in securely, but not so emphatically that it can't be removed.

The correct type is a matter of opinion, but Danforth and CQR (pronounced "secure," also known as a plough) are favored for holding in mud or sand. Both are good all-rounders, the CQR being marginally better in sand and weed, the Danforth being marginally better in mud. In addition, the Danforth folds flat for storage, but since storage space is usually freely available on a houseboat and the anchors are not aboard that often, it really becomes a chocolate or vanilla choice. Both anchors drive into the bottom as a horizontal pull is applied.

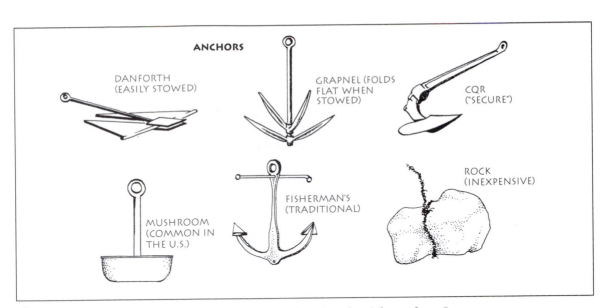

Figure 13-10. **Don't skimp when it comes to choosing the right anchor. Opt for one that suits the bottom conditions and size of your houseboat.**

The traditional fisherman anchor, or Admiralty type, is better than the CQR or Danforth on rocky or weedy ground, although far less effective in mud or sand. As weight comes on the anchor, the stock tips the anchor over, and the down-fluke drives into the bottom. In tidal areas where the boat will dry out, it is possible to come down on top of the upright fluke. "This very thing happened some years ago in Gravesend Bay, New York, when Mr. Pierre Lorillard's valuable houseboat settled on the sharp fluke of her anchor and punched a hole through her bottom and filled with water."

Other, less popular anchors have their uses for smaller vessels: the grapnel for holding on rocky bottoms, the mushroom in mud, and the rock just about anywhere—if it's big enough.

No matter which anchor you use, it should have at least 10 feet of fairly heavy chain shackled on to change the pull from vertical to horizontal. In addition, the scope, or length of the anchor rode, should be equal to seven times the water's depth at highest tide.

CHANGES

Houseboats are not always popular. The history of houseboating—once the socialites abandoned them—is sprinkled with such reaction. Let's face it, houseboats are a minority, a small minority, a very small minority.

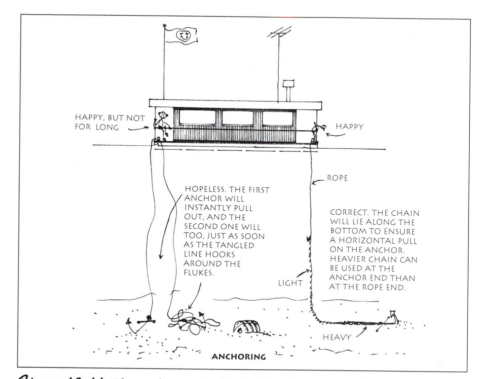

Figure 13-11. The anchor on the far right has been properly laid, with the weight of the chain pulling the anchor along the bottom and enough line to equal seven times the water's depth at highest tide. The resulting horizontal pull makes the anchor dig in even deeper. The two on the left would only be good for snaring sharks. At the first tug from a wind-pushed houseboat, the extreme left one would lift up, and out. In the example to its right, the rope would snare around its fluke, and it too would rip out. Admiral Bedford advised his sailors that wrapping a rope around the fluke would guarantee being able to extract it, at a pull, from possible enslavement at the bottom.

The use of the sea and air is common to all, and neither Nature, nor use, nor custom, permit any possession thereof.

Queen Elizabeth I to Sir Francis
Drake.

The disfavor shown the concept of living permanently afloat may have a lot to do with the nature of the coastline. Good mooring sites are infrequent, and there is increasing demand for them by all boat users, recreational as well as domiciliary. There are more recreational boaties than there are liveaboards and, in the normal manner with which these things are done, biases and emotive mutterings can replace facts.

The reason generally given for disfavoring houseboats is a fear of pollution. Mention that you live on a houseboat, and the first question usually will be, "whaddaya do about your toilet?" It's a good question, but it must say something about people ashore when it's the first thing that pops into their minds.

It's too easy to project pollution problems onto a small, easily identifiable target, particularly if those doing the projections are part of the smug majority whose bathrooms and factories and cities regularly spew forth an unimaginable load of, for want of a better word, crap.

According to the *N.Z. Herald*, Sydney, Australia, every day pours 1.3 billion liters of sewage directly into the Pacific Ocean—enough to be photographed clearly by satellite, and enough to permanently close Malabar Beach. Not that it's only cities: Figure 13-12 shows a sign erected by a tiny holiday community in New Zealand; look what they've done to our beach, Ma! Imagine the furor if houseboaters did that.

In this book we've tried to devise houseboats that are as self-sufficient and nonpolluting as possible. We try to generate our own power and deal with our own wastes in a responsible fashion. How many ashore can say that?

Figure 13-12. Land-dwellers' sense of responsibility.

Figure 13-13. **Start 'em young.**

This is how the world goes . . . you are going to have to make it different, you are going to have to stop listening to your parents. If you go on obeying your parents, the world will never be a better place.

Jacob Bronowski, *The Origins of Knowledge and Imagination*. New Haven: Yale University Press, 1978.

If a house-on-land had more validity, more reality, than a houseboat; if a house-on-land were somehow superior . . . but it is not. It is merely different. If most people had the sense to live afloat, then a house-on-land would be an oddity. Likewise, an igloo is an oddity—but not in the Arctic. The very fact that it is different, means that *it is not the same.*

If a houseboat is anything, it's an escape. If, once afloat, we enjoy some of the conveniences and comforts of houses ashore, then we may well feel disposed to bless our boat with the name Houseboat.

There's one thing you should know, you few builders who go out on to the water. It is impossible—utterly impossible—to effect change, and at the same time to keep the status quo. It can't be done. Yet change is vital. We have to uproot the way it's been.

Houseboats aren't an easy fix, but they hint of a new approach. It doesn't necessarily mean that houseboaters are better people—or that they should pretend they are. It simply means that they feel dissatisfied with the way things are—either personally, or generally.

Happy building!

Plans to Build From

Designing your own houseboat can be the most rewarding part of the building process. Still, some seem more comfortable working from a designer's plans. Indeed, if the houseboat is meant to live a mobile rather than a stationary life, a skilled boat designer's expertise is almost essential. Boat design is both art and science; unlike houseboats, boats from unskilled designers are seldom satisfactory—and often outright horrors.

These plans are from an assortment of well-regarded yacht designers whose work is eclectic enough to embrace the decidedly un-yacht–like world of houseboats. If you find one that suits you, write the designer for more information.

Retreat

Length on Deck:	18 feet
Length on Waterline:	14 feet
Beam:	7 feet
Draft:	5 inches
Designer:	William Atkin; plans available from John Atkin, PO Box 3005, Noroton, Connecticut 06820

In his *Fourth Book of Good Boats* (International Marine, 1984), noted boat-nut Roger Taylor wrote this about *Retreat*:

About the cheapest way to live afloat is in a small houseboat or "shantyboat deluxe," as designer William Atkin called his creation Retreat. *In 1944 he said this 18-footer could be built for $200. We know she'd cost a lot more than that today, but she'd still be inexpensive and fairly easy for almost anyone to build. She's plain looking but practical, and her appearance is helped by the different levels of house top and "porch" railing.*

The accommodations are fine for one person. Although there is not standing headroom in the sleeping area, a person 6 feet tall can stand in the galley and sitting area. There is room for chairs on the porch, where you'd spend plenty of time in fair weather. With her identical ends, you could anchor from either one bow or the

other, exposing the porch to the breeze in hot weather or sheltering it in cold weather.

Of course, Retreat *is intended for still, protected waters, and she'd be ideal for shallow creeks. You could put her where no deep-draft boats can go. You'd have privacy and a better view than a great many luxury homes. In most cases she could be propelled by an oar or a quant (note how each is stowed on the house side). Atkin even envisioned moving the boat on wheels and towing her behind a car to change to a distant locale.*

Although this craft is not as richly named as the notorious Potomac River houseboat-of-ill-repute, Aquatic Temptations, *I think* Retreat's *name is most appropriate. She enables you to take an inexpensive breather and back off temporarily from the stress of living ashore.*

Retreat

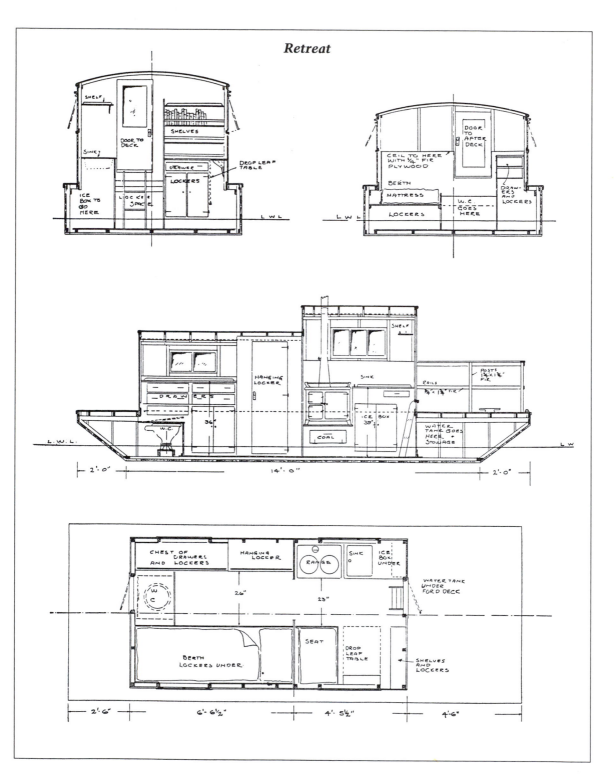

Rufus

Length on Deck: 33 feet
Beam: 11 feet
Draft: 1 foot 3 inches (leeboards up)
Designer: George Buehler, PO Box 966 Freeland,
   Whidbey Island, Washington 98249

Retreat is a mostly a stationary house-boat, although as Henry Spruks showed us in Chapter 13, an outboard on brackets, with a pair of leeboards for directional stability, can move her sedately along. *Rufus* is meant to move under sail and power, although she's unlikely to set any speed records. Iconoclast George Buehler has built his reputation designing rugged, salty-looking boats that are easily built using materials no more exotic than you can find in the neighborhood lumberyard. His plans catalog is worth sending for even if you don't want to build a boat; it's better reading than the *National Lampoon*.

Here's what George has to say about *Rufus*:

Some years ago I designed Rufus *for a guy who lived along the Intracoastal Waterway in Florida. I had a lot of fun thinking it up, and I mean to own one myself some day. I've thought of building it way up the Columbia River and floating down to Astoria; or maybe building it at the headwaters of the Mississippi and floating down to New Orleans. Of course,*

it would be a fine craft for quiet fjords just about anywhere.

The idea was a cheap and simple-to-build floating camp, with a small inboard or a "power" outboard, like a British Seagull, and a big sail to loaf along downwind. The hull is just a plywood box covered with fiberglass cloth and epoxy, and would be no challenge to build.

The house is set well back from the hull to give lots of deck space. Since I designed it, I've thought I might extend the house clear out to the side decks and back to the stern, leaving the foredeck as the helm. One guy said he was planning to build it that way and attach a diving board to the back of the house roof, which sounds pretty good to me. This would open up the interior considerably and give room for permanent bunks rather than the fold-down system shown here. However, as drawn the extra deck space is nice for lolling about in warm climates, and gives holds on each end for crab pots, fishing gear, and the like. And folding up the couch to make a bed sounds like more hassle than it actually is.

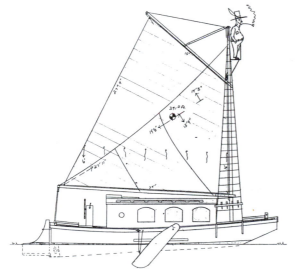

Rufus

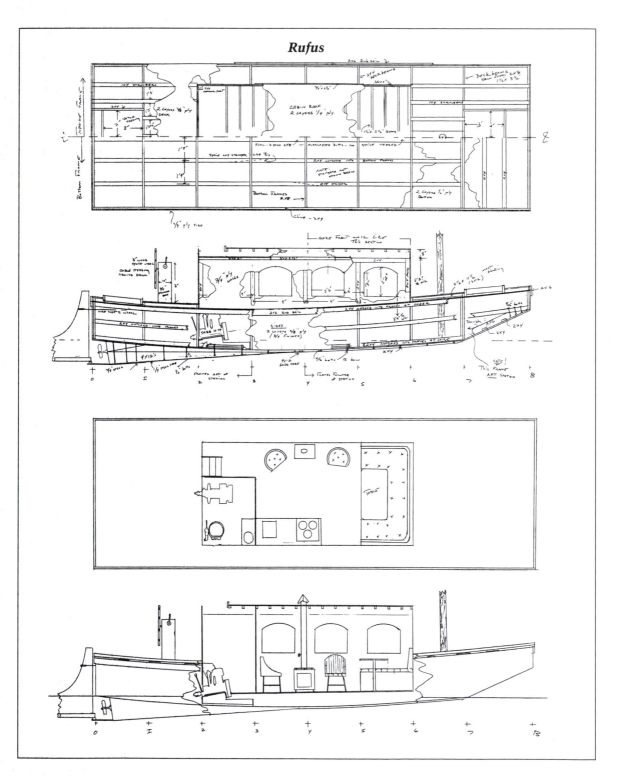

Scow Sloop

Length on Deck: 32 feet
Length on Waterline: 28 feet
Beam: 11 feet 9 inches
Draft: 2 feet 3 inches, board up
Designer: Reuel Parker, PO Box 3547,
                                 Fort Pierce, Florida 34948-3547

With her flat bottom and straight sides, *Rufus* is more house than boat. This V-bottom scow sloop, from Florida designer Reuel Parker, is more boat than house—although as you can see from the accommodation plans, she's spacious, even yacht-like, below decks.

Parker's specialty is shallow-draft cruising boats, easily built from plywood covered with epoxy and fabric, that draw heavily on traditional workboat designs. This boat derives from the old Gulf Coast scows, once a common sight along the Southeast Coast hauling produce and lumber to market. She's been considerably refined to make her faster and easier to handle.

Parker believes this design embodies the most boat possible for the money and says this hull can also be built as a powerboat, with or without a small pilothouse, as a Chinese junk (!) complete with aft cabin, or as a gaff-rigged yawl.

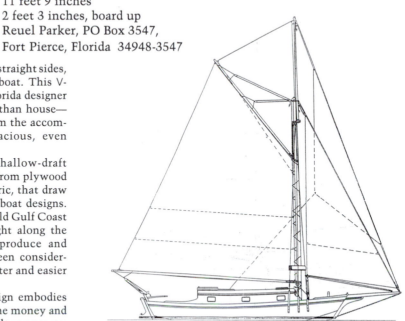

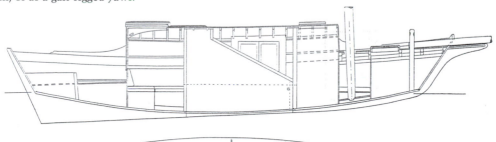

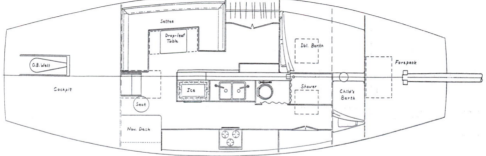

Suggested Reading

BOATBUILDING BOOKS

These books will be of great assistance to any builder wishing to eschew a barrel-type raft in favor of a "conventional" hull, or to expand his or her knowledge of things nautical. Most are available from International Marine (Blue Ridge Summit, Pennsylvania 17294-0840; 1-800-822-8158), or from an enlightened neighborhood bookstore with the good judgment to carry books about boats.

Boatbuilding: A Complete Handbook of Wooden Boat Construction, Howard I. Chapelle. New York: W. W. Norton & Company, Inc., 1941 and 1969.

Long known as the boatbuilder's bible, this is a complete handbook of wooden boat construction.

Boatbuilding Manual, 3d ed., Robert M. Steward. Camden: International Marine, 1987.

This is the standard industry manual for wooden boats.

Boatbuilding with Plywood, Glen L. Witt. Bellflower: Marine Glen L. Designs, 1962.

Everything there is to know about plywood and how to build with it.

Boatbuilding with Steel, 2d ed. (including *Boatbuilding with Aluminum* by Thomas Colvin), Gilbert C. Klingel. Camden: International Marine, 1991.

Steel is an inexpensive material, but very strong. Mr. Klingel's enthusiasm and explanations make it easy. Working with aluminum is also included.

Boatowner's Energy Planner: How to Make and Manage Electrical Energy on Board, Kevin Jeffrey with Nan Jeffrey. Camden: International Marine, 1991.

Everything you need to know to plan and install a self-sufficient and highly sophisticated electrical system.

Cold-Moulded and Strip-Planked Wood Boatbuilding, Ian Nicolson. Dobbs Ferry: Stanford Maritime/Sheridan House, Inc., 1983.

A complete book on the subject. Cold-moulded veneer is strong and light.

The Essential Knot Book, Colin Jarman. Camden: International Marine, 1984.

Includes the most important knots and splices you'll use aboard your boat.

Modern Boatbuilding Materials and Methods, Steve Sleight. Camden: International Marine, 1985.

For high-tech boatbuilding, GRP, Kevlar, etc., as well as finishing and varnishes. A complete book for modern building techniques.

Solar Boat Book, rev. ed., Pat Rand Rose. Berkeley: Ten Speed Press, 1983.

Details of living afloat as self-sufficiently as possible—solar heaters, solar cookers, solar water stills.

HOUSEBOAT BOOKS

Some of these books are out of print but may be found in libraries and used bookstores. Some are current. All of them provide interesting reading.

Crocodile Creek: The Cry in the Night, Colin Hawkins and Jacqui Hawkins. New York: Doubleday, 1989.

A delightful story, with large, humorous pictures, to read to kiddies at bedtime. Baby crocodile (with a new tooth coming through) chews through the mooring ropes of the family houseboat—will they crash over Fatal Falls?

Crocodile Creek: The Crockers on Holiday, Colin Hawkins and Jacqui Hawkins. William Collins, 1989.

Another crocodile family houseboating book. In this tale, they sail for Australia, stopping along the way at France, Spain, and Italy. Mum Croc gossips with neighbors, while Dad Croc tries to shear sheep. Then they meet the Flying Doctor, have a barbecue, and sail home again.

Floating Homes: A Houseboat Handbook, Ted Laturnus. British Columbia: Harbour Publishing.

Photographs and anecdotes from the world of houseboating.

Houseboats, Ben Dennis and Betsy Case. Smuggler's Cove Publishing.

A photographic essay of waterborne houses.

Houseboats and Houseboating, Albert B. Hunt. New York: Forest and Stream Publishing, 1905.

Long out of print. Who knows, a copy may be found in a rare-book store. It's well worth looking.

Old Glory, Jonathan Raban. William Collins, 1981.

A solo adventure down the Mississippi in a riverboat.

Shantyboat: A River Way of Life, Harlan Hubbard. Lexington: The University Press of Kentucky. Copyright 1953 and 1981 by Harlan Hubbard.

The building of a shantyboat and the consequent discoveries of the artist/author while drifting down the Ohio and Mississippi rivers. Absolutely must reading.

Waterhouses: The Romantic Alternative, Ferenc Maté. West Vancouver, British Columbia: Albatross Publishing House, 1977.

A photographic exploration of houseboats in North America and Europe by a well-known marine photographer.

Water Wagon, Rube Allyn. Saint Petersburg: Great Outdoors Publishing Co., 1952.

An entertaining and adventurous tale of one man's construction of a 21-foot houseboat the experts laughed at, and his ensuing adventures throughout Florida.

Illustration Credits

Unless otherwise noted, photographs are from the author's collection.

Chapter 1
Chapter opening art: Jackie O'Brien; Figure 1-9: The Cincinnati Historical Society; Figure 1-11: Modern Mechanix Publishing Co.; Figures 1-12 and 1-13: Holiday Mansion, Salina, Kansas; Figure 1-14: National Library of Australia, P.J. Phillips Collection; Figure 1-17: Alexander Turnbull Library, the National Publicity Studios Collection, Wellington, New Zealand.

Chapter 2
Figure 2-1: Mark Mitchell photo, *N.Z. Herald.*

Chapter 3
Figure 3-1: Roy Bisson photo, World Expeditions, Sydney, NSW; Figure 3-17: *Sunday Mail*, Brisbane, Australia.

Chapter 4
Chapter opening photo: Bernard Wides.

Chapter 5
Figure 5-2: *N.Z. Herald*; Figure 5-5: Jackie O'Brien.

Chapter 9
Chapter opening photo: Bernard Wides; Figure 9-3: photograph reprinted from *Boatowner's Energy Planner* by Kevin Jeffrey, International Marine, 1991. Courtesy Jack Rabbit Marine.

Chapter 11
Sidebar art: reprinted from *Shantyboat: A River Way of Life*. Copyright 1953 and 1981 by Harlan Hubbard, University Press of Kentucky.

Chapter 13
Sidebar photo: Henry Spruks.

Index